The Complete Book of Puppetry

The Complete Book of Puppetry

David Currell

Publishers PLAYS, INC. *Boston*

To my mother

Preface

This book really began to take shape in 1961; the actual writing was to come much later but already the foundations were being laid, for this was when I first met Gordon Staight, a puppet master with remarkable ingenuity who gave me considerable guidance and encouragement. To Gordon my sincerest thanks are due, for without his inspiration and help I would not be in a position to write this book today.

Everybody who has ever exchanged views on puppetry with me, or given information or assistance, has played some part in the shaping of this book, especially the members of the British Puppet and Model Theatre Guild, the Educational Puppetry Association, the Puppeteers of America, and UNIMA, the international organisation. To all of these friends my thanks are offered, and in particular to Jan Bussell and Ann Hogarth for their hospitality in so kindly opening their extensive puppetry collection to my use in gathering photographs and information; to Barry Smith for his invaluable assistance with the photography; to Miss K. R. Drummond for her expert advice on the bibliography; to Daniel Llords, John Thirtle, Ian Allen and V. Basetlíková, Assistant Cultural Attaché to the Czechoslovak Embassy in London, for information as well as photographs; to all those (listed separately) who have so generously contributed photographs for my use in this book.

Special thanks are extended to Mr and Mrs A. R. Philpott (Pantopuck and Violet) for considerable help, suggestions and photographs; to Panto again for so kindly consenting to read the manuscript and giving his expert opinion; and finally to Ian Herbert, General Editor at Pitman Publishing, and Georgina Bannister who designed and sub-edited the book, for their continuing help throughout the project.

D. C.

Contents

1 Introducing puppetry

Throughout the world the puppet show is a popular entertainment. Sometimes it is an ancient heritage, a last reminder of an age long past; sometimes a medium for the contemporary artist's experiments with shape, colour and movement. For centuries it has been used to relate myth and legend and enact simple traditional farces. Now, as well as undergoing a tremendous revival as entertainment for both adults and children, it is becoming more and more widely used in education and as therapy.

What exactly is a puppet? Perhaps it might best be described as 'an inanimate object moved in a dramatic manner by human agency', a definition which includes a wide range of figures, but not dolls and automata.

The puppeteer is an artist, a unique combination of sculptor, modeller, painter, needleworker, electrician, carpenter, actor, writer, producer, designer and inventor who in the course of preparing a show calls upon a host of diverse skills. He may take on all of these tasks himself and, with luck, achieve a high degree of artistic unity. Alternatively, he may be just one of a group or company, pooling their many and varied talents.

Puppetry itself is essentially a folk art which from time to time has become a fashionable craze. Because of its ephemeral nature its history must be largely a matter of conjecture. Its origins, which like those of most of the arts are confused, are generally thought to lie mainly in the East. Certainly puppetry in Asia was highly sophisticated at a very early date and Asia is the source of many of the ideas and techniques of the puppetry of the West. Cult figures with moving parts survive from the very earliest times, but whether or not these were used in a 'dramatic manner' can never be definitely known.

In all the early Mediterranean civilisations and under Roman rule the puppet drama undoubtedly flourished and vestiges of this dramatic tradition may possibly have survived the Dark Ages. (The characters of the *Commedia dell' arte* may well owe something to it.) In the Middle Ages wandering showmen travelled all over Europe with the puppet show and puppets were widely used to enact the scriptures—until they were banned by the Council of Trent.

Since the Renaissance puppetry in Europe has continued as an unbroken tradition, though experiencing many rises and declines in popularity. In seventeenth-century England it reached the height of popular appeal as the only entertainment allowed by Parliament; and again in eighteenth-century France when *Ombres Chinoises* not only flourished as a fairground entertainment but were also a fashionable craze amongst artists and nobles. Puppetry has always been popular in Italy, and the magnificent Sicilian Orlando marionettes are one of the most famous puppet traditions of the West.

In the nineteenth century the puppet show was taken to America by emigrants from many European countries and their various national traditions were the foundations for the great variety of styles to be found there today.

In contrast to the changes and developments which are taking place in Europe and America the Far Eastern countries cling to their ancient, unchanging traditions. In Burma, a dancer's skill is still measured by his ability to imitate the movements of the marionette and in Japan the Bunraku puppets, which once overshadowed the Kabuki in popularity, survive unaffected by the general, if ambivalent, turning towards the West.

Throughout its long and world-wide history the puppet show has remained essentially characteristic of the country that produces it, reflecting something of the national temperament and psychology of different peoples. Compare for example the elaborate refinement of shadow puppets, most popular in the East, with the earthy knock-about glove puppets of the West. Similarly, within Europe itself, the main protagonists of the traditional farces—Karagöz of Turkey, Caspar of Germany, Guignol of France—embody many aspects of the national character.

The types of puppet in use today fall into five main categories: glove puppets, rod puppets, shadow puppets, marionettes and the figures of the toy theatre.

The glove or hand puppet is, as the name implies, used like a glove on the operator's hand; the rod puppet is held and moved by a rod, usually from below but sometimes from above. Sometimes a combination of hand and rod is used for the control of one puppet.

Glove puppets are usually quite simple in structure but a rod puppet may vary in complexity from a simple shape supported on a single stick to a fully articulated figure with moving eyes and mouth.

Shadow puppets are flat cut-out figures held by a rod or wire against a translucent illuminated screen. The figures of the toy theatre are cut-out two-dimensional figures moved by wires off stage.

The marionette is a puppet on strings, suspended from a control held by the puppeteer. Its construction can vary from the extremely complex to the very simple; from a figure with any number of moving parts controlled by a multitude of strings to a simple figure with only a few strings.

Glove and rod puppets are usually presented from within a booth. The traditional covered booth is still used for 'Punch and Judy' but the open booth is becoming more and more popular, affording as it does far greater scope for performances and a wider viewing angle for the audience.

Marionettes are also increasingly presented on an open stage with the puppeteer in view of the audience. The traditional marionette stage with

2

a proscenium front to hide the operators is still used, but size, portability and setting-up time are factors which influence the trend towards open-stage performances.

Of the various types of puppet the marionette is obviously the most versatile and lends itself to the greatest number of uses and variations of construction. Its performances can be of unique grace and charm but fast and forceful action is generally ruled out by the danger of tangles. The glove puppet, although limited in gesture to the movement of one's fingers, is ideal for quick, robust action and the live hand inside it gives figures a unique flexibility of physique.

Rod puppets, like marionettes, offer a great potential for creativity in design and presentation. The range of swift and subtle movements possible makes the rod puppet ideal for sketches that depend on precision timing. Shadow puppets are often used to illustrate a narrated story, a use for which their nature ideally suits them; however, the traditional Greek and Turkish shadow shows demonstrate the adaptability of the shadow puppet to direct dialogue and vigorous knock-about action.

It is perfectly possible, of course, to combine or alternate the use of different types of puppet in one performance. The combination of marionettes with rod puppets is particularly satisfactory as the stylised movement of the rod puppet is closely related in effect to that of the marionette. Shadow play, which can be used very successfully to show scenes and actions taking place in the distance while three-dimensional figures carry on the main action in the fore-ground, can also be used to illustrate linking narrative in a three-dimensional show and for such things as dream and memory sequences.

The combination now occurring more frequently of masked human beings and puppets has aroused both interest and controversy as it is not considered by the purists to be puppet theatre at all. However that may be it looks as if it may well become an accepted part of theatre for children.

Probably the best advice that can be given to anybody starting on puppetry is to try anything: try to be creative; experiment with materials; experiment with various methods of control. The method of construction best suited to any particular puppet can be decided only by the puppeteer as he makes his puppet and explores the possibilities open to him. (An excellent way of starting to explore materials and the possibilities of construction at the same time is to make a 'junk-box' puppet from whatever materials may be to hand.)

The two main aims when creating a puppet are to construct a figure that embodies the character you wish to convey and to operate it so that its movements convey character and emotions to the audience.

The puppet is an essence and an emphasis of the character it is intended to reflect. The puppet artist has to create and interpret character, not imitate it: he selects those characteristics that he considers most suitable to express the personality he has imagined. He has considerable freedom for not only does he design the costumes of his actors, he also creates their heads, faces, body shapes, etc.

Whatever the puppet represents, it must be distinctly and boldly

3

modelled, for delicate features, however beautiful, will be lost on the puppet stage. The puppet that lacks bold modelling and exaggerated design will appear nondescript to an audience only a matter of feet away.

The artist studies natural form but he does not simply copy what he sees; he interprets it by searching for the underlying structures and then working on these. So must the puppet maker. To take the example of the face, he must look to the basic structure, to see what is happening 'behind' the face and how it gets its form.

Study different people in all kinds of moods, not with the idea of copying a particular head or body shape but to see how it 'works'. Take the person in a thoughtful mood: what is it in his face and bearing that characterises his mood? Now he looks happy, but what changes have occurred to his face? What is it that produces the happy expression? What makes that same face look sad? And so on. This kind of study leads to greater understanding not only for the artist and sculptor but also for the puppeteer.

It is an excellent plan to keep a scrapbook of drawings, pictures, ideas, etc. Pictures of animals, clowns (for make-up), people in period costume, magazine articles on eye make-up or hair styles are just a few examples of useful reference items.

To convey character through movement the puppeteer, just as when trying to convey character through appearance, must study human beings. People at rest and people in motion, people when gay, when sad, when bold, when shy, when weary. He must consider the character of his creation and see that the movements of the puppet are in keeping. Will he walk slowly with a stoop? Will he have a brisk walk, or a weary shuffle? Will he glide across the floor? What about all his other gestures? They must all fit into the total picture, making a unified study.

This is not to say that the puppeteer must attempt to reproduce human movement. He will be far more successful if he draws upon stylised movements in keeping with the character of the puppet.

It has been suggested that the puppeteer would do better to study the formal movements of the dancer rather than the naturalistic movements of the actor, for the great variety of human gestures can never be matched by a puppet. The process that concerns the puppeteer is simplification, selection of the movements that best convey the required character.

It is essential to avoid unnecessary movements: this is part of the process of simplification. No jerking of the head to every syllable of speech, no continual waving of the hands in the air, nor any of the other useless gestures so commonly employed.

The way in which a puppet moves is as important in conveying character as its actual appearance and the puppeteer must learn not only to operate his figures skilfully but also to make its actions significant of mood and character. Extremely useful investigations can be made at an early stage with a simple shape such as a handkerchief. Attach a string to it. What can this 'puppet' do with just this simple control?. If another string is added, how much more can be achieved? If one of these strings is moved, how does this affect the shape and its movements? This sort of investigation may be repeated with any number of strings on a great variety of objects. Attach a wooden rod or a springy piece of wire to an object and carry out similar experiments. Then, what about a combination of methods? Wire and string, hand and rod, and so on, make interesting mixed methods of control to be explored.

Throughout this book stress is laid upon the importance of giving only the merest suggestion of movement and leaving the audience to interpret this in their own minds. They will readily imagine the puppets to be doing the most marvellous things. This will be understood expecially through the suggested experiments: the objects used are so limited, so restricted in their movements, yet even a coat-hanger on one or two strings is capable of holding our attention, of fascinating us, and we will readily see significance in its movements. The art of suggestion is an important element of the puppeteer's skill.

An essential part of good performance is practice. The puppeteer must practise (with or without a mirror) until he perfects the manipulation and control of his puppet. No two puppets are the same; each has its own characteristics and each its own idiosyncracies of movement, so every puppet requires fresh thought and further practice.

A large part of the success of any puppet show depends upon *showmanship*—the capacity to exhibit puppets to the best advantage. Some aspects of showmanship have particular importance for the 'variety' entertainer but, by the very meaning of the term, it is bound to be relevant for every show.

The puppet showman must learn how to interest his audience from the start and sustain this interest above a certain level allowing for the inevitable fluctuations of attention.

Good timing is vital. Without it jokes fall flat, important lines are lost and the show is marred. Lines must not be rushed; sensible pauses are as important as the lines that precede or follow them. An entrance or a gesture can do as much if it is well timed as it can lose if it is badly timed.

Long speeches, long 'variety' acts, bore the audience. (If the puppet is part of a 'variety show' he will do all he can in a very short time and it is fatal to stretch out the act by repetition.)

Just as important as his own dexterity is the puppeteer's ability to assess and respond to the reactions of his audience. No two audiences are the same and the performer should be able to cater for differences in taste and humour, to play upon the points that the audience take up and pass quickly over those they do not; to sum up the situation very quickly and adapt himself to it.

Adaptability is particularly vital when performing for children, for they participate with the most delightful and unexpected comments and the puppeteer can make use of these to enhance his performance. They know what they like and it is fatal to try to impose upon a show a pre-arranged pattern if it is obviously heading in a different direction. The performance must move with the audience.

Showmanship is an art in itself; it is an art that can be acquired through practice and experience. It cannot be taught; it can only be learned, but one golden rule is: always leave the audience wanting more.

2 Puppetry past and present

Puppetry is a visual and dramatic art which has continued for thousands of years. Exactly when or where it originated is not known, and even its comparatively recent history in many countries is obscure.

In one country puppetry may be a living folk art; in another it may be used as a means of teaching simple or illiterate people; in a third it may be considered a high art form. In one manner or another it is practised throughout most of the world by young and old.

This chapter gives in outline something of what is known of the development of puppetry throughout the world, and also brief descriptions of the work and activities of contemporary puppeteers.

Puppets in ancient times

The origin of puppetry remains the subject of dispute.

Some authorities claim that puppetry was practised in India as long as four thousand years ago. It is widely held that puppets were in use before human actors as religious taboo forbade impersonation. Supporting evidence for this is found in the fact that the leading player in Sanskrit plays is titled *sutradhara* which means *the holder of strings*.

In China puppetry is thought to have begun some two thousand years ago and marionettes were in use by the eighth century AD. There seem to have been several types of 'puppet' in ancient times, among them 'living puppets'—which may have been children acting as puppets —and 'water puppets'—possibly akin to the Vietnamese figures which perform on wooden rafts floated on a lake and are controlled from a distance by a complexity of strings. Some authorities, however, suggest that shadow puppets were the earliest form of puppet used in China; they certainly date back well over a thousand years.

The Greeks used puppets possibly as early as 800 BC. Undoubtedly puppetry was a common form of entertainment by the fourth century BC. Marionettes were the type of puppet used, as can be deduced from the fact that the Greek word for puppet is *neurospastos*, *neuron* meaning cord. Glove puppets may also have been in use, the Greek work *koree* meaning both a long sleeve that covers the hand and a small statue.

The first puppeteer known by name is Potheinos, a Greek who performed in the theatre of Dionysys in Athens. He is referred to by Athenaeus, a Greek writer of the second century, in a miscellaneous work called *The Deipnosophists*, but nothing is said of the content of his performance.

Puppetry was certainly established in Rome by 400 BC when there start to appear references to puppets in the writings of the time. The nature of these references point to the use of marionettes and glove puppets but the allusions are not specific so we know nothing of the nature of the performances. When the Roman Empire came to an end in the fifth century the circuses fell into disuse and the entertainers were driven out. Among them were the puppeteers who then wandered over Europe with their shows.

Puppets in Western Europe

Puppets were used all over the Mediterranean in ancient times and it seems reasonable to assume that the tradition was kept alive through the Dark Ages by wandering entertainers.

By the thirteenth century puppetry was well established in many parts of Europe. It has since experienced many changes in popularity which at times has rivalled that of the live theatre.

Free exchange between the countries of Europe has produced in them

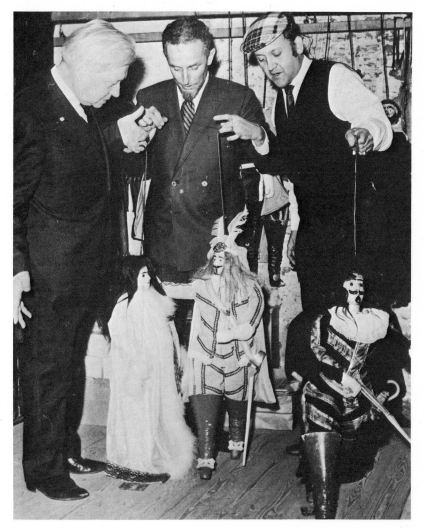

Figure 1   Belgian marionettes of José Geal operated by (left to right) Sergei Obraztsov (USSR), Daniel Llords (USA) and José Geal

7

similar trends and styles in puppetry. The Belgian puppets, for example, are very similar to the large Sicilian marionettes and most countries have a counterpart of Mr Punch. In Holland he is Jan Klaasen (originally Pickle Herring), in Belgium Tchantches, in Spain Don Christoval Polichinello, and so on.

Today there is a rapidly increasing number of professional puppeteers although the majority continue to be either amateur or semi-professional.

Italy

In Italy at the end of the fifteenth century there appeared a form of drama known as the *Commedia dell' arte*. Amongst the stock characters of these plays were buffoons, or *zanni*, who went under such names as Pulcinello, Arlecchino, Scaramuccia and Burattino. The travelling entertainers often had puppet representations of the characters but it is not possible to determine whether they appeared first as puppets or live actors. In fact the term *burattini*, meaning glove puppet, was in use before the dramas of the *Commedia dell' arte* emerged.

One of these buffoons, Pulcinello, travelled as a puppet character throughout Europe and became a popular figure in many countries though taking on other names and adapting to the nature or styles of the region. It is from this character that Punch derives.

By the end of the fifteenth century puppets seem to have become well established as a popular form of entertainment in Italy. The types of puppet used were marionettes, probably supported by a rod fixed to the head with the limbs manipulated by strings or fine wire; *marionnettes à la planchette* which were jigged to music; a type of rod puppet which moved in grooves made in a plank; and glove puppets.

In the late eighteenth century Italian *fantoccini* (puppet) plays, which incorporated a great many spectacular effects and ingenious tricks and transformations, were tremendously popular and travelled widely throughout Europe and to England.

In recent times the popularity of puppets was greatly influenced by the famous *Theatro dei Piccoli* of Vittorio Podrecca which, founded in Rome in 1930, flourished for over twenty years and travelled extensively.

Today there are still many street shows to be seen in Italy, especially during Saint day festivals, and beach shows are still quite common. The puppets used are mainly glove puppets.

Sicily

Sicilian marionettes are renowned for their magnificent productions which dramatise the conflict between Christianity and Islaam. The most famous of these plays is *Orlando furioso*, Orlando originating from an eighth-century knight called Roland.

The legend of Roland, which evolved over several hundred years, was finally embodied by the Italian poet Ludovico Ariosto in his poem, *Orlando furioso*, in 1532. Orlando, the perfect knight, is the leader of the Paladins (the twelve peers who accompanied King Charlemagne) but is distracted from his duty by his love for Angelica. After many adventures, Angelica marries another and Orlando goes mad, hence the

Figure 2 A 19th century
Sicilian Orlando Furioso

title. Eventually Orlando returns to Charlemagne's camp, is cured of his madness and in battle kills Agramante, King of Africa and leader of the Saracens.

This story, made up of hundreds of smaller episodes, was improvised by puppeteers until it became the story it is today—a tale of knights, witches, giants and dragons. The Orlando marionettes became more popular in Sicily than anywhere else and Sicily has become the permanent home of this traditional puppet drama.

The Sicilian puppets are made of wood and have beaten armour, shields and swords. Some may be over three feet high, their height being determined by their rank. A heavy rod passed through the puppet's head from above supports the whole body and another rod works the sword arm. The shield arm is moved by a string. By lifting and turning

Figure 3   Karaghiosis

the one centre rod, the puppet walks and can even be beheaded.

The first reference to the story of Orlando being played by puppets dates from the sixteenth century, but this type of puppet had been in use since Roman times.

The most famous contemporary puppet performer is Signor Emanuele Macri, whose theatre is at Acireale, near Mount Etna.

Greece

Today in Greece shadow puppet shows are the most popular, featuring a Punch-like character, Karaghiosis (or Karaghioz), introduced to Greece by the Turks. The figures, approximately two feet high and traditionally made of leather, are now often made from plastic or acetate. The shadow screen may be up to twenty feet long and five feet high. The lighting is arranged from below the screen and the figures operated from behind.

One of the best known contemporary Karaghiosis puppeteers is Spatharis, a talented performer whose father and grandfather were both Karaghiosis performers. His latest venture is the establishment of a museum which he proposes to open in the Amaroussion area of Athens in the near future.

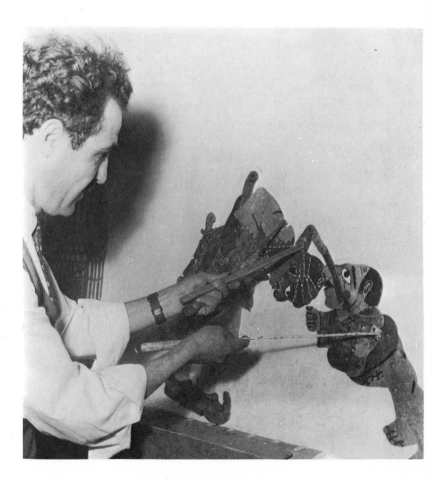

Figure 4   Spatharis manipulating Karaghiosis (right) and Veligekas, the brave man of the Turkish Pasha

10

*Figure 5   Rod puppets of
Richard Teschner, showing the
early influence of the Javanese
wayang golek puppets*

*Figure 6   A later rod puppet by
Richard Teschner*

*Figure 7   Madonna and Child by
Richard Teschner*

Austria

The most important contribution of Austria to the development of puppetry was made comparatively recently by Professor Richard Teschner who considerably influenced the development of rod puppetry in Europe. Inspired by the Javanese *wayang golek* figures, he developed his own very intricate type of rod puppet, often with a complicated system of control strings inside the supporting rod. From 1925 until his death in 1948 Teschner presented shows in his *Figurenspiegel* theatre, the proscenium of which was a gold-framed concave lens surrounded by the signs of the Zodiac.

The Salzburg Marionette Theatre presents some of the most beautiful puppetry spectacles the world has ever seen, with productions ranging from *Don Giovanni* and *Die Fledermaus* to *The Tempest* and *Rumpelstiltskin*. Performances, which have been given since 1913, include operas, operettas, ballet, plays, musical plays and pantomime. The company employs hundreds of craftsmen, designers, musicians, etc, to meet the demands of these elaborate productions.

Figure 8   Mozart's Il Seraglio
*by the Salzburg Marionette
Theatre*

Figure 11   An old German marionette: the dwarf flower seller transformed into the wizard

Germany

Since the beginning of the nineteenth century Germany has shown a special affinity with the puppet theatre. In 1802, Christoph Winter founded in Cologne the Haenneschen Puppet Theatre which, over a century and a half later, still performs in the original style with a distinctive type of rod puppet. The puppet is supported by an iron rod, the end of which is held in a thick wooden rod which stands on the floor. Nowadays both legs hang free but in older figures the rod passed through one leg. One arm is controlled by a wire, the other hangs loose.

Figures 9, 10 (Left) Scenes from Mozart's The Magic Flute *by the Salzburg Marionette Theatre*

Figure 12   Clown Gustaf with his horse Alize Zizipée: marionettes by Albrecht Roser

Figure 13   Albrecht Roser's Clown Pünktchen

Figure 14   Professor Doctor Freidreich Wilhelm Ambrosius of Albrecht Roser

In 1858 Joseph 'Papa' Schmid acquired a small Munich Theatre, the Heideck Theatre, in which he performed with such success that in 1900 a new theatre was built for him by the Municipal authorities.

In 1905 the Munich Artists' Theatre was founded by Paul Brann and in 1911 Ivo Puhonny's theatre at Baden-Baden. Max Jacob, who, until his death in 1967, was the President of UNIMA, had one of the finest German puppet companies, the Hartstein Puppets, later to become the Hohnsteiner Troupe. Today one of the most active German puppeteers is Albrecht Roser of Stuttgart, a skilful performer who has travelled the world with his puppets and gained experience of many varied styles of production.

Germany's traditional puppet play is *The History of Doctor Faustus*. Puppets have performed the play ever since it was first published in 1587. Originally these performances included a comic character called Hanswurst (Jack Sausage) but after the publication of Goethe's *Faust* in 1832 he was replaced by a rather less vulgar character called Kasper, or Kasperle. The popularity of Goethe's *Faust* had a reviving effect on the puppet show and Kasper survives to this day as a counterpart of Punch.

Germany has the finest collection of puppets and puppet theatre exhibits in the world, housed in the Munich City Theatre Collection.

France

The fourteenth-century *Li romans du bon roi Alexandre* (in the Bodleian Library) contains an illustration of hand puppets used in a portable booth with castle turrets on either side, the arrangement termed a *castellet* or *castello*.

Marionnettes à la planchette were used in France before the sixteenth century and puppet theatres existed in Paris by the beginning of the seventeenth century.

In the eighteenth century marionette operas were so popular that bitter rivalry arose with the live theatre and in 1720 an attempt was made to have the puppet productions restricted by law. This failed, and puppet performances continued with added vigour and even greater popularity.

Shadow puppets, called *ombres Chinoises*, were also popular in the eighteenth century, not only as fairground entertainment but also among artists, and a theatre founded in 1776 by Dominique Seraphin was much patronised by the fashionable world. Again, at the end of the nineteenth century, a shadow theatre flourished in the Chat Noir club of Rodolphe Salis.

In about 1630 Italian travelling showmen brought Pulcinello to France where he became Polichinelle, and gradually acquired the exaggerated physical characteristics of Punch. Polichinelle's popularity, however, was surpassed by that of Guignol, a glove puppet dressed in the style of a Lyonnais silk weaver and of typically Lyonnais character, who appeared at the beginning of the nineteenth century. Guignol in fact became so popular in France that the name is now the common French term for 'glove puppet'.

Figure 16   Guignol (right) and Gnafron (c 1906)

Figure 17   Papotin by André Tahon

15

Figure 18   Danse Russe *by André Tahon*

Today in France the trend is towards experimental puppetry. In the hands of Yves Joly, for example, the most unlikely objects become 'puppets'. An outstanding exponent of 'black theatre' puppet technique (see page 168) is Georges Lafaye, but probably the best-known to the public, through his numerous television and stage appearances, is André Tahon with his famous snail and caterpillar act, his delightful mice, Papotin, and a host of other creations.

Puppets in Eastern Europe

Figure 19   A rod puppet bear from the Hungarian State Puppet Theatre's production of Petrouchka

Most countries of Eastern Europe had an early tradition of travelling showmen who included puppets in their entertainment. In these countries too there was a Punch-type character: in Russia he was Petrouchka (or Petrushka), in Hungary Vitez Laszlo, in Czechoslovakia Kasperek, in Rumania Vasilache and in Yugoslavia Pavliha.

With a few exceptions, puppetry in East European countries did not develop very much until the twentieth century but when the development began it progressed at an impressive rate. Now there are thousands of amateur puppeteers and many State puppet theatres employing large numbers of professionals. One of the largest of these theatres is the Hungarian State Puppet Theatre, Allami Bábszinház, founded in 1949 in Budapest, and the Rumanian Tandarica Theatre in Bucharest has won international acclaim for its puppet presentations.

East Germany, of course, shares many traditions with West Germany but with obvious influences from the Soviet Union.

Poland

Polish puppet theatres date back at least to the fifteenth century. The traditional *szopka* theatres were first used in the churches and then, in

Figure 23 Three robbers by
Frieder Simon

the seventeenth century, played in the streets. These small, portable stages were used for Nativity plays rather like medieval miracle plays. Each tiny puppet is held by one small rod or wire which moves in grooves in the stage floor, the stage usually being constructed to represent a church. This form of puppetry is still practised.

In the last twenty years more than thirty State puppet theatres have been formed. Their presentations, which are of a high technical standard, are mainly for children, drawing upon Polish poetic fairy tales and some foreign material.

Today it is not unusual to see live actors and puppets in the same play and 'black art' technique is commonly practised.

Czechoslovakia

Czechoslovakia had a long tradition of marionette presentations but since the Second World War has been more concerned with rod puppetry. Considerable work has also been done in the sphere of 'black art' presentations and some of the 'black' theatres of Prague have received world-wide recognition.

One of the most famous Czech puppeteers this century was the late Joseph Skupa whose father-and-son creations, Spejbl and Hurvinek, are known throughout the world. The Hurvinek and Spejbl Theatre in Prague was forced to close during the Second World War and Skupa was imprisoned in Dresden when it was discovered that he had continued to perform secretly. He escaped during a fire in 1945 and after

Figure 24 A Polish szopka

Figure 25 A Polish rod puppet from the State Theatre Lalka, Warsaw

the war re-opened his theatre which still presents puppet productions today.

One of Joseph Skupa's pupils, the late Jiří Trnka, won international acclaim for his puppet films. Although his early ventures in professional puppetry were a failure, his later outstanding work on cartoons, puppet films and book illustrations earned him the title of National Artist.

The greatest influence on the development of modern puppetry in Czechoslovakia is attributed to Professor Doctor Jan Malik, who was for forty years the Secretary-General of UNIMA, the international puppetry organisation. A holder of the State Prize Laureate, his career has covered the roles of author, editor, producer and director.

The puppet companies are subsidised by the State and since 1948 the puppet theatre has enjoyed equal status with the live theatre. Puppeteers sit on the State Theatre Council. A Chair of Puppetry has been established and a four-year course is offered for training in all aspects of puppet theatre.

For the past twenty years, the town of Chrudim has held annual festivals for amateur puppeteers and 1971 saw the establishment of an

20

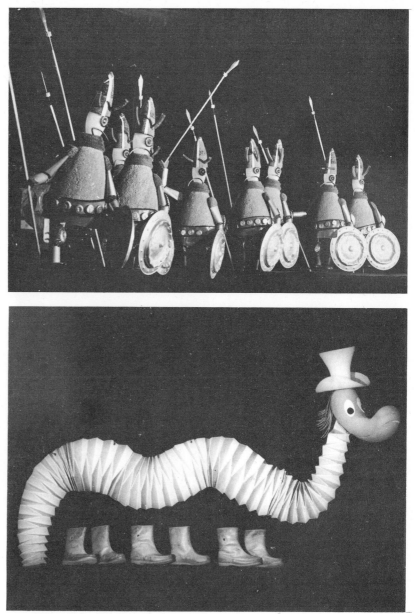

Figure 28 Kidnapping in Tiutiulistan *by the Polish State Puppet Theatre Guliwer, Warsaw*

Figure 29 *Kasparek of Czechoslovakia*

Figure 30 *A puppet from the Black Theatre of Prague of Hana and Joseph Lamka*

international museum, the *Musée international de la marionnette* (MIM). Already a notable collection of exhibits is being built up and this promises to be one of the finest collections of puppets and related material in the world.

Russia

Russia's only puppeteers before the Revolution were the travelling Petrouchka men, the last of whom, Ivan Zaitsev, died in 1930. Zaitsev was the first puppeteer to receive the Soviet title Merited Artist.

Early experiments in puppetry had an emphasis on performances for children but today there are presentations for audiences of all ages.

21

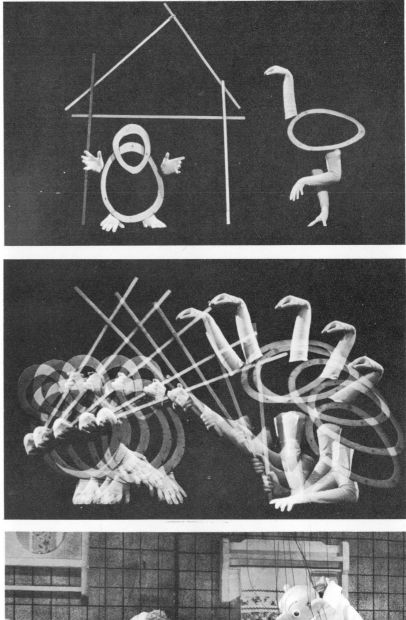

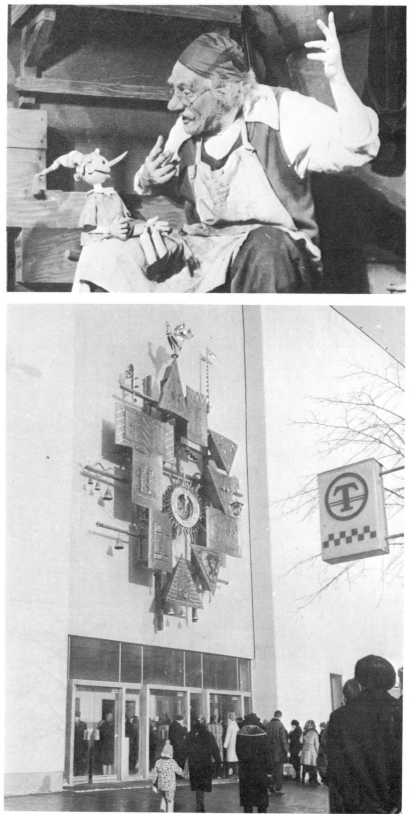

Figure 33 A scene from The Adventures of Burattino *by the State Central Puppet Theatre, Moscow*

Figure 34   Two characters from A Straw Hat *by the State Central Puppet Theatre*

Figure 35   The new State Central Puppet Theatre, Moscow

Figure 36   The Turkish Karagöz (left) and Hacivad

Especially through the influence of Richard Teschner of Austria, the Russian interest in rod puppetry grew and Russia is considered to be one of the leading countries for this type of presentation.

The finest puppeteer Russia has ever had is generally thought to be Sergei Obraztsov, an expert in all forms of puppetry. Originally a teacher and actor, then solo puppet performer, in 1931 he became the Director of the first State Puppet Theatre, now the State Central Theatre in Moscow which is one of the largest puppet companies in the world with some 350 members.

The State Central Theatre, still directed by Obraztsov, has recently been rehoused in a magnificently equipped puppet theatre with two auditoriums—one for children and one for adults. There are two performances a day for children and evening performances for adults. This theatre also has a museum and is now a training centre for actors and directors.

Throughout the Soviet Union there are over a hundred permanent State puppet theatres as well as the thousands of puppeteers with travelling companies.

Puppets in Asia

In general, puppetry in the Eastern countries is very unlike that of Europe. The Asian puppet theatre often has close connections with human dance and drama and frequently draws upon classical literature or religious sources for its themes.

There is a great variety of puppetry styles in Asia. Every type of puppet is to be found and there are many unique types of presentation.

Turkey

The traditional Turkish puppet show is a shadow puppet knock-about comedy. The plays centre around a Punch-like character called Karagöz ('Dark-Eye').

The Turkish shadow figures are only six to twelve inches high, and the screen is about five feet wide. The figures are traditionally made of tough camelskin, specially treated to make it translucent and brightly coloured with dyes, but modern materials for construction are now to be found as well.

The origins of these puppets is unknown but it is possible that they came from India or Arabia. The script, like that of Punch, is traditional and was never written down. The plays are presented most frequently during Ramadan; for twenty-eight days there is a different Karagöz play each night.

India

All forms of puppetry are practised in India, the type varying with the area. An interesting style of marionette is to be found in Southern India: the figures are made of wood and are approximately four feet high with an unusual stringing arrangement. The main control, to which head and waist strings are attached, consists of a cloth-covered ring which fits onto the puppeteer's head. Rods held by the puppeteer are used to control the puppet's hands.

In contrast, the *Kathputli* marionettes of Rajasthan have a very simple control. The puppets have carved heads and bodies with stuffed cloth arms; instead of legs, they have long skirts which twirl and sway expressively. The control is a single loop of string, one end of which is attached to the puppet's head, the other to the back of the waist. Occasionally an extra string is added to control the arms. The Rajasthani marionettes have high-pitched voices produced by the performers speaking through bamboo and leather reeds.

The *tolu bommalata* (there are a variety of spellings) shadow puppets are found in the Andhra region and may be the origin of the Javanese *wayang kulit* puppets. The name *tolu bommalata* means *the play of high-fashioned toys*, the figures being made of intricately pierced deer or goatskin, treated to make it translucent, coloured with dyes and held by split cane. The arms are controlled by thin canes whilst the legs hang free. The figures are all over five feet high, relative size being governed by the character's importance. The shadow screen is usually made of two saris, fastened together and attached to poles.

Figure 37 An old Rajasthani
Pan *figure*

The plays, frequently performed throughout the night every night for a few months, are often taken from the Hindu epics, *The Mahabharata* and *The Ramayana*, both written some two thousand years ago. These great works lend themselves to puppet productions, containing as they do supernatural beings, gods, magical monkeys and other similar ingredients for successful puppet entertainment.

In recent years the traditional styles of puppetry have been practised increasingly by part-time puppeteers. As elsewhere, puppetry's educational possibilities have been recognised and puppets are used in the villages to teach the people about health and hygiene as well as to entertain.

Burma

Puppetry in Burma is given full recognition as a serious form of art. The traditional puppets are marionettes which may have as many as fifty or sixty strings, although the majority have far fewer. The characters of the traditional show are always the same; they include votaresses,

Figure 38 A Rajasthani marionette operated by only one loop of string

Figure 39 An Indian shadow figure from Andhra

a horse, two elephants (one black, one white), a tiger, a monkey, parrots, a necromancer, a yogi, a king, a prince, a princess, two prince regents (one white faced, one red faced), four ministers, an astrologer, a hermit, clowns and ogres.

The stage is a bamboo platform with curtains to hide the puppeteers. The acting area is divided into a court and a forest, one on either side of the stage. The characters are referred to as either 'left' or 'right' puppets, depending on which side of the stage they take; the 'left' are ugly and evil whilst the 'right' are good and honourable.

The plays number hundreds, drawing mainly upon the *jatakas*, the stories of the Buddha's previous incarnations, either as animal or human. They are concerned chiefly with virtuous life and constantly stress moral retribution.

These marionette productions were created and developed by U Thaw, a Minister of Royal Entertainment in the eighteenth century. They have had a considerable influence on the human dance drama, to the extent that the dancer's skill is measured by his ability to recreate convincingly the movements of the puppet.

27

Figure 40 Burmese National Dancers and Puppets: the skill of the dancer is measured by his ability to recreate convincingly the movements of the puppet

Thailand

Thailand's form of shadow play, the *Nang*, is said to have come originally from India. There are no individually operated puppets, the characters and scene being cut in the same large piece of hide which is fastened to two poles. These scenes are held against a large white screen and the shadows cast by firelight are used to accompany the narration of the story. Although the characters remain static, the performers holding the 'scenes' dance.

The plays are based upon Thai dance dramas and musical accompaniment is provided by percussion and stringed instruments.

A similar form of presentation is also found in Cambodia though now mainly on special occasions only.

Vietnam

Vietnam has for centuries used all the familiar types of puppet and also one that is unique—the 'water puppet'. Each puppet is between thirty

and thirty-six inches high and is manipulated by a long bamboo pole with a complexity of strings. A raft forms the stage, which floats on a lake. The puppeteers operate the puppets from approximately twenty to thirty feet away and often have to stand in the water, behind a screen, for many hours whilst performing. The audience watches these presentations from the waterside.

For the plays, the puppeteers have drawn upon traditional material—often religious or didactic—but now more modern themes such as warfare and resistance are blended with the traditional ones as propaganda and morale boosters.

China

Chinese puppets are usually small but very elaborate. The marionettes are made of wood, ivory, or bone and sometimes have as many as forty strings, though this is not common. The use of rod puppets is increasing as a result of Russian influence.

An old style of glove puppet presentation, *Ku Li Tzu* ('the Coolie

Figure 41 The Fishgirl and the Official: 17th century Chinese shadow puppets

Show'), is still in existence. The tiny puppets perform in a small booth styled like a house; it is fastened on the end of a pole that is used to carry it about. For the show, this fitup is propped against a wall and drapes attached to the booth are released so that they hang down and hide the puppeteer. Sometimes the drapes are tied around the puppeteer's ankles.

There appear to be two main traditional types of shadow puppet: the Peking shadows, intricately made of leather from the belly of a donkey and just over twelve inches high; and the Cantonese shadows which are larger and of thicker leather.

The leather is treated to make it translucent and then dyed to produce delicate colouring. The faces, which are stylised, are always in profile. Those of heroes, rulers and women are mostly cut away, leaving only a thin outline, whilst those of other characters have only a few features cut away. With the large number of characters in each play, the puppet maker must be able to produce a great variety of heads that are immediately distinguishable.

Each figure is controlled by three wires (held in bamboo rods); the wire that supports the figure is fastened by thread to the front of the neck and is held by the operator in one hand while, with his other hand, he holds the rods that control the puppet's hands. Heads are often interchangeable. Limbs hang freely, usually in two sections with joints fastened by knotted thread.

The shadow screen is made of white translucent cloth or strong paper

Figure 42   A 'Good Honest Dragon' (Chinese)

approximately five feet wide and three feet high. It is supported by a framework of bamboo poles with bright drapes hung around the screen. Scenery is extremely simple, and symbolic rather than realistic. Light, traditionally from lanterns, is increasingly provided by electricity.

A shadow puppet company usually consists of up to eight performers, some also acting as musicians. Their plays are akin to the classical theatre's productions, not raucous comedy like Punch and Judy. Traditional themes from Chinese history and legends still survive, but contemporary plays contain much propaganda with workers and peasants among the heroes.

Japan

Japan's puppets are centuries old, having originated, probably, in Korea. Originally they were used mainly for religious presentations but by the middle of the sixteenth century puppet shows had assumed sufficient dramatic form to draw audiences with performances of *noh* plays and *kyogen* comic interludes at religious festivals.

By the middle of the eighteenth century *Bunraku* puppetry completely overshadowed the *kabuki* as popular entertainment and the human theatre regained its position only by emulating the puppet drama. Towards the end of the century, however, the puppet theatres went out of fashion and most closed. Today small shows of all types (drawing upon Japanese and European material) are to be found in the provinces, and the Bunraku puppets still survive, aided by various subsidies.

Bunraku puppets are usually between three and four feet high and are manipulated by three men. The leading operator, the *omo-zukai*, with his left hand holds the puppet in front of his body and works the head, mouth, eyes and eyebrows; with his right hand he operates the right arm and hand of the puppet. He has two assistants: the *hidari-zukai*

Figure 43   A puppet from the
Bunraku Puppet Theatre of Japan

Figure 44   A Bunraku
performance

who works the left hand and arm, and the *ashi-zukai*, the junior assistant who manipulates the legs.

All three work with perfect co-ordination and precise timing. Usually they all wear black gowns (*kurogo*) and black hoods, the black costume traditionally representing invisibility or 'nothingness'. In some presentations the main manipulator may wear a brightly coloured robe but, except in gay dance dramas, this is usually regarded as unorthodox.

Less important characters are usually simpler to operate and may have only one or two puppeteers. The Bunraku puppeteers only manipulate the puppets and do not speak. In addition to certain realistic movements there are exaggerated and stylised actions that are unique to Bunraku and detailed rules and forms to be adhered to in conveying all emotions.

The plays presented are often by Chikamatsu Monzaemon (1653-1725). He is said to have been the finest dramatist Japan has ever had, specialising in *joruri* plays for the puppet theatre. As the puppets act, the *joruri* (a story in the form of a dramatic epic poem) is told by the *tayu* (the narrator). He explains all the dramatic elements: the story, the action and the personality and psychology of the characters of the play. Musical accompaniment and atmosphere are provided by a *samisen* player.

The roles of *tayu* and *samisen* do not exist just to support the puppets' acting: each stands in its own right and Bunraku depends upon the perfect harmony of these arts with that of the puppet.

Java

Javanese puppetry is famous for its beautiful *wayang* figures. The term *wayang* is a general term referring to the theatrical performance and is qualified by a further word which defines the particular type of puppet.

Figure 45 Wayang golek *wooden rod puppets of Java*

A great variety of presentations is encompassed by this term; the main ones are as follows.

Wayang golek, wooden rod puppets. This style of puppet probably came to Java from Bengal with the spread of Hinduism.

Wayang klitik, flat, wooden rod puppets with leather arms. The figures are carved in low relief and exquisitely painted. This type of presentation is not often seen today.

Wayang kulit, shadow puppets, the most common of all the *wayang* figures. They are about two feet high and are made from delicately patterned buffalo hide, the design being chiselled out of the leather and then the whole figure painted and gilded. Every aspect of the puppet's design is set down by tradition and is related to the character portrayed. Thus the audience gathers all the necessary information about the puppet's character simply from its appearance. Even the angle of the head is significant.

The Javanese puppeteer, the *dalang*, presents his shadow show from dusk to sunrise. The role of the *dalang* has been likened to that of the

Figure 46 Arjuna, a Javanese
wayang kulit *shadow puppet*

priest as in Java puppets are thought to be the incarnation of ancestral spirits, and thus the *dalang* is a medium between these spirits and his audience. He manipulates the puppets, speaks all the dialogue, and conducts the *gamelan*, the percussion orchestra which sits behind him.

The *dalang's* cotton screen, or *kelir*, is supported by bamboo sticks and is about five feet high and up to fifteen feet long. Two long stems of banana plant, placed along the bottom of the screen, are used to hold the puppets' rods when they are off stage, the good characters on the right, the evil on the left.

Until recently it was traditional for the men of the audience to sit behind the *dalang* and watch the actual puppets whilst the women sat in front of the screen and watched the shadows cast by the light of an oil lamp on the beautiful figures.

Puppets in Britain and America

Great Britain

Puppets were known in England by the fourteenth century, possibly introduced by French entertainers in the thirteenth century. By the time of Elizabeth, marionettes and shadow puppets were in use, although glove puppets were the most popular as they were easy to pack and carry around. During this period vagrancy was a serious problem and acts were passed which made these wanderers criminal. Actors and puppeteers were included unless they could find a patron amongst the nobility or were granted a royal licence.

In 1642, with the outbreak of the Civil War, the theatres in England were closed. Puppet performances, however, were not restricted. Thus the eighteen years of the Parliament were a period of unsurpassed popularity for the puppet theatre.

When Charles II returned to England in 1660 entertainers from the continent, including puppeteers, came with him. These puppeteers brought with them a character called Polichinelle, originally based on the Italian Pulcinello. In England Polichinelle became Punchinello, a name soon shortened to Punch. At that time Punch was a marionette, not a glove puppet.

By the early eighteenth century puppetry was a fashionable entertainment for the wealthy, the puppet show being one of the places at which to be 'seen'. Punch, by then an established and popular character, was included in all manner of plays and had now acquired a wife, Joan, later to become Judy. Later in the century, when interest in puppetry was flagging, the Italian *fantoccini* marionettes made a timely arrival. With their tricks and 'transformations', the *fantoccini* plays gave fresh impetus to the art of puppetry. This was accompanied by new interest in shadow play through the influence of the French *ombres Chinoises*.

Figure 49 The Cures: collapsible clowns from a 19th century English troupe (probably the Tiller-Clowes)

By the end of the eighteenth century the novelty of tricks and transformations began to wear off and Mr Punch came back into the limelight, now as a glove puppet performing for parties and in the streets. By 1825 Punch was at the height of his popularity and the story he played had taken on a standard basic form. Until now puppetry had been an adult entertainment but by 1820 the puppeteers were catering for children.

Marionette performances were still to be seen but as the permanent theatres closed they, like the glove puppets, took to the streets. Their success here was only short-lived and they soon performed in the pleasure gardens, following the example of Punch and Judy for whom this had proved to be a profitable venture. Also to be seen after dark were the street *galanty* shows, a form of shadow show, presented in a Punch and Judy booth, but with a white sheet across the proscenium, illuminated by candlelight.

The travelling marionette companies now took up the melodramas of the live theatre as well as presenting the old traditional tricks in pantomime-style shows. Toward the end of the nineteenth century the

puppets' popularity had risen once again and reached a point when England's marionette troupes were considered to be the best in the world. Great companies toured the globe with wagons carrying large theatres for elaborate productions. This popularity was to decline again, however, with the arrival of the cinema.

The twentieth century has seen yet another revival, and with the advancement of scientific knowledge there has been a parallel development in the techniques and materials used in puppetry, both in construction and in presentation. Interest in the toy and model theatres in the early part of the century led to the formation of the British Model Theatre Guild in 1925 by H. W. Whanslaw and Gerald Morice. This

37

Figure 58   Unicyclist by John Thirtle (the Playboard Puppets)

organisation, which subsequently became the British Puppet and Model Theatre Guild, is still very active.

In 1943 the Educational Puppetry Association was formed. Considerable credit for the success of the E.P.A. must be given to A. R. Philpott (the puppeteer 'Pantopuck'), a man of many talents and a leading authority on all aspects of puppetry, and his wife, Violet, whose own *Cap and Bells* company presents some of the most charming, lively and imaginative puppetry that can be seen today.

There is also a flourishing British Centre of UNIMA, the international organisation. The president of UNIMA is Jan Bussell, a first-class puppeteer and Chairman of the British section. Jan and his wife Ann Hogarth, regarded by many as the finest marionette manipulator in the world, have been presenting their *Hogarth Puppets* for over forty years.

It is highly likely that the very near future will see the establishment of a National Puppet Theatre Centre, which will provide many facilities including a puppet museum, workshops, library and a theatre with puppet entertainment of the highest international standard.

Figure 59   A scene from The Winkleburg Armourer *by Gordon Murray for BBC television*

Figure 60   Melody Angel from Captain Scarlet and the Mysterons

Figure 61 Arctic Adventure, *a* Joe 90 *episode*

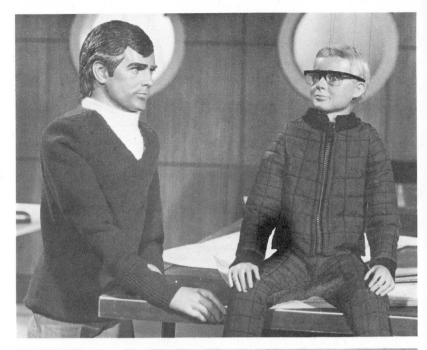

Figure 62 Camberwick Green *a 'stop-action' television series by the Gordon Murray Puppets*

Figure 63 Wispa the Wizard by *the Da Silva Puppet Company, Huntingdon*

Figure 64 The Fisherboy from The Arabian Nights *by the Theatre of Puppets*

Figure 65 Chinese Kites, *an item from* Playspace *by the Theatre of Puppets*

There are two permanent puppet theatres of note in Britain: the *Harlequin Theatre* at Colwyn Bay, directed by Eric Bramall and Christopher Somerville, experts in puppet technique and manipulation, and John Wright's *Little Angel Theatre* at Islington in London. The *Little Angel* has been the training ground for a number of well-known puppeteers and here the beautiful presentations cater successfully for both children and adults. Puppet theatres have also been established within recreation halls and arts centres, the most active of these being that directed by John Blundall in the Midlands Arts Centre for Young People, Birmingham.

It is impossible to mention all the puppet performers who deserve acknowledgement of their skills and talents. They range from 'suitcase puppeteers', who can pack all of their equipment into one or two cases, to those who are fortunate enough to have their own permanent theatre. Their presentations vary from the old traditional acts, such as Punch and Judy and the fantoccini-type shows to pantomimes, plays, ballet, opera and experiments in modern art forms.

Others are actively engaged in making puppet films, especially for television, where puppets have cut themselves a fairly large slice of viewing time. Apart from educational television, they are to be seen frequently in the programmes for young children, in the 'space-age' series, often referred to as *supermarionation*, and in variety shows.

The tremendous possibilities of puppetry, not only as an art form but also as an educational and therapeutic agent, have been realised in recent years, and are being thoroughly explored by teachers, social and medical workers and many professional bodies.

43

The first American puppeteers were the Indians, the puppets they used probably a development of the mask. The Northwest Coast Indians are known to have used beautifully carved cedar wood masks in religious ceremonies of a dramatic nature. The Hopi Indians of the American Southwest also used both human and animal figures in forms of puppet drama. In these and many other societies a development from the mask to the marionette may be clearly discerned.

There is no one tradition that typifies American puppetry for it has drawn upon the puppetry styles of many nations. When in 1524 Cortes went to Honduras in search of gold there was a puppeteer in his entourage. The first English-style marionette show that can be traced in America was presented by a puppeteer named Holt in New York in 1738 and was *The Adventures of Harlequin and Scaramouche*.

When Maximilian became Emperor of Mexico in 1864, Guignol was introduced to the American continent. In the nineteenth century the Greeks came to North America with Karaghiosis, and immigrants from all parts of Europe brought with them their own styles and traditions. Such were the influences upon American puppetry, but the presentations were very much 'patriotic' affairs, with the Greek showmen playing in Greek and for Greeks, and so on. Only with the third and fourth generations did the puppeteers begin to play to audiences of a more international flavour.

Towards the end of the nineteenth century a few American puppeteers began to gain international recognition. Probably the most outstanding of these was Walter Deaves. One of his world tours lasted seven years and it was he who developed the idea of having an elaborate puppet theatre, with boxes for the puppet audience and a puppet orchestra, in which to present puppet shows on the vaudeville stage. In fact, the whole fitup could fill a live theatre stage.

By the twentieth century it was recognised that puppetry was capable of being a much more intellectual form of artistic expression than it had previously been and European fashions influenced the puppeteers to produce plays rather than variety. One of the foremost performers of the age was Tony Sarg (1880-1942), the son of a German consul. Sarg set out as an illustrator in London, took up puppetry and moved to New York in 1915. Although he designed and operated his puppets, they were in fact made by other puppeteers. His productions were so successful that the majority of American puppeteers followed his lead.

Remo Bufano (1894-1948), born in New York of Italian parents, was one of the experimental puppeteers who developed their own individual styles during this period. Probably his most successful creations were the giant marionettes which he designed and made for Robert Edmond Jones' production of *Oedipus Rex*.

Bufano was a travelling performer with no permanent theatre, like most puppeteers of the period. By the late twenties there were about a dozen large travelling companies in North America but most were destined to close with the Depression.

One of the leading puppeteers this century was Paul McPharlin, a key figure in the formation of the Puppeteers of America organisation

Figure 66   Giant Bird by Majorie Batchelder McPharlin for Weapons of Lightning, *a Navajo Indian play by Virginia Lee Comer*

Figure 67   The Kuklapolitans by Burr Tillstrom

Figure 68   The Frost Giant and the Spirit of Spring from Holiday on Strings *by Bil Baird*

Figure 69   A scene from Ali Baba and the Forty Thieves *by Bil Baird*

Figure 70   Zsa-Zsa and Ali
Baba in Ali Baba and the Forty
Thieves

in 1937. He wrote *The History of the Puppet Theatre in America* which
was completed by his wife, Marjorie Batchelder McPharlin, also an
accomplished puppeteer and a Vice-President of UNIMA.

After the Second World War, American puppeteers began to delve
into the possibilities of 'modern puppetry'. Many of the large puppet
companies had disappeared but a new army of solo performers emerged,
often performing in full view of the audience in the now familiar
cabaret-style or open-stage presentations.

Developments were made in educational and therapeutic puppetry
and many puppeteers, among them Bil Baird and Burr Tillstrom, kept
pace with modern trends in television, advertising and films.

Burr Tillstrom with his creations Kukla and Ollie began making
television shows—*The Kuklapolitans*—in 1939. He was among the first
of the television performers and went from strength to strength. Today
the Kuklapolitans still hold their position in American puppetry.

Bil Baird at one time toured with Tony Sarg, then formed his own
show which he has directed for nearly forty years, performing for night
clubs, films and television. He has established himself as an international
puppeteer of high repute and his book, *The Art of the Puppet*, is a
magnificent work.

One of the biggest impacts on television puppetry in recent years has
been made by Jim Henson, a Past President of the Puppeteers of
America, with his *Muppets*—a cross between monsters and puppets.
They are a central feature of *Sesame Street*, a programme intended for
children of pre-school age, more particularly those who are culturally
deprived, but watched by viewers of all ages. It is a noisy, fast-moving,
humorous way of conveying basic concepts from numbers and counting,
to good social habits. The show uses human actors, life-sized puppets
and cartoon characters. The script appears 'ad-libbed' but is carefully
contrived and the presentation techniques are a breakaway from traditional television puppetry. *Sesame Street* is now seen in fifty countries
and has been a success in all of them.

Many puppeteers have developed spectacular and impressive styles
of live presentation, like Daniel Llords, the solo marionettist, talented
showman and Past President of the Puppeteers of America. With his
famous *Llords International Concertheatre for Adults*, Daniel Llords has

Figure 71   Two soul-less characters from Stravinsky's The Firebird, *as conceived by Daniel Llords for his* Concertheatre

made many world tours and represented the Puppeteers of America at international festivals.

This, of course, is only a part of the American scene today, for the United States also has its 'suitcase puppeteers', party performers, open-air shows, and all the other styles familiar in Western Europe. There is still to be found the great variety of styles which reflects international influence upon American puppetry.

3 Puppetry in education

In recent years the considerable attention given to the possibilities of 'education through art' has made puppetry a very popular subject in schools.

Nursery and infant schools (four to seven years)

Involvement in puppetry, which affords children a chance to give their imaginations free rein, to enact and come to terms with experiences of everyday life, may help considerably towards their satisfactory emotional and social development. Acting through puppetry a child may shed many of his inhibitions, portraying, perhaps, what he would most like to be or the embodiment of his most terrible fears.

Some teachers, when introducing young children to puppet making, prefer to start a few at a time, letting others join in gradually (but the constructional side must not be allowed to drag on for too long). Others prefer to drum up enthusiasm and start the whole class together in one concerted effort. If the method of construction is suited to the capabilities of the children they should need the minimum of help. This is not to say that they will need no help, for they will almost certainly need somebody with whom to discuss methods, particularly if they come up with constructional ideas of their own, as often they do.

'Junk-box' or cloth puppets are ideally suited to the needs of young children. They are easy to make and give great scope for individuality of expression in design and use of materials.

Some children may not want a 'stage' but others may like to be hidden, sometimes because of shyness but often because it makes the show seem more professional and gives them a feeling of importance. The mere fact of there being a division between operators and audience has a great significance. A table top can make a very acceptable stage. Equally well, a stage can be cut from a cardboard box and stood on a table, or a clothes horse covered with a few drapes. The latter is particularly satisfactory as it is easy to erect, yet probably feels the most authentic of simple fitups. A proper stage can be made and how this is done is discussed in the appropriate 'presentation' sections.

At this age children usually like to perform plays—not scripted, of course—on themes of their everyday experience, or of fairy tales and other favourite stories. Their 'ad-libbed' performances are often full of vitality. But to whom shall the performances be given? It is usually a matter of small groups performing for their own pleasure or to the rest

Figure 1   John, four years, with simple rod puppets

Figure 2 (Below) Infant school children with 'sock' glove puppets

Figure 3 (Right) An impromptu glove puppet performance by nine-year-olds

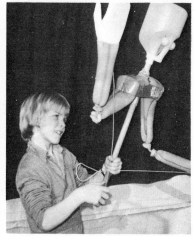

Figure 4 Luke manipulates Horace, a junk-box rod puppet

Figure 5 Mask puppets made by children in an Indian village near Madras

of the class, but sometimes it is feasible to perform to other classes. Other younger children will be filled with awe by the efforts of their elders but older children may expect more in terms of action and plot than the young performers can provide.

The junior school (seven to eleven years)

In the junior school puppetry may be used in a number of ways. It may be a small group activity with the children performing just for their own enjoyment or to the class; or part of a class project; or perhaps a big production to entertain the whole school or parents.

49

Sometimes puppetry may bring together a number of different subjects such as English, drama, poetry, art, music and social and environmental studies.

With project work, puppetry may be used as a means of sharing the findings of research or for a play connected with the topic. It can also be used very effectively to teach foreign languages, English for immigrant children (children who are inhibited about venturing to speak in a foreign

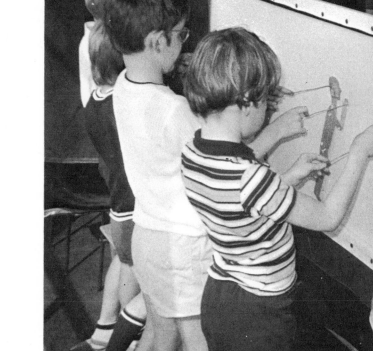

Figure 7 Junior school children operating shadow puppets with illumination from a window behind the screen

Figure 8 Mark and Diana manipulate junk-box marionettes with only four strings

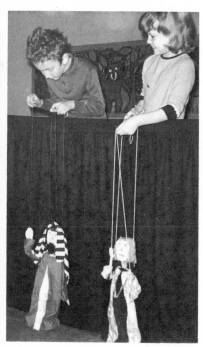

tongue will often do so more freely through a puppet) and to convey the principles of civics, road safety, hygiene, dental health, etc.

Whatever the prime purpose of a puppet production it will always in a practical sense involve aspects of English, drama and art.

All types of puppet—glove, rod, shadow and marionettes—can be made by children of this age. Teachers tend to favour glove puppets, but rather because of tradition than because these puppets have any inherent advantages over the others.

Frequently it suits the requirements of the situation to make junk-box puppets. Children will provide endless ideas for utilising odds and ends but at this age their inventiveness often outstrips their abilities, so discussion with the teacher is very important. At the same time, requirements for some special effect (such as fire) provide a challenge for the children's ingenuity.

As to preparing the performance, there is a range of possibilities: the children may make their puppets and then 'act' impromptu; if the play is to be performed for a special occasion, they may prepare it by impromptu acting until a situation with good dramatic possibilities arises, then work on this theme; a child's story may provide a rough outline and the children can explore the possibilities of this for a play; a

51

Figure 9   The Laundryman and his Wife from The Secret of Fire, *a play by ten-year-olds*

published story may be adapted, involving a process of selection of important points and developments to obtain a scenario; or a child or group of children may script a play. If the play is to be learned word-for-word it may lack the vitality which free speech gives, even within a limited situation. Moreover, forgotten lines and technical hitches can result in terrible confusion if the performers are not used to improvisation.

These difficulties may be surmounted by using a tape-recording but the problems of making a good recording in classroom conditions and the disadvantage of ruling out improvisation and variation make this a method not to be recommended. In addition, the recorded voice does not have the same power to hold the attention, particularly of young children.

The number of puppets in any show is bound to be limited; there must be room on stage for the puppets to move and room back stage for the manipulators to handle them. It is not necessary, though, to have a large number of puppets to involve the whole class. The children who are not performing can take care of the scenery, props, lights, coloured filters, sound and visual effects, curtains and background music; and a stage manager, or two, are necessary to direct operations. In a fairly elaborate production there is no need to invent jobs to occupy spare helpers.

It is possible of course to have one child manipulating the puppet and another speaking the part, but this is not recommended as a way of involving more children, nor indeed for any other reason. The manipulators should be truly 'involved' in the play and this is much more likely if they speak the parts they perform. The movement of the figures and their speech will be far more expressive.

If, nevertheless, it is intended to have separate speakers and manipulators, it is most important that the speakers should *see* the characters on the stage or speech and action may easily become disunited.

It is very important always to be aware of, and explore, the full potential of puppetry in any situation and not to fall back on formal and stereotyped methods, situations and figures. The great value of puppetry for children is that it gives them opportunity to express themselves and allows them to explore materials and techniques, and also that it is fun.

It is in the hands of the children themselves that the true value of puppetry in education lies.

The secondary school (eleven and over)

Puppetry in secondary schools has previously been largely an out-of-school activity but its value as a means of bringing together children of differing abilities, talents and ages is now fairly widely recognised.

At this age children are able to take advantage of the tremendous scope for experimentation that puppetry offers, with endless possibilities for lighting, design, sound effects, characterisation, etc. The small scale of all these activities has the great advantage not only of being suitable for children but also of making the activities considerably cheaper.

Topical sketches of school life (for which rod and rod-hand puppets are ideal) are popular for this age. Shadow puppets provide excellent opportunity for experimentation with shape, colour and 'effects', and 'variety' acts with marionettes are amusing. For plays, all sorts of puppets can be used.

Colleges of education (teacher training colleges)

In colleges of education puppetry may be studied within a curriculum course concerned with methods of teaching a particular subject or as part of a main course such as Art and Crafts or Drama. It is a popular topic for a special study or thesis within Art, Drama, Art of Movement and English courses as it is often closely related to aspects of these. Such studies would be much more interesting and worthwhile if the information were more frequently obtained by personal creative experiments in puppetry rather than taken from books.

In considering puppetry as an educational tool, we have already seen how it lends itself to being incorporated in the teaching of many subjects

Figure 10   An African teacher displaying puppets made from local materials at a course conducted by Dora Beacham of the Educational Puppetry Association

Figure 11   A puppet head made entirely of banana fibre by an African student

and how it furthers the integration of the curriculum and stimulates interest and creativity. However, it must be remembered that, from the child's point of view, it is puppetry itself that is the attraction.

Before embarking on a teaching practice, students often ask for 'information about puppetry' so that they can 'teach it to the children'. It must be remembered that it is an art that is acquired or learned rather than taught and, for it to be of maximum value, the children should be given the opportunity to put into practice their own ideas. The student teacher should be prepared to give advice and discuss methods; the best way to equip himself for this is to spend a few hours trying various materials and types of puppet at quite a simple level (especially 'junk-box' puppets). This will foster a better understanding of both the nature of the puppet and the practical problems for the children.

It is also useful for students to make a simple stage. Developing a stage to meet one's particular requirements and overcoming the problems that arise is a valuable exercise important to the art of presentation.

4 The puppet head

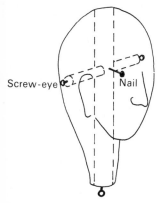

Figure 1   A dowelling 'cross' built into the head

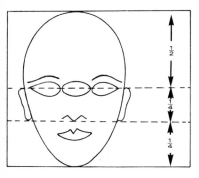

Figure 2   A guide to suitable proportions for the head. Top of ears align with eyes. Bottom of ears align with nose. The eyes are approximately one eye's width apart

The techniques discussed in this chapter may be used to make heads for marionettes, rod puppets or glove puppets.

If masks are to be used—to show change of character or the process of ageing for example—these can be made by casting, rubber being a particularly suitable medium.

Note   If a head is to be used for a marionette, the ears should be strong enough for attaching head strings to them. If they are not (or if it is a cloth or rubber marionette), build a dowelling 'cross' into the head. This cross consists of a large dowel with a hole drilled across it to accommodate a smaller dowel which is glued and nailed in place (*figure 1*). This provides strong fixtures for three screw-eyes: one to join the neck to the body and one behind each ear for head strings.

Proportions for the head

The head can be divided into four approximately equal parts: the chin to the nose; the nose to the eyes; the eyes to the hair line; the hair line to the top of the skull. Thus the eyes are approximately halfway between the chin and the top of the skull (although they are often in fact slightly nearer to the top). The top and bottom of the ears are normally in line with the top and bottom of the nose.

It is a common mistake to make the eyes too high in the head or too close together, foreheads too low and ears too high or too small for the head. Ears should be studied from the side and from behind: they contribute to characterisation more than is generally realised.

These guide lines to proportions for the head are not intended as anything more than a basis on which to work. As with the overall proportions of a puppet (and a human being), it is the variations from the norm which are usually most significant. For example, the eyes are shown as approximately one eye's width apart, but the spacing in fact depends upon the width of the nose and the characterisation required. The age of a character affects the proportions of the head, and the addition of hair can completely change its apparent shape.

When considering head proportions, pay special attention to the bulking of hair on the head. Keep this in mind from the initial stages of head making, as the shape of the skull may need to be related to the bulk of the 'hair'. This contributes to the eventual size and shape of the head and, obviously, thick fur and dyed string will have different influences upon size, shape and, therefore, character.

55

Figure 3/1 A head for a marionette

Figure 3/2 A head for a glove puppet

Figure 3/3 A head for a rod puppet

A sock or stocking head

Take a sock or stocking and stuff it with *either* an old tennis ball, *or* a piece of fabric or foam rubber. (Foam rubber may cause a lumpy surface if the pieces are too large.)

If the head is intended for a marionette, knot the sock and then cut it off at the heel (*figure 3/1*); if for a glove or rod puppet, cut off the sock at the heel then glue and tie it round a conical cardboard neck tube or a rod (*figures 3/2* and *3/3*).

Stitch or glue on features.

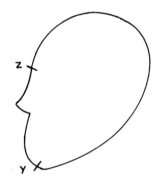

A felt head

Cut out two side pieces (*figure 4/1*) and a central gusset (*figure 4/2*). Place the two side pieces together and oversew them together between the chin and the top of the nose (Y to Z).

Make crossed cuts in the gusset as marked (*figure 4/2*). This is for the neck.

Oversew the gusset to the two side pieces (Y to Z) leaving a gap in the seam to allow the head to be stuffed.

Stuff the head with foam rubber (or any other suitable material) and stitch up the seam.

Make a conical tube of material for the neck (*figure 4/3*). Insert the narrow end into the head gusset and stitch it firmly in place.

Stitch or glue on features.

Figure 4/1   The felt side shape

Figure 4/2   The head gusset

Figure 4/3   The conical neck tube

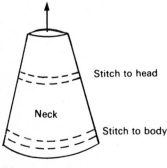

Into head

Stitch to head

Neck

Stitch to body

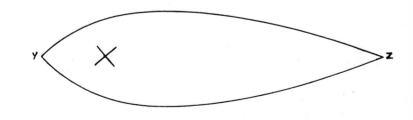

Figure 5   Wolf and Rabbit, cloth glove puppets by Ian Allen of the Playboard Puppets

Figure 6   Rosie Dear from To See the Queen: *a rod puppet with head and hands cut from foam rubber by Violet Philpott*

Figure 7/1   The cardboard shape with 'ribs' glued on

Figure 7/2   Braces glued between ribs

Foam rubber heads

Foam rubber heads can be made very quickly. If the features are to show up on stage bold modelling is essential.

Either build up the head in layers, glued together, around a rod or cardboard tube, *or* trim to shape a block of foam rubber using sharp scissors. Cut out the centre of the head through the bottom of the neck to accommodate a rod or cardboard tube.

Enhance the modelled features with felt, fur, pearl buttons, etc.

A cardboard head

This type of head is extremely strong and particularly suitable for animal characters.

Draw the profile shape on strong cardboard and cut it out.

Glue on cardboard 'ribs' to give the head its shape (*figure 7/1*). Strengthen the ribs with strips of cardboard glued on as braces (*figure 7/2*).

Cover the whole shape with layers of thin card (*figure 7/3*).

Cover the cardboard with cloth, fur, or a thin layer of plastic wood, having first smeared the card with glue. If moving eyes or mouth are desired (see pages 64, 65 for how to make these), cut away the cardboard as necessary.

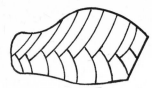

Figure 7/3 Shape covered with strips of thin card

A Polystyrene head

Polystyrene (Styrofoam) is an excellent medium for the puppeteer as it is very light. Blocks of it can be shaped into heads, and even large hands, by melting or cutting it. Be sure to use fire-resistant Polystyrene.

Make the basic shape with a heat gun, a rasp, a hand saw or any hot implement. Carve finer details with a sharp craft knife.

Cover the surface of the Polystyrene with carpenter's pearl glue and small pieces of brown paper, or newspaper.

If the neck is to be hollow line it, too, with glue and paper.

Cover the last layer of paper with a coat of glue, then sand it.

Note Exercise care over choice of glues to be used with Polystyrene. Many glues will dissolve it.

Carving a head

Wood carving is an art in itself and the reader is recommended to consult books specifically concerned with the subject. A useful book is John Wright's *Your Puppetry* (Sylvan Press, London, 1951).

However, many puppeteers with no special knowledge of carving make beautiful wooden heads, having developed their own individual techniques through practice. One needs only a few sharp knives (or a small craft knife with interchangeable blades), a selection of small files and glasspaper. With the softer woods a considerable amount of modelling may be done with glasspaper. The illustrations (*figure 8*) show the main stages often followed in carving a head.

Suitable woods to use are lime, birch, pear, holly, mahogany, sycamore and, today, jelutong is a particularly popular choice.

Figure 8 Carving a head

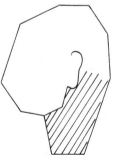
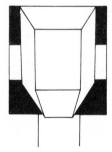

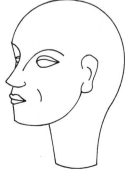

Figure 9 Rapunzel, a carved marionette from the Little Angel Marionette Theatre, London

Figure 10 Grossmutter
Figure 11 Mephisto
Carved puppets by Frieder Simon, the Larifari Theatre, DDR

Modelled and moulded heads

The following heads are all made by one or other of these two methods.
1 A head is modelled in plasticine (plastilene) and then covered in some material (eg plastic wood) that will form a shell. This is then split, the plasticine removed and the shells joined together again.
2 A head is modelled in plasticine and a plaster mould then made of it. The mould is used to cast a head in some suitable material such as rubber.

To model the head, make a modelling stand of suitable proportions by screwing together a dowel and a block of wood (*figure 12*) and model the basic form of the head around the dowel. It is unwise to model very fine detail as this will tend to be lost in the following process. Modelling can be heightened at the finishing stage.

Necks

Modelled heads for glove puppets must have bell-shaped necks (then the body fastens more securely) and the hole in the neck should be oval to accommodate two or three fingers (*figure 13/1*).

Marionette and rod puppet heads can be modelled either with necks, in which case there is a joint between neck and body (*figure 13/2*), or without necks, in which case there is a joint inside the head (*figure 13/3*). Occasionally the neck is made separately from head and body and there is a joint inside each (*figure 13/4*).

59

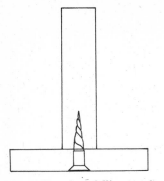

Figure 12   A modelling stand

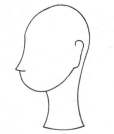

Figure 13/1   Neck for a glove puppet

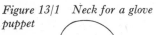

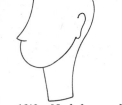

Figure 13/2   Neck for a rod puppet or marionette

Figure 13/3   Neck for a rod puppet or marionette

Figure 13/4   Neck for a marionette

A plastic wood head

Plastic wood is a pliable material which, when left exposed to the air, sets hard and can be cut, drilled, sanded, etc just like wood. It is easier to work with if you keep your fingers moist or smeared with petroleum jelly.

Cut out cardboard ears and fasten them in the plasticine model (*figure 14/1*). It is easier to build the ears on card and these solid ears are very strong. Smear the plasticine (but not the cardboard ears) with petroleum jelly to prevent the plastic wood sticking to it.

Cover the head with a fairly thick layer of plastic wood, applying it in small pieces (*figure 14/2*). When working on the ears, smear the cardboard with glue, then add the plastic wood. Model finer details with modelling tools or any other suitable implement (such as a small knife blade or even the end of a paintbrush).

When the plastic wood is dry (twenty-four hours is sufficient), cut open the head, making the cut behind the ears and over the top of the skull (*figure 14/3*).

After removing the plasticine, glue the two hollow shells together again. Any gaps that may be caused by the two shells shrinking at different rates can be filled in with plastic wood. Smooth the head with glasspaper.

Note   Not all glues can be used with plastic wood. Bostik No. 1 glue, a clear multi-purpose adhesive, or Sobo, a white resin glue, are both recommended.

A papier maché head

Make the head in exactly the same way as a plastic wood head.

To prepare the papier maché

Tear newspaper into very small pieces and soak them in a bucket of water. Rubbing the paper and heating the bucket will help the paper to disintegrate.

When all the paper has turned to pulp, drain off the excess water. Mix powder-paste with the pulp and add water to produce a consistancy like porridge.

After modelling the head, it may be warmed to dry it, but carefully and slowly. When dry, the head may be sanded lightly and cracks filled in with more pulp.

A plaster and bandage (or paste and paper) head

Make the head in the same way as a plastic wood head.

Cover the modelled head with either ordinary surgical bandage or book muslin (mull), using plaster filler as an adhesive, or thin paper stuck with cellular paste. Muslin is preferable to paper as it stretches over modelled detail more successfully.

First cover the plasticine head with overlapping 1 in squares of damp tissue paper. This will prevent sticking. Then apply 1 in squares of muslin or paper, the squares overlapping slightly. If muslin is used, two layers are enough; if paper, a minimum of four. Press each layer firmly into the previous one.

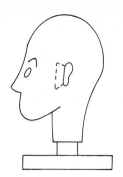

Figure 14/1 Plasticine model with cardboard ears

Figure 14/2 Model covered with plastic wood

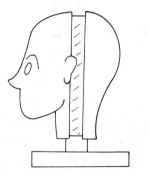

Figure 14/3 When dry, the head is cut open and the plasticine removed

When the plasticine has been removed glue together the two halves of the shell and cover with another layer of muslin or paper.

Detail can be built up with finely teazed cotton wool saturated in plaster filler and further shaped with a knife or glasspaper. This technique, also known as the *Alabastine* method, was evolved by Pantopuck (A. R. Philpott).

A Celastic head

This is made in the same way as a plastic wood head.

Celastic is the trade name of an impregnated woven cloth which can be bought by the yard in varying thicknesses. The name has become a general term used by puppeteers to describe all brands of this material. It is strong, unbreakable, waterproof, very light and fast drying.

Dip strips of Celastic in acetone or the Celastic medium and cover the plasticine model with them. If thick Celastic is used, butt the strips together rather than overlap them.

Whilst the first layer is still damp (but not sticky), add another layer. Continue until the required thickness is reached.

After removing the plasticine, join the shells with Celastic and acetone.

The head may be sanded. If this leaves a 'fuzz' on the head, apply a coat of lacquer and sand again when dry.

To cover any uneven patches paint on a thick cream of pumice powder mixed with lacquer and sand when dry.

If the Celastic medium is used, the head may be built up on a Polystyrene shape. The Polystyrene need not be removed. (N.B. Acetone dissolves Polystyrene.)

It is also possible to cast a Celastic head (see *A fibreglass head*, page 63).

A rubber head

This is made by casting the modelled head in liquid latex.

To make a plaster mould

Smear the plasticine model with petroleum jelly.

Put thin metal (eg tin) strips in the plasticine, over the head and down the sides in front of the ears. The strips should overlap each other by about $\frac{1}{8}$ in to form a fence (*figure 16/1*).

Mix up the plaster (adding the powder to the water), fairly thinly at first. A chemical action takes place and it will thicken very quickly.

Hold the back of the head in your hand and, working on the other half, scoop the liquid plaster out with a spoon and fill in all the hollows (*figure 16/2*). When it starts to set, the plaster will turn creamy; at this stage pour it all over the half of the head. The plaster should be about $1\frac{1}{2}$-2 in thick.

Allow this half to harden for about thirty minutes, then remove the metal strips with tweezers.

Make a few shallow holes in the clean edge left by removing the metal strips (*figure 16/3*).

Figure 15   Eagle Beak, a marionette with head made of plastic wood, by the author

Metal strips overlap each other

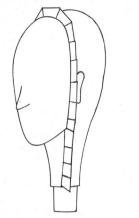

Figure 16/1   The plasticine model with metal strips inserted

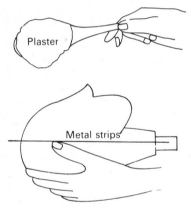

Figure 16/2   Making the first half of the plaster mould

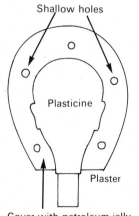

Figure 16/3   Making the second half of the mould

Cover the edge of the cast with petroleum jelly and take a cast of the other half of the head.

When the mould is hard, take the two halves apart and remove the plasticine. The second half of the cast will have knobs around the edge to fit into the holes in the other half; this allows the two shells to be aligned accurately for casting the rubber head. Clean the inside of the mould carefully with a rag soaked in methylated spirit (wood alcohol). Clean the ears, nose and other awkward cracks with loops of fine wire.

Leave the moulds to dry out for about a week, by which time they should no longer feel cold and heavy.

To make the rubber head

Secure the two halves of the mould together with strong rubber bands and cover the join with plasticine.

Pour the rubber into the mould through the neck until it is approximately a quarter full. Roll the mould to fill in all the cracks and continue to roll it as it is being filled to remove air bubbles.

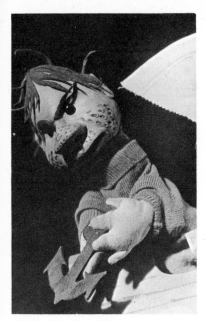

Figure 17   Snitchity Titch by Ronnie Le Drew

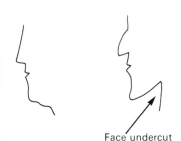

Figure 18/1   A face not undercut

Figure 18/2   A face undercut

Figure 19/1   Hollow eye sockets

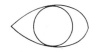

Figure 19/2   Wooden bead glued in eye socket

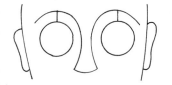

Figure 19/3   Wooden balls suspended from the eyebrows

Top up the level of the rubber as it drops slightly.

The longer the rubber is left in the mould, the thicker the head will be. An hour gives a suitable thickness. At the end of this time, pour the excess rubber in the centre of the mould back into the container to be used again.

Leave the rubber in the mould to dry. Twenty-four hours is usually ample but it depends on the thickness of the rubber, so be careful not to open the mould before the rubber is dry.

Put a little powder in the head, through the neck, and blow it around inside. This prevents the inner surfaces of the rubber sticking together.

Pull the plaster mould apart and remove the head. If there is a 'flash', or ridge, around the head from the join in the mould, trim it off with sharp scissors.

Allow the head to dry for at least a further twenty-four hours before painting it.

A fibreglass head

Fibreglass matting is supplied in various grades and may be used either to make a shell on a model (1), or to cast a head in a plaster mould (2).

1   Cover the model with a layer of damp tissue paper to prevent the fibreglass sticking to the plasticine.

Saturate pieces of fibreglass matting in polyester liquid resin, press out all air bubbles and then press the matting onto the model with the pieces overlapping. Use 'finishing matt' for the first layer so that the inside of the head is smooth. Build up the head and features in coarse matt, then apply a final layer of fine-quality matt.

To remove the plasticine, cut open the head with a sharp knife before it is completely hard. If it is allowed to get too hard, a saw will be needed to cut it.

Join the two hollow shells with saturated matting, then sand the head (and file it if necessary), and paint it.

2   It is essential that there is no 'undercutting' in the original model (*figures 18/1* and *18/2*) or the hard fibreglass head will lock in the mould and it will be impossible to remove it without breaking the mould.

Take a plaster cast of the plasticine model as described for the rubber head, dividing the head in front of the ears.

Separate the mould, clean it, and allow to dry thoroughly.

Coat the inside of each half with a fibreglass 'separator' to prevent the head sticking in the mould.

Saturate pieces of the matting in polyester liquid resin, press out air bubbles, then press the matting into the moulds with the pieces over-lapping.

When dry, remove the two casts from the moulds and join them together with further pieces of saturated matting.

For a better surface, apply a fine-grade 'finishing fibre' to the head.

Eyes

Eyes can be modelled and painted with the other features, or they can be suggested in one of the following ways.

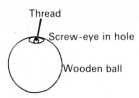

Figure 19/4   Attaching the thread to the wooden ball

Figure 19/5   Sticky black paper pupil on a pearl button

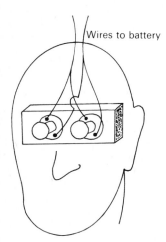

Figure 20/1   Fixing the eyes in the head

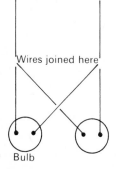

Figure 20/2   Connecting the bulbs

Hollow eye sockets can be painted black and varnished (*figure 19/1*) or covered with metallic spangles.

Deep slits can be made in the eye socket to produce heavy shadow; the shape of the eyeballs can be cut out and a small wooden bead (often black), glued top and bottom, placed in the centre of the hole (*figure 19/2*).

Painted wooden balls can be suspended from the eyebrows on fine, strong thread (*figures 19/3 and 19/4*).

Sticky black paper (for the pupil) can be glued on to a large pearl button. This is especially effective for animals (*figure 19/5*).

Illuminated eyes

Fit torch (flashlight) bulbs into the eye sockets. Screw the bulbs into bulb holders fixed to a block of wood; fasten the block into the head before the two pieces are joined together (*figure 20/1*).

Connect the bulbs in parallel (*figure 20/2*) for maximum brightness. The battery and a small switch may be contained within a hollow body (but there must be access to change the battery). The wires run into the body through the neck.

If the lights are to be switched on and off during the performance, the switch must be attached to the control.

Moving eyes

Moving eyes are most often made for marionettes, occasionally for rod puppets, but seldom for glove puppets. Eye movement can be most expressive but is only effective for intimate performances as it will not show from a distance.

Make the eyes from two wooden balls (the size depends on the size of the head) with a hole drilled through the centre of each ball. Pivot the balls on a piece of strong galvanised wire (12 or 14 gauge), using $\frac{1}{2}$ in diameter dowelling to give the necessary spacing between the eyes.

Build the balls and wire into the plasticine model (figure *21/1*) and model the head over this shape, leaving the eyeballs uncovered and the ends of the wire projecting though each side of the head. When the head is cut open and the plasticine removed, remove the balls and fix a screw weighted with lead into the back of each ball (*figure 21/2*). This acts as a counterbalance to open the eyes after they have been closed. They are closed by means of a string attached to the end of each screw.

Replace the balls in the head, cut the wire to the required length and secure it in the head by covering the ends with the same material as that used to model the head.

To stop the eyes opening too far, fix a thin dowel rod across the head for the screws to rest on.

If the eyes jam in the head this can usually be put right by running a sharp knife around the inside of the eyelids.

Paint the eyes on the wooden balls when the face is painted.

Figure 21/1   Wooden eyes built into a plasticine base before the head is modelled

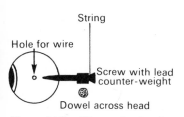

Figure 21/2   The mechanism for opening and closing the eyes

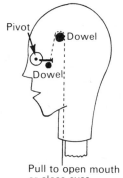

Figure 21/3   Moving eyes for a rod puppet

Control

For a marionette, the eye strings pass through two holes in the head. To prevent the thread fraying, it is a good idea to glue a piece of plastic drinking straw into the hole.

For a rod puppet, the strings pass over another dowel, fastened across the head, and then run down to the control (*figure 21/3*).

A moving mouth

A moving mouth is not very often required and, indeed, can be a liability. It must not move indiscriminately with no regard to speech, yet it would be impossible (and undesirable) to move it with every syllable. Its most effective use can be to give a gasp or similar reaction.

Moving mouths, like moving eyes, are most appropriate to marionettes but can be made in rod puppets.

The method described is usually the most practical way of making moving mouths. Other methods, used in the construction of specific types of puppet, are decribed on pages 71 and 72.

Model a head over a plasticine base.

When the head is cut open and the plasticine removed, carefully cut the mouth (ie the lower lip and chin) from the head in an L shape (*figure 22/1*).

Glue a wooden block inside this L-shaped piece (*figure 22/2*) and strengthen the bond with the material used to make the head.

Drill a hole through the block and pivot it on a piece of galvanised wire (12 or 14 gauge). Drill holes in the sides of the head to accommodate the ends of the wire.

Attach a string to the back of the block for opening the mouth (*figure 22/2*). The weight of the block acts as a counterbalance to close the mouth. A screw weighted with lead may be attached to the back of the block to increase the weight (*figure 22/3*).

Control

As with moving eyes, the string passes through the top of the head for a marionette, and over a dowel secured in the head then down to the control for a rod puppet.

Painting and finishing the head

For painting the head Reeves Polymer Colours, or a similar type of paint, are recommended. These can be matt or shiny, depending on whether they are mixed with water or the Polymer medium. The latter *must* be used when painting rubber.

It is a good idea to paint the head under artificial light if the show is to be lit.

To obtain a flesh colour, mix red, brown, yellow and white, or use a ready-mixed flesh colour and add to this.

If eyeballs are painted pure white they will tend to look bare so add a dash of yellow to produce a 'warm' or creamy white. It can be effective to ignore the iris and pupil and paint the whole eyeball a dark colour

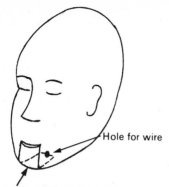

Hole for wire

L shape cut from the head.

Figure 22/1   The shape cut from the head

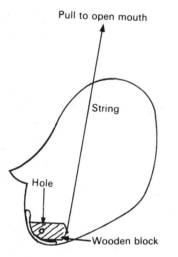

Pull to open mouth

String

Hole

Wooden block

Weight of block closes mouth

Figure 22/2   The mechanism with a wooden block as a counterweight

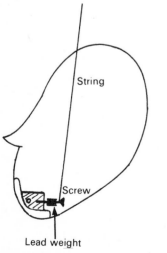

String

Screw

Lead weight

Figure 22/3   The mechanism with a lead counterweight

(eg black, blue, purple or green). Eyebrows can be painted or made from the same material as the hair.

Polymer varnish can be applied to the lips and eyes for emphasis.

Hair can be modelled and painted but it is usually more effective to glue it on using materials such as knitting wool, rug wool, fur, fur fabric, dyed string, embroidery silks or 'hair' from a nylon ponytail (available in a variety of colours from Woolworth's and various drug stores).

Note   The head should not be painted until it has been joined to the body as some joints necessitate more work being done on the head.

Figure 23   Madam Butterfly by Ken Barnard

5 The glove puppet

Construction

The head

Glove puppet heads can be made as described in Chapter 4.

The 'glove' for the body

Cut out two body shapes (*figure 1/1*) from any suitable material. Make the body long enough to reach almost to your elbow, and take care to tailor the glove to your hand as it must be a comfortable fit for successful manipulation.

Place the two shapes together, wrong side to wrong side, and stitch, leaving the bottom and the neck open. Reverse the glove and attach the head at the neck, either by gluing or tying.

Bend a length of galvanised wire (12-14 gauge) into a loop with a portion of it forming a hook (*figure 1/2*). Place the loop in the bottom of the glove and stitch up the hem so that it contains the loop. The hook enables you to hang up the puppet in the booth and the loop holds the bottom open for speedy insertion of your hand during a show.

Fit a costume over the glove (made to approximately the same dimensions). This helps to conceal the hand shape and reduces the effects of wear.

Hands

Hands may be made as an integral part of the glove, as described above. Alternatively they may be made separately in a different colour material, or by one of the more complicated techniques described in Chapter 8.

To make a cloth hand, first cut out two shapes, mitten-shaped or with fingers (*figures 2/1* and *2/2*). Stitch the two shapes together inside out and then reverse. Where appropriate, stuff the fingers with foam rubber. Glue or stitch the hands to the glove body.

When hands are made by a more complicated technique, glue a strong cardboard 'cuff' to the hand (*figure 2/3*) and cover the card with whatever material is used for the hand. (With rubber hands, the cuff can be moulded with the hand and, if necessary, lined with card to stiffen it.) Glue the cuff inside the puppet's cloth arm and, for manipulation, slip your finger inside the cuff. This method permits greater character in the shape of the hands but usually at the expense of expressive gesture and easy handling of props.

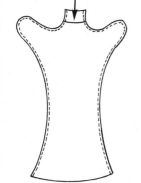

Tie or glue onto the neck here

Figure 1/1   The body shape

Figure 1/2   The loop and hook bent from one piece of wire

Figure 2/1   Mitten-type hand

Figure 2/2   Shaped hand with seams inside

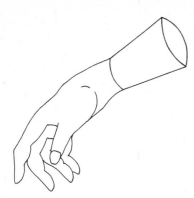

Figure 2/3   Modelled hand with a cardboard cuff

Figure 3   (Right) Robber, by Frieder Simon

Figure 4   (Below, left) Granny, by Ian Allen

Figure 5   (Below, centre) Timmo Tarin, by Violet Philpott

Figure 6   (Below, right) Clown, by John Thirtle

A glove puppet with legs

If legs are required, they are best made as cloth tubes stuffed with cloth or foam rubber. Stitch the legs to the 'glove', inside the jacket.

Cut the feet from a chunk of foam rubber then cover them with glued-on material (such as felt). Glue and stitch the feet on to the legs.

The legs are not controlled; they swing freely.

In order to conceal your arm when you manipulate a glove puppet with legs, make the glove long enough to reach your elbow. Use of a dark material helps it to recede (*figure 7*).

Animal puppets

You can make a simple glove with an animal head, covering the glove with a human costume, fur or fur fabric. Alternatively, a complete animal body that rests on your wrist and forearm may be made of cloth and stitched to the glove (*figure 8*).

Stuff the body and hind legs with fabric or foam rubber.

A puppet required to maintain a particular body shape (such as a fish) may be made by covering a framework made from card (stuck, stapled or Cellotaped into shape), or by covering a framework of wire netting covered with foam rubber (*figure 9*).

Leave a U-shaped hole under the body for inserting your hand and fasten a dowel inside the body to hold on to when manipulating the puppet.

A sleeve animal puppet may be just a simple sleeve of material with head attached. Often the head has a moving mouth (*figure 10*). A stuffed body and dangling legs may be attached to the sleeve.

Two-handed glove puppets are made on the same principle as sleeve puppets, leaving underneath a hole large enough to insert your crossed arms (*figure 11*). The body is often stiffened by lining it with buckram, foam rubber or even newspaper.

Figure 7   A glove puppet with legs

Figure 8   A glove puppet that sits on the arm

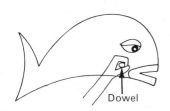

Figure 9   An animal puppet made from cardboard

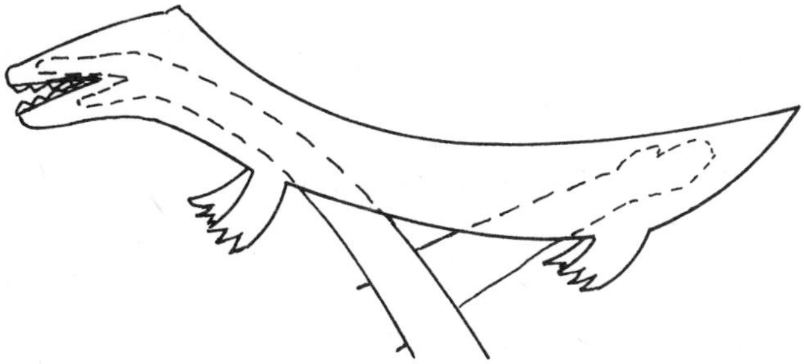

Figure 10 (Right)   A sleeve puppet

Figure 11 (Above)   A two-handed glove puppet

69

Figure 12 (*Top*) *Bandicoot and the Crocodile from* The Birthday Cake *by Violet Philpott*

Figure 13 (*Above, left*) *Ferdy, by Julie Gosling*

Figure 14 (*Right*) *Moose and Mouse, by John Thirtle*

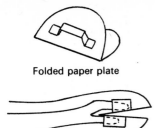

Folded paper plate

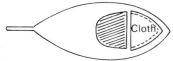

Figure 15   A simple moving mouth

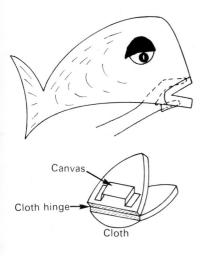

Canvas

Cloth hinge

Cloth

Cloth

Figure 16   A moving mouth made of wood

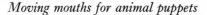

Moving mouths for animal puppets

A moving mouth, which is employed at the expense of leg movement, may be made by one of the following methods.

1   A folded paper plate or an egg box makes an excellent pair of jaws. Glue a strip of stepped cardboard (*figure 15*) on top of, and underneath, the jaws. Slip your fingers and thumb under these strips to move the mouth. Glue the jaws into the material head.

2   Cut out two pieces of plywood for the jaws. Glue and tack a cloth hinge to the plywood. Tack strips of canvas to the plywood to slip your fingers into to hold the puppet and control the jaws (*figure 16*). This is a stronger method of construction, particularly suitable for use with a cardboard, or wire and foam rubber, body.

Catalan glove puppets

This type of puppet (*figure 17*) is now rarely used as it is heavier and more difficult to manipulate than an ordinary glove puppet. Traditionally the head, neck and shoulders are carved from one piece of wood, but a head may be made by one of the methods described in Chapter 4 and attached to a separate wooden shoulder block. Drill holes in the shoulder block for the first three fingers and use your thumb and little finger to control the arms. These are made from cardboard tubes glued to the hands (see page 68).

The rod-hand puppet

Made on exactly the same principles as a glove puppet, the head of this puppet is moved by a rod inserted in the neck. The thumb and index finger move the hands and the other three fingers grasp the rod (*figure 18*).

Junk-box glove puppets

Glove puppets can be made by the junk-box method. A few examples are illustrated (*figures 19-22*).

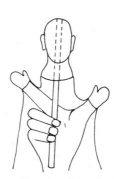

Figure 17   A Catalan glove puppet

Figure 18   A rod-hand puppet

Figure 19   A simple glove puppet: an old ball with features made from felt, buttons and a toothpaste tube cap

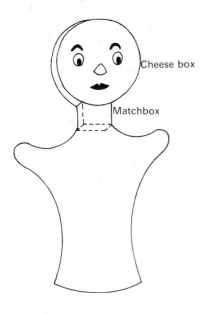

Cheese box

Matchbox

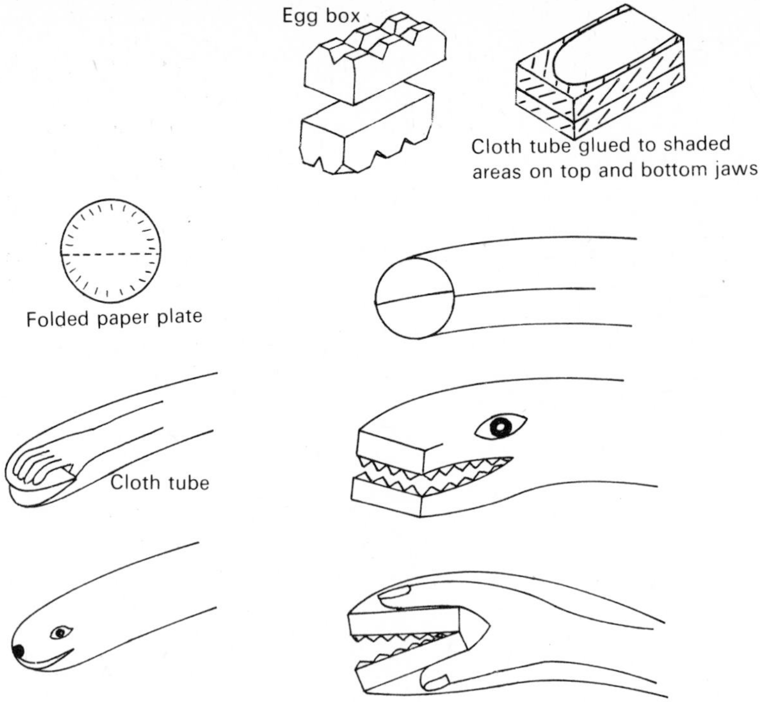

Egg box

Cloth tube glued to shaded
areas on top and bottom jaws

Folded paper plate

Cloth tube

*Figure 20   A cheese box puppet
head*

Figure 21   A simple sleeve puppet

*Figure 22   A sleeve puppet with
snapping jaws*

Figure 23/1

Figure 23/2

Control

Basically, the method of controlling a glove puppet is very simple
although it needs a considerable amount of practice to achieve convincing movements. The glove type of body is usually manipulated with
the hand in one of the three positions illustrated (*figures 23/1,23/2, 23/3*),
the first two of which are preferred by most people.

Animal puppets with moving mouths are held by the puppeteer's
whole hand in the head, with the thumb moving the lower jaw (*figure
23/4*).

To improve manipulation, practise ordinary movements such as
stroking the head, putting the hand to the mouth, rubbing the eyes,
nodding and shaking the head, bowing, falling, and picking up and
putting down various objects. Whilst experimenting with movement,
study gestures and try to relate them to emotions.

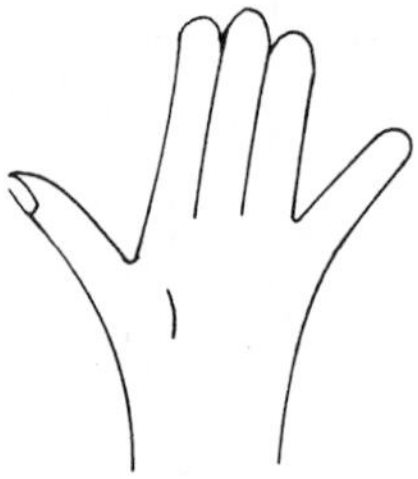

Figure 23/3

Figure 23/4   Animal mouths

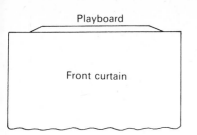

Figure 24/1   The booth set up

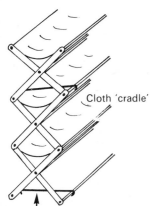

Figure 24/2   An airer with cloth cradles attached

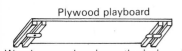

Figure 24/3   Securing the playboard to the airers

Figure 24/4   The playboard and front curtain rail

Figure 25/1   The booth set up

Presentation

It is possible to perform with just a clothes horse or some form of simple screen but a specially made fitup is obviously more satisfactory. For comfortable manipulation, the top of the screen should be just above the puppeteers' heads.

An open booth made from collapsible clothes airers

This is a useful fitup which requires the minimum of construction and setting up. The main elements are two collapsible clothes airers which support a playboard and a front curtain (*figure 24/1*).

To prevent the two airers collapsing, hook lengths of strong galvanised wire between the bars (*figure 24/2*). Use wires of different lengths to raise or lower the height of the fitup.

Make the playboard from a piece of plywood of suitable dimensions. Screw two strips of wood to each end of it to prevent it from moving when placed on the airers. Screw a small piece of wood to one of the wooden strips at each end of the playboard; and turn it to secure the playboard to the airer (*figure 24/3*).

Support the front curtain rod (a long dowel rod) by hooks screwed into the tops of the airers (*figure 24/4*).

Attach fabric between the bars of the airers to make cradles to hold equipment (*figure 24/2*).

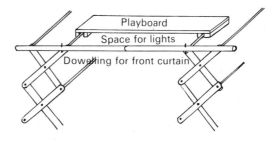

The standard open booth

This type of booth (*figure 25/1*) is becoming more commonly used, particularly for indoor performances. It allows for a wider viewing angle and greater scope for action and scenery than the traditional proscenium booth, and it packs away just as easily.

The minimum width suggested for this fitup is 5 ft. This will serve solo performers well and is practicable for group work too, although larger dimensions are preferable.

2 × 1 in timber is suitable for the booth; if a smaller size is used for lightness, cutting away may weaken the frame.

The framework is in four pieces which are hinged together. It opens out to form a three-sided fitup (*figures 25/2* and *25/3*). The propshelf, which is hinged in the centre for packing, holds the frame rigid by being bolted to each section. This frame is supported by four 1 × 1 in legs

73

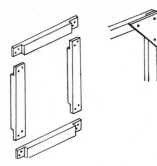

Figure 25/2   One section of the framework

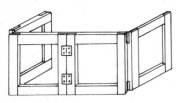

Figure 25/3   The four sections hinged together

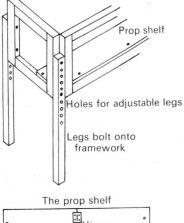

Prop shelf

Holes for adjustable legs

Legs bolt onto
framework

The prop shelf

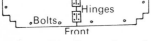

Hinges

.Bolts.

Front

Figure 25/4   Supporting and securing the framework

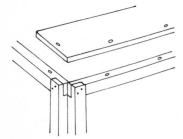

Figure 25/5   The playboard bolts onto the frame

which are bolted to each corner of the fitup (*figure 25/4*). So that it is possible to adjust the height of the fitup, drill a series of holes for the bolts through the legs.

If a playboard is required, it is hinged for packing and bolted on to the framework in the same way as the propshelf (*figure 25/5*).

The back screen is bolted on to two lengths of wood which are themselves bolted on to the main framework. For easier packing, the screen may be hinged and held firm by a plywood plate, screwed to one half and hooking over a screw in the other half (*figure 25/6*). The openings in the screen may be any shape, size, or type required, and may have a hinged door or a draped curtain.

For a multi-purpose screen it is usually best to paint it black but, however it is painted, matt paint is strongly recommended as glossy paint will reflect light and may distract the audience.

A plain dark curtain may be used in preference to a solid back screen.

Cover the framework with fairly heavy drapes. All drapes can be attached to the booth with Velcro tape (sewn to the curtains and glued on to the booth) or with large press fasteners (sewn to the curtains and tacked to the booth).

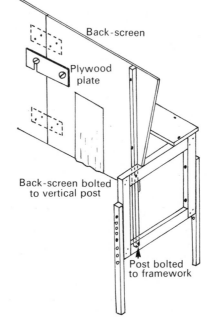

Hinges on other side of screen

Back-screen

Plywood
plate

Back-screen bolted
to vertical post

Post bolted
to framework

Figure 25/6   The back-screen

*Figure 26   Starosta and Ňafron,
in* Ginolovy Trampoty, *an open-
stage presentation of the State
Central Puppet Theatre, Prague*

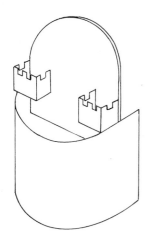

Figure 27   A castellet, or castello

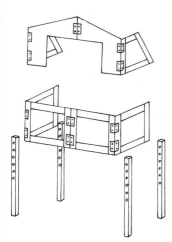

Figure 28/1   The separate parts

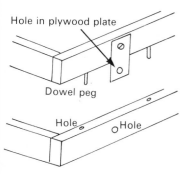

Hole in plywood plate

Dowel peg

Hole   Hole

Figure 28/2   Joining the sections

A castellet or castello

This type of glove-puppet booth dates back at least as far as the fourteenth century. It was made to represent a castle for the enactment of
chivalric episodes and, although originally a bow-fronted fitup, may
be any shape desired.

The feature of interest to us today is the use of scenery, such as
turrets, to provide a second acting level and give a greater feeling of
depth to the scene. A painted back cloth usually lacks the effect of depth
achieved with this technique, which is capturing the attention of contemporary puppeteers in their experiments with split acting levels.
The fitup is constructed in the same fashion as the standard open booth.

The proscenium booth

This is a larger version of the type of booth traditionally used for Punch
and Judy. The lower part of the booth is constructed in exactly the same
way as the open booth. It differs in that there is a hinged upper section
which has two plywood shapes in the centre, forming the proscenium
(*figure 28/1*).

The proscenium is held firm by a plywood plate screwed to one half
and hooking over a screw in the other half, as for the back screen of an
open booth.

The two folding sections are joined to each other by dowel pegs which
are glued into holes drilled in the sides of one section and which also fit
into holes drilled in the other section. They are held together by a plywood plate which is screwed to one section and bolted to the other
(*figure 28/2*).

Screw a plywood shape (at least $\frac{1}{2}$ in thick) to each side of the top
section to hold dowel rods from which the back cloths hang (*figure 28/3*).

75

Figure 28/3   The booth set up

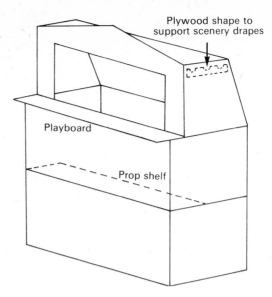

Plywood shape to support scenery drapes

Playboard

Prop shelf

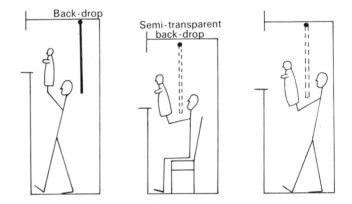

Back-drop

Semi-transparent back-drop

Figure 28/4   Positions for operating the puppets

Cover the framework with a fairly heavy material. Draw curtains may be added to cover the opening (see Chapter 8).

The height of the booth depends upon the method of manipulation to be used (*figure 28/4*). It is restricting to perform sitting down and performing with your head behind a semi-transparent back drop allows you to see the puppets clearly but places restrictions upon the background scenery. Performing standing with the playboard above your head is the most common and recommended practice.

A booth and scenery combined

This is a fitup in which the booth *is* the scenery (*figure 29*). It can be very effective—especially in schools.

Imagine the captain in the cabin popping his head out of the porthole only to see the ship's cat shoot out of the funnel! This sort of thing is ideal for children.

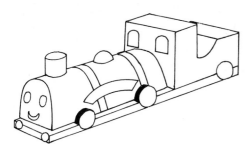
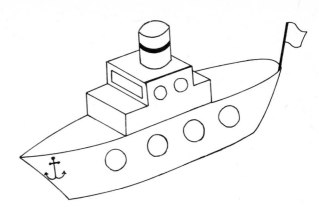

Figure 29   Two examples of booths made from cardboard for classroom use

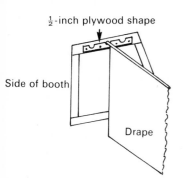

½-inch plywood shape

Side of booth

Drape

Figure 30/1   Suspending a back-drape

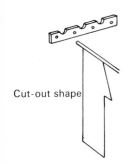

Cut-out shape

Figure 30/2   Suspending a solid scenery drop

The booth can, of course, be any object desired and, aside from school use, the idea offers much food for thought for the amateur and professional puppeteer.

The booth is made in the same way as other large 'models'—from large cardboard boxes, cut open and made into the shape.

Scenery

For the open booth

In the open booth, painted drapes may be hung over the back screen, or a variety of screens can be made and used for different performances. This type of booth is not however intended for elaborate scene changes but is excellent for continuity in plays, so it is suggested that usually the back scenery be kept constant throughout the performance. For variety sketches, a dark curtain, suspended from a rod, might be preferred to a wooden back screen.

For a proscenium booth

In the proscenium booth there are a number of possibilities for scenery.
1   Drapes may be suspended from a dowel rod. Each end of the dowel fits into a groove in the plywood shapes screwed to each side of the booth (*figure 30/1*). If the puppeteer is to stand behind, rather than below, the drape, he should use a semi-opaque material so that he can see the puppets.
2   Background scenery can be made extremely effectively by cutting out the shapes in thin plywood, or hardboard. Separate pieces or one long piece may be used. There are two suitable methods for holding this cut-out scenery in the booth.

Nail the tops of the shapes to a batten, or dowel rod, which is held by the two plywood plates in the sides of the booth (*figure 30/2*), or incorporate an extra vertical strip in each of the top side sections (*figure 30/3*). Fasten two screws to each strut and cut inverted keyhole shapes in the scenery to fit over the screws (*figure 30/4*).

If a cut-out background is used a back cloth of some description will be needed—usually a sky cloth. Fasten it to the angled struts of the top

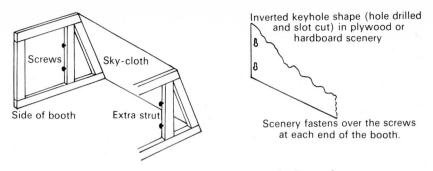

Inverted keyhole shape (hole drilled and slot cut) in plywood or hardboard scenery

Scenery fastens over the screws at each end of the booth.

Figure 30/3   Supporting cut-out background scenery

Figure 30/4   Cut-out background scenery

section (*figure 30/3*) so that it has a slight slant; this is helpful for illumination. (In fact it is well worth while having special lights to illuminate the sky cloth.)

Making and securing cut-out scenery in any booth

Scenery cut from plywood, or strong card, may be attached to the front or sides of any booth. A few techniques are suggested.
Slots   Cut out plywood shapes with a coping saw, leaving a strip projecting downwards to fit into a slot in the booth (*figure 31/1*). Cardboard shapes, cut out with a sharp knife, should be tacked to a strip of plywood.

Figure 31/1   Attaching small items of scenery to the frame of the booth

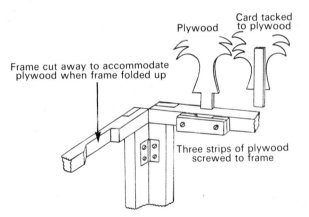

Card tacked to plywood

Plywood

Frame cut away to accommodate plywood when frame folded up

Three strips of plywood screwed to frame

Stage 1 Stage 2 Stage 3

Figure 31/2   Stages in making a scenery slot in the playboard

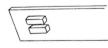

Figure 31/3   Blocks of wood screwed underneath the playboard on each side of the slot to hold scenery securely

The slot to hold the scenery is made by either of these methods.
1   Screw three strips of plywood to the frame of the booth (*figure 31/1*). (If this method is used the top side piece of the frame must be cut away to accommodate the extra blocks of wood when the sections are folded up.)
2   Make a slot in the frame of the booth, or the playboard, by drilling a series of holes in a line (*figure 31/2*). If a slot is cut in a thin playboard, screw two small blocks of wood underneath it, one on each side of the slot, to steady the scenery (*figure 31/3*). This method is also useful for holding a long strip of scenery which fits on to the front of the booth instead of a playboard (*figure 31/4*).
Dowels   Cut away the top half of two dowels and tack the cut-out

78

scenery to them (*figure 31/5*). The dowels fit into holes drilled in the playboard or the frame of the booth.

Clamps or bolts Large items of scenery which must be securely fastened may be screwed or nailed to a wooden block which is held firmly on the playboard or frame by a 'G' clamp (in America, a 'C' clamp), or a wing nut and bolt (*figure 31/6*).

Spring clips Properties which are required to stand firmly on the playboard may be held in place by a large spring clip, obtainable from stationers. Screw, glue, or otherwise fasten the clip underneath the prop (the method will depend on what the prop is made of). Fasten the clip over the edge of the playboard (*figure 31/7*).

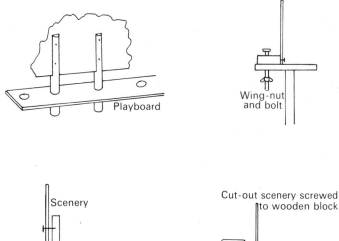

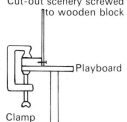

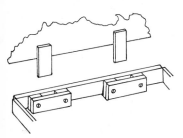

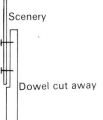

Figure 31/4   Scenery used instead of a playboard

Figure 31/5   Dowels attached to scenery fitted into holes in the playboard or the frame of the booth

Figure 31/6   Scenery clamped or bolted to the playboard

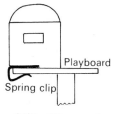

Figure 31/7   The use of a spring-clip to hold properties on the playboard

6 The rod puppet

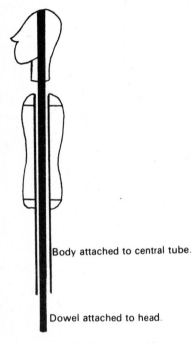

Body attached to central tube.

Dowel attached to head.

Figure 1   A rod puppet with a turning head

Figure 2   The simplest rod puppet

Construction

The head

Rod puppet heads can be made as described in Chapter 4.

The body

The body is constructed so that it can be supported by a central rod which may be free to turn, or may be fixed.

In order that the head may turn independently of the body, it is necessary to have a tube of some description to support the body. The tube may be aluminium, thick cardboard (such as the centre of a bale of material) or any other strong tubing. The dowel attached to the head turns inside this tube (*figure 1*).

The simplest form of rod puppet

This consists of a head, central rod and a gown tied around the rod (*figure 2*). It has neither shoulders, arms, nor legs but is surprisingly effective. The material of the robe plays a very important part: for example, a stiff satin material will give a very different movement from a soft cotton fabric.

A simple rod puppet with shoulders, arms and hands

Rod puppets of the simplest sort may be given shoulders made from a cardboard box, stuffed with newspaper.

Make holes in the box to accommodate the central supporting rod and securely glue and tape the box in place (*figure 3/1*). Alternatively, wind tape or strips of glued paper around the rod below the box; this supports the shoulders, yet leaves them free to turn (*figure 3/2*).

Make arms and hands by one of the methods described on pages 117, 118.

A simple nodding puppet

To make a puppet that will nod, first glue a long dowel in the head.

Cut out a plywood shoulder block (with a coping saw) and drill a hole in the plywood to accommodate the dowel. Glue the shoulders on to the dowel and pad them with foam rubber (*figure 4*).

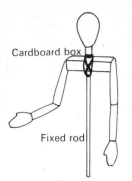

Cardboard box

Fixed rod

Figure 3/1   A puppet with a fixed rod

Rod free to turn

Figure 3/2   A puppet with the rod (and head) free to turn

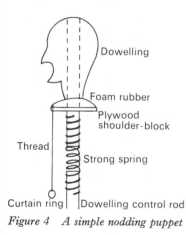

Dowelling

Foam rubber

Plywood shoulder-block

Thread

Strong spring

Curtain ring | Dowelling control rod

Figure 4   A simple nodding puppet

Fasten one end of a strong spring (eg a coil of spring steel) on to the dowel and the other end on to the control rod.

Attach a length of thread to the front of the shoulder block. Tie a large curtain ring on to the end of the thread. Pull the thread to make the puppet nod.

A plywood and canvas body

The body is made from two plywood shapes joined by a tube of canvas, or some other strong material.

Drill a hole in the centre of each piece of plywood to accommodate a rod or tube. Secure the rod or tube in the shoulder piece with strips of glued paper or card (*figure 5*).

Tack the body on to both pieces of plywood and gather in the waist with thread.

Glue foam rubber on to the shoulder piece to give it more shape.

A buckram or cardboard body

The body is constructed from strong pieces of cardboard or buckram, glued together (*figure 6*).

Build the shape on a wooden shoulder block. Fasten the central rod or tube to the shoulders with strips of glued paper or card, as described above.

A carved body

Although it is not a very common practice to do so today, the body may be carved. To reduce the weight, cut open the body and hollow out the centre with a chisel.

Glue the central rod or tube inside the body and secure further with strips of glued card (*figure 7*).

Arms and hands

The techniques described for making marionette arms and hands (see pages 117, 118) are suitable for rod puppets, or the hands may be cut from a large sponge or a block of foam rubber. Puppeteers have a variety of preferences for wrist or elbow joints. It is usually preferable that rod puppets should have somewhat more restricted joints than marionettes for purposes of control.

A leather joint

The leather joint permits considerable flexibility whilst maintaining good control. This is a neat method for a bare arm. The wrist has sideways movement and the elbow vertical movement (*figure 8*).

81

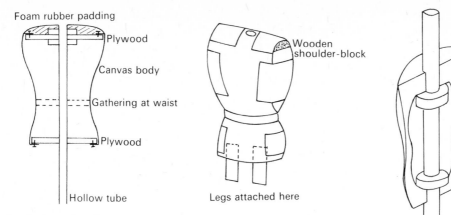

Foam rubber padding

Plywood

Canvas body

Gathering at waist

Plywood

Hollow tube

Wooden shoulder-block

Legs attached here

Figure 5   A plywood and canvas body

Figure 6   A buckram, or cardboard, body

Figure 7   A carved body

Figure 8   Leather joints

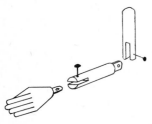

Figure 9/1   Wooden 'tongues' in slots

Figure 9/2   Screw-eyes pivoted in slots

An open mortise and tenon joint

This joint, which tends to restrict a marionette's arms, is a useful joint for rod puppets (*figure 9/1*). A variation on this joint uses screw-eyes instead of the wooden 'tongues' (*figure 9/2*).

Interlocked screw-eyes and string joints

Although there seems to be general agreement that a more restricted joint gives greater control over the rod puppet, some puppeteers still prefer interlocked screw-eyes (*figure 10/1*), or simple string joints (*figure 10/2*).

Hands without wrist joints

Occasionally hands are built on to the arms without any flexible wrist joint. In this case, the fingers must be in an interesting position to compensate for the lack of wrist movement.

Rope arms

Arms may be made of rope (*figure 11*). This gives a desirable firmness in the arm yet allows total flexibility of movement. Corrugated cardboard may be glued and wound around the rope to give more shape to the arms.

Figure 10/1   Interlocked screw-eyes

String (or dowel)

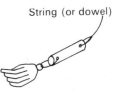

Figure 10/2   Screw-eye and thread

Figure 11   Rod puppets designed by John Blundall for use with 'black light' technique in Pinocchio *at the Midland Arts Centre Puppet Theatre*

Figure 12   A rod puppet without legs

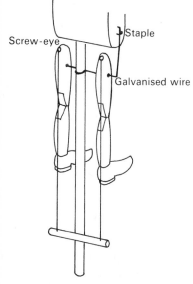

Figure 13   A screw-eye hip joint

Screw-eye

Staple

Galvanised wire

Figure 15   A hip joint for legs controlled by strings

Figure 14   A leather, or canvas, hip joint. The leather thong is pushed through the slot, glued and tacked down.

Figure 16   A rod-hand puppet

Legs and feet

It is not essential for the rod puppet to be given legs, especially if it is a large figure. Rod puppets are often visible only to waist or hip level (*figure 12*).

If the puppet is to have legs and feet they may be made in the same way as those of a marionette (see pages 118-121). Interlocked screw-eyes (*figure 13*), or a leather or canvas joint (*figure 14*), are particularly useful for rod puppets.

Usually the legs dangle freely; occasionally they are controlled by strings from below. In the latter case suspend them from a length of 12 gauge galvanised wire (*figure 15*). Allow a fair length of leg above the wire to facilitate good leverage for moving the legs.

The rod-hand puppet

There are a number of variations on rod-hand puppets (see also Chapter 5) but the example given here is the most common (*figure 16*).

Figure 17 (Right) *Duchess Grognon, Envy and Fairy Chrystallina from* The Chrystal Palace *by the Theatre of Puppets*

Figure 18 (Below, left) *Princess Shari from* The Arabian Nights *by the Polka Children's Theatre*

Figure 19 (Bottom, left) *Peter and the Bird from the Caricature Theatre's production of* Peter and the Wolf

Figure 20 (Below, right) *Herr Musikmeister from* The Pied Piper of Hamlin *by Ted Harold*

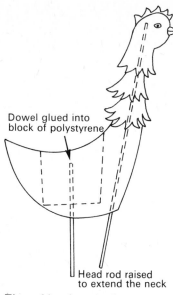

Dowel glued into
block of polystyrene

Head rod raised
to extend the neck

Figure 21 An animal puppet

The puppet has a central rod but no body, only a robe. The puppeteer holds the rod in one hand and slips his other hand, usually gloved, through a slit in the puppet's robe. The slit may be elasticated if desired.

This type of puppet is also used for two-man operation, with one puppeteer controlling the head and the other providing the hands.

Animals

Animals can be made from a wide variety of materials. A common technique is described below (*figure 21*).

The head

The head may be built with the body, all in one piece, or it may be made separately by one of the methods described in Chapter 4. Sometimes it is painted but it is usually covered with the same material as the body.

If the head is to move, the head rod is inserted through the bottom of the body and is used to turn the head and raise or lower it by lengthening the neck.

A nodding head

Build a strip of plywood or aluminium into the neck. By means of this projection, pivot the head on the head rod (*figure 22*).

Attach a length of galvanised wire (12-14 gauge) to the back of the head. This runs down the head rod (through screw-eyes) and is used to nod the head.

This technique is usually not as effective as the one described above.

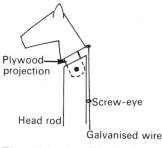

Plywood
projection

Screw-eye

Head rod

Galvanised wire

Figure 22 A nodding head

Figure 23 A dog from Happy Bunny *by the Pinokio Puppet Theatre, Łodź, Poland*

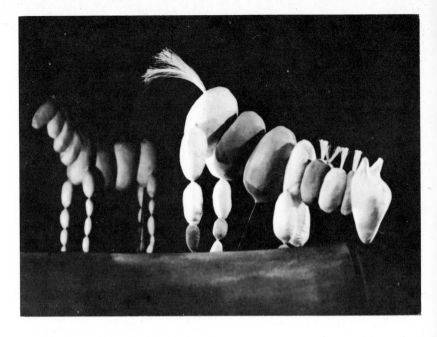

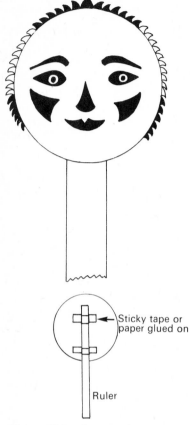

Sticky tape or paper glued on

Ruler

Figure 25/1   A paper plate puppet with coloured paper or felt features

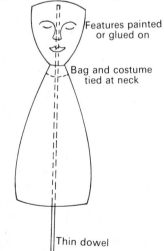

Paper bag stuffed with paper

Features painted or glued on

Bag and costume tied at neck

Thin dowel

Figure 25/2   A paper bag rod puppet

86

The body and legs

Construct the body around a block of Polystyrene (Styrofoam). Around this base make a frame of strong cardboard, or chicken wire, covered with foam rubber. Cover the body with fur or fabric. Make the legs in the same way as animal marionette legs (see pages 122, 125). Glue the supporting rod into the body at the point where the body is well balanced on the rod.

Junk-box rod puppets

Rod puppets can be made by the junk-box method. A few examples are illustrated (*figures 25-27*).

Control

The main feature of a rod puppet control is the central rod which supports the figure. Additional controls are added to move the head, hands and, occasionally, legs.

Moving the head

Two sorts of central rod have been described in the constructional section (page 80).
1   A rod passed through the body is attached to the head (*figure 28/1*). This requires only one-handed control but the head does not move independently of the body.
2   A tube is incorporated in the body inside which turns a rod fixed to the head (*figure 28/2*). The head can be moved using two- or one-handed control.

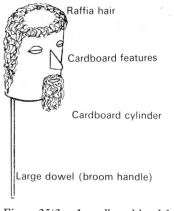

Raffia hair

Cardboard features

Cardboard cylinder

Large dowel (broom handle)

Figure 25/3   A cardboard head for a rod puppet

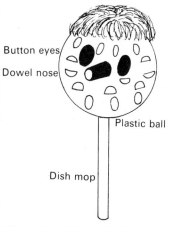

Button eyes

Dowel nose

Plastic ball

Dish mop

Figure 26   A 'junk-box' marot

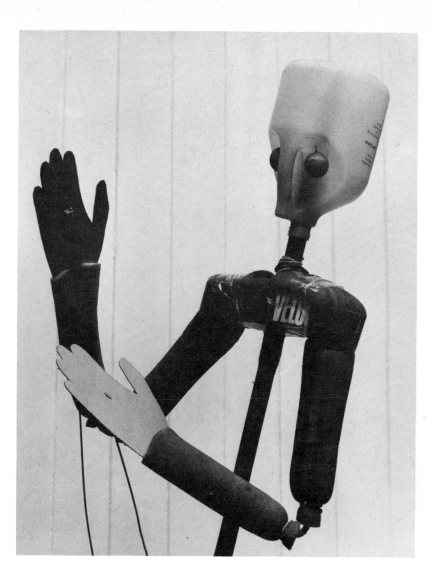

Figure 27   Horace, a junk-box rod puppet

Two-handed control

Hold the central tube with one hand and turn or raise the head rod with the other.

A short dowel glued into the end of the head rod will prevent the rod coming out of the tube (*figure 28/2*).

One-handed control

Cut a rectangular shape from the tube where your thumb would rest (*figure 29/1*).

Through the rectangular hole drill a hole in the dowelling head rod. Bend a length of 12 gauge galvanised wire into a thumb rest and glue the ends of the wire into the hole in the dowel. Hold the tubing below the thumb rest and use your thumb to effect all the head movements (*figure 29/2*).

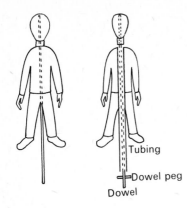

Tubing

Dowel peg

Dowel

Figure 28/1   The central rod fixed to head and body

Figure 28/2   The central rod turns inside a tube

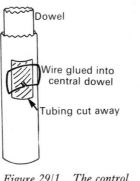

Dowel

Wire glued into central dowel

Tubing cut away

Figure 29/1   The control

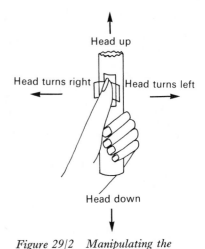

Head up

Head turns right   Head turns left

Head down

Figure 29/2   Manipulating the control

Screw-eye or thread

Galvanised wire

Figure 30/1   Galvanised wire

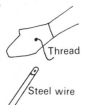

Thread

Steel wire

Figure 30/2   Steel wire

Figure 30/3   Galvanised wire attached to the wrist

Controlling the hands

Constructing the control

The hands are controlled by two lengths of thick (12 gauge) galvanised wire or, preferably, steel wire. It is advisable to drill a hole in a length of dowelling and glue the wire into the hole. The dowel is easier to grip than the wire.

To attach the wire to the hand, make a small loop in the end of galvanised wire (*figure 30/1*) or, with steel wire, beat the end flat and drill a hole in it (*figure 30/2*). Then attach the wires to the hands by means of thread or screw-eyes.

If the hand is attached to the arm without a flexible wrist joint, an alternative method is to drill a hole through the arm, push the wire through, and bend over the end (*figure 30/3*).

A useful device for holding one hand wire whilst manipulating the other is a small hook on each side of the central rod, level with the puppet's feet. If it is a dowel rod, screw hooks into it. If it is a tube, bend a strong piece of galvanised wire into the shape shown (*figure 31/1*), then glue and bind it to the tube. Make a small loop in each hand wire (*figure 31/2*); this fits onto the hook and holds up the hand, permitting it to swing slightly, when it is not being manipulated.

Wire 'hooks'

Figure 31/1   Galvanised wire bent into the hook shape to hold the hand wires

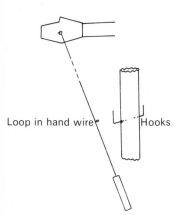

Loop in hand wire   Hooks

Figure 31/2   Hooks screwed into dowelling

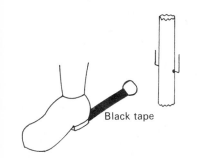

Black tape

Figure 34   Restricting leg movements

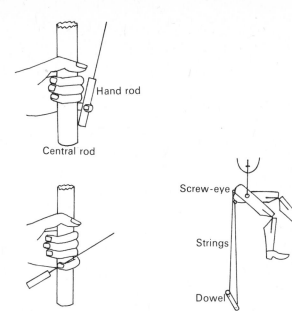

Hand rod

Central rod

Figure 32   Holding the hand rod for simple gestures

Screw-eye

Strings

Dowel

Figure 33   A leg control

Using the control

Either hold the central rod with one hand and the two hand wires with the other, *or* hold one of the wires with the little finger of the hand that holds the central rod (*figure 32*). This leaves your other hand free to control the other hand wire. If the hooks described above (*figure 31*) are attached to the control, these may be used to hold the hand wires as necessary.

It is quite common practice to allow one arm to hang limp whilst the other is being manipulated but this is not a recommended technique.

Controlling the legs

Very often the legs are allowed to dangle loosely. If, however, a leg control is required, attach screw-eyes to the tops of the legs (pivoted on a wire as described on page 83) and tie thread to the screw-eyes. Attach the other ends of the strings to a dowel rod which is 'paddled' to produce a walking movement (*figure 33*).

There may be times when dangling legs need to be prevented from swinging. The hooks for hand wires on the central rod (*figures 31/1, 31/2*) can also be used for this purpose. Glue and tack a strip of black tape to each heel of the puppet; stitch a small ring on to the end of each tape (*figure 34*). Slip the rings over the hooks to restrict leg movement.

You may also move the legs individually by holding the tape.

Nodding

The head, without a neck, is pivoted on the central rod by means of a thin dowel or strong (12 gauge) galvanised wire fastened in each side

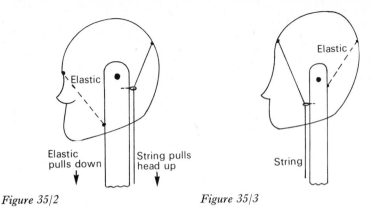

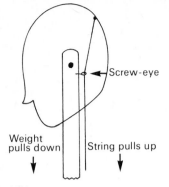

Figure 35/1

Figure 35/2

Figure 35/3

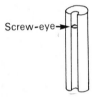

Figure 36   A central dowel grooved for the control string

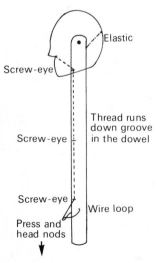

Figure 37   A lever control for nodding

of the head. There are alternative methods for controlling the movement.

1   Pivot the head so that its weight pulls it forwards, and attach a string inside the back of the head to lift it (*figure 35/1*).

2   Pivot the head so that it balances on the rod. Attach a string to the back of the head to lift it; fix a piece of strong elastic between the front of the head and the control rod to provide a counter-pull to nod the head (*figure 35/2*).

3   Attach the string to the front of the head and the elastic to the back of the head (*figure 35/3*).

Whichever control technique is used, it is advisable to groove the head rod for the string (*figure 36*).

A lever control

When the dowel alone is used as the central rod, the string should run through a screw-eye and down the rod to a lever made of galvanised wire which is fixed in the dowel (*figure 37*). Press the lever to move the head.

A control for all head movements

When the dowel turns inside a central tube it is possible to modify the usual one-handed 'thumb' control (see pages 87, 88) to effect all head movements, including nodding.

Take a piece of 12 gauge galvanised wire, at least as long as the central rod, and bend one end into a thumb rest (*figure 38/1*).

Cut a slot in the central dowel to accommodate the short end of the wire (*figure 38/2*).

Put the dowel inside the tube and push the long end of the wire through the opening in the tubing and up the groove in the dowel. The short end of the wire fits into the slot in the dowel (*figure 38/3*).

Bend the top of the wire into a small loop and attach the nodding string (*figure 38/4*).

Turn the head by moving the lever from side to side with your thumb; raise and lower the lever to nod the head.

90

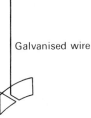

Galvanised wire

Figure 38/1 Galvanised wire bent into a thumb rest

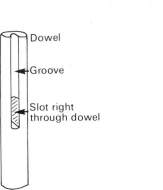

Dowel

Groove

Slot right through dowel

Figure 38/2 The dowel is grooved and slotted to take the wire

Figure 38/3 The control assembled

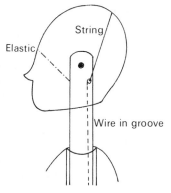

String

Elastic

Wire in groove

Figure 38/4 The top of the rod

Presentation

The Booth

The open booths described for the glove puppet can be used for rod puppets too, but rod puppets tend to need slightly larger dimensions. Suggestions for alternative structures which conform to the specific requirements of rod puppet performances are offered in this section.

It may be necessary, especially with lightweight frameworks, to use some kind of stage weight to stabilise the fitup.

The simplest fitup

For simple explorations, such as those in which children might participate, a clothes-horse draped with curtains, or a sheet, is satisfactory, although cramped conditions do not make for good puppetry.

Figure 39 Back stage at the State Puppet Theatre, Moscow

Figure 40 Puppets and puppeteer from Twelve Months *by the Czechoslovak Joy Theatre*

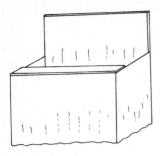

Figure 41/1   The booth

Figure 41/2   The framework

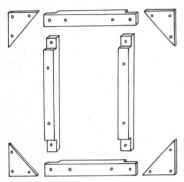

Figure 41/3 . Constructing one section of the frame

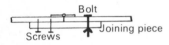

Figure 41/4   The joint in the cross-bar

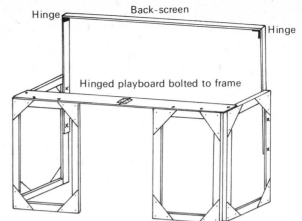

A standard fitup

In its simplest form this fitup consists of a front screen to hide the operators, and a back drop against which to operate the figures (*figure 41/1*). Some puppeteers dispense with a back screen but this is not really wise as it is unusual at engagements to find a suitable background against which to perform.

The frame consists of four main sections, hinged together in pairs. These form the corners of the booth (*figure 41/2*). Each section is made from four lengths of wood, glued and screwed together with half-lap joints. It is advisable to use triangular plywood plates to hold the section rigid (*figure 41/3*).

A plywood playboard bolts on to the frame (*figure 41/2*). The length of the playboard determines the width of the booth. The playboard can be hinged in the centre if it is too long for transporting.

The back screen is supported by three lengths of wood—two uprights hinged to a cross bar. Bolt the uprights on to the back of the framework. If necessary, hinge the cross bar in the centre and hold it rigid by a length of wood screwed to one half and bolted to the other (*figure 41/4*).

Attach the curtains with Velcro tape, glued to the booth and sewn on to the drapes, or by press fasteners, tacked to the wood and sewn on to the drapes.

An elaborate booth with two acting levels

This booth has two acting levels, both of which may be used for rod and glove puppets (*figure 42/1*). The framework folds up into a box for carrying puppets, props or drapes.

The basic frame consists of twelve main sections (*figure 42/2*), each of which is made in the same way as those for the previous fitup. The sections (which are here numbered for convenience) are hinged together so that they fold up for transportation (*figure 42/3*).

Screw a sheet of plywood, or hardboard, on to each of the outer sections (nos. 1 and 12) when the frame is folded up, so making a useful box for carrying equipment. This is held together by a strap (*figure 42/4*).

On to this framework are bolted a number of simple units for supporting drapes and scenery.

Figure 42/1   The booth

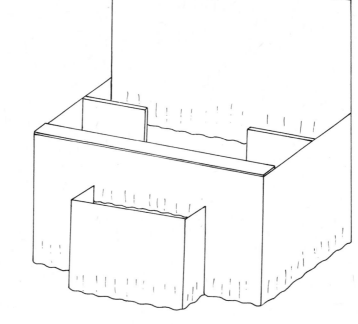

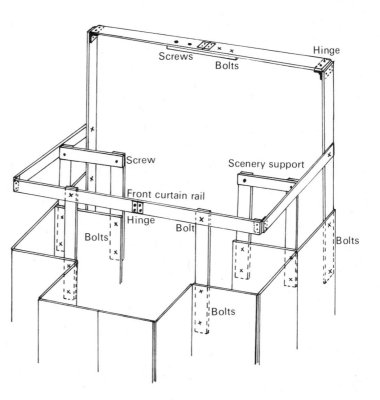

Figure 42/2   The basic frame

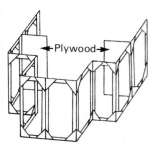

Plywood

Figure 42/3   Plan of the fit-up, showing how the sections fold up into a box for puppets, props or curtains

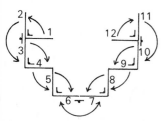

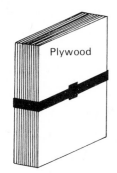

Plywood

Figure 42/4   The basic framework folded up

Figure 42/5   The back-screen

93

1   The back screen is supported by four lengths of wood which are hinged together. The centre joint has a joining bar to hold it rigid, as described for the previous fitup. The two end lengths of wood form the vertical posts which bolt on to sections 2 and 11 (*figure 42/5*).

2   The front curtain rail is in four parts, hinged together. It is bolted to the back screen supports and to two vertical posts which bolt on to sections 4 and 9 (*figure 42/5*).

3   Three battens are screwed together (two vertical posts and a cross bar) to form a scenery support for the side of the booth (*figure 42/5*). The two vertical posts bolt on to section 1 (another set bolts on to section 12).

4   The playboard is made of plywood and is hinged in the centre. It bolts on to the front curtain rail.

Attach all drapes with Velcro or press fasteners, as for the previous fitup.

Figure 43   Snow White and the Seven Dwarfs *by the Naive Theatre, Czechoslovakia*

Figure 44   Split acting levels are used in this production, O Zwyrtale Muzykancie, *by the Lalka Puppet Theatre, Warsaw*

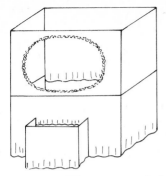

Figure 45/1   The screen attached to a booth

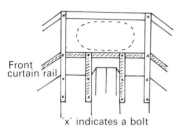

Front
curtain rail

'x' indicates a bolt

Figure 45/2   Supporting the screen (viewed from inside the fit-up)

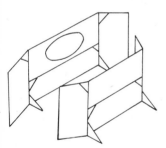

Figure 46/1   Front and back screens used without a booth

Figure 46/2   The framework to support the screens

Figure 47   Simple but effective scenery for 'Winter' in What the Four Seasons Are Talking About by the Pinokio Theatre, Poland

A front masking screen

This technique makes use of a high front screen with a large, oval shape cut from it (*figure 45/1*). The surround can be decorated. The screen is used purely for effect, helping to create a particular atmosphere or setting for the presentation.

If the screen is to be used with a booth it is supported by a curtain rail hinged together in four parts. The rail is bolted to the back screen supports of the booth and to two other vertical posts. These posts bolt inside the front of the existing fitup (*figure 45/2*).

Scenery and back drop are used as usual.

If the screen is to be used without a booth then a back screen also is made (*figure 46/1*).

Both screens are supported by collapsible frameworks, each consisting of two uprights, two cross bars (jointed, as necessary) and two triangular plywood supporting plates bolted to the uprights (*figure 46/2*).

Side pieces may be hinged to the main screen frame. Bolt a strip of wood on to a triangular plywood plate. The plate is hinged to the vertical post of the framework (*figure 46/2*).

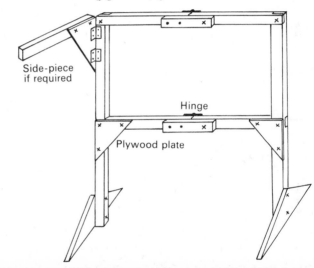

Side-piece
if required

Hinge

Plywood plate

95

Figure 48 A scene from The Fair Maguelone *by the Theatre of Puppets*

Scenery

The back cloth

A simple black back cloth is often the most satisfactory for rod puppet performances, although a scenic back cloth can be used. Remember that, with an open booth, the back cloth cannot be changed during the performance.

Projected scenery

A translucent screen is used instead of the usual back screen so that the scene can be projected on to the screen from behind the booth (see Chapter 10 *Lighting and sound*).

Arrange the stage lighting so that no strong light falls directly on to the screen.

This method allows the setting to be changed as often as desired and is particularly suited to the style of the rod puppet.

Cut-out scenery

Plywood scenery cutouts are attached to the playboard or the frame of the booth as described for glove puppets (see pages 78, 79).

Properties

Props which the puppets are required to carry may be fastened to rods, preferably thin steel, and held in the puppets' hands. Slot the playboard to allow props on rods to be placed upon it (*figure 49*).

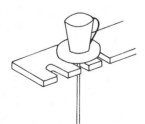

Figure 49 A slotted playboard for props on rods

7 The shadow puppet

Figure 1   A shadow figure with the body and shoulders slightly turned

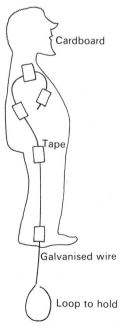

Figure 2   A simple shadow puppet

Shadow puppets are flat, cut-out figures that are held by a rod or wire against a translucent screen whilst some form of light is shone on to them. As the puppets move, the audience on the other side of the screen watches the shadows of the figures. Shadow puppets are traditionally made of parchment or hide but they are now usually made of strong card or, sometimes, translucent acetate. They are not difficult to make or to operate and, even if only roughly cut, look surprisingly delicate and intricate on the shadow screen.

Shadow puppets are controlled from below or behind, usually by means of wires, and occasionally from above by strings. It is most common to support and move the figure by one main wire. Extra wires or strings are added, if required, to control the movement of the limbs and head.

The puppet figures are represented by convention partly in profile, partly straight on. The Javanese *wayang kulit* figures, for example, are designed with the head and legs depicted as a side view whilst the body is viewed from the front. Although this sounds strange, it is acceptable on the shadow screen. It can also help towards characterisation to employ this technique, as shown in *figure 1* where the head, legs and feet are in profile and the shoulders and body slightly turned.

Lighting for the shadow screen is discussed in Chapter 10 *Lighting and sound*.

Construction

Simple shadow puppets

Draw the shape of the figure (usually a side view) on a piece of cardboard.

Cut out the shape with scissors.

Tape the figure on to a piece of galvanised wire, a ruler or knitting needle. It is now ready to use (*figure 2*).

Articulated shadow puppets

Draw on cardboard the parts of the figure. The pieces that are to move must be designed to overlap for joining.

Cut out the shapes (*figure 3/1*) and join the separate parts: either with string, threaded through holes in the card and knotted on either side

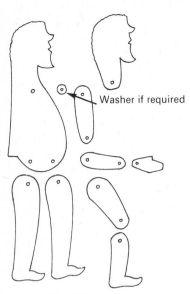

Figure 3/1   The separate parts

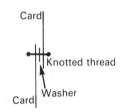
Washer if required

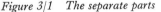

Card

Knotted thread

Washer

Card

Figure 3/2   A string joint

Figure 3/3   A paper-fastener joint

Figure 3/4   Correct method for joining the parts

(*figure 3/2*), or with rivet-type paper fasteners (*figure 3/3*). The pieces must be joined in layers, one on top of the other as shown in *figure 3/4*. If joined as shown in *figure 3/5*, they will lock together.

To restrict the movement of joints, tie the moving parts (*figure 3/6*).

Washers between the moving parts are sometimes thought to give greater flexibility. (Make the washer from the same material as the figure.) However, provided reasonably smooth card and good quality thread (eg No. 18 carpet thread) is used, a washer will not usually be needed.

Decoration

Shadow puppets can be decorated by cutting small slits or other shapes, or by punching holes in them. The Javanese *wayang kulit* shadow figures, the Indian shadows and the beautiful, intricate, Chinese shadow puppets all use these methods and it will help to study these. The amount of cutting away that is possible depends on the material used.

If a design is cut in an articulated figure it is advisable to cut away as much as possible of one of the overlapping parts to allow the design in the other part to show (*figure 5*). Leave sufficient material in both parts to allow the usual joint to be made.

Colour

Colour can be introduced by covering cut-out shapes in cardboard figures or scenery with coloured acetate or cellophane paper.

Alternatively, the puppets and scenery may be cut from fairly thick plain or coloured acetate. Plain acetate may be coloured with glass painting colours or with Letrafilm shapes. (Letrafilm is a self-adhesive, translucent, coloured film.) The use of plain acetate permits many colours to be combined in the same figure. Join moving parts with strong thread.

A mixture of materials

One figure may be made from a number of different materials. For example, imagine an animal with head and tail made of a rigid material, such as cardboard, but with the body in between made of a stretchy fabric (*figure 6*). Such puppets allow a variety of movements and also present the opportunity to experiment with the shadow created by different textures.

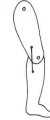

Figure 3/5   Incorrect method for joining the parts

Figure 3/6   String used to restrict leg movement

Figure 4 Chinese shadow puppets from the collection of Jan Bussell and Ann Hogarth

A cut-away design

The overlapping part

Figure 5 Decorating overlapping parts. The shaded parts are cut away

Figure 6 A mixture of materials

Two-dimensional wire puppets

Wire is becoming more widely used for making shadow puppets. Bend the wire to the outline of the required shape; whilst it retains the basic shape, it will also give a certain amount of spring. This offers interesting possibilities for shadow play. The head illustrated (*figure 8*) can change in shape, character or mood.

Three-dimensional wire puppets

There have been many recent experiments with three-dimensional objects and figures, exploring the possibilities of the 'puppets' as seen from various angles. Solid objects with perspex or acetate parts have interesting properties to explore but one of the most fascinating forms of three-dimensional shadow play is that which uses wire puppets.

Make the figures by bending galvanised wire to the required shapes. Join separate parts by interlocking small loops made in the wire (*figure 9*). Control the figures in the same way as a rod puppet, by three wires—a central control and two hand controls—leaving the legs to dangle freely.

Lighting the screen for three-dimensional puppets

Three-dimensional puppets may be used to create two- or three-dimensional shadows. The three-dimensional shadow technique has many possibilities and can be extremely effective but it relies entirely upon the audience wearing special glasses so its importance in the shadow theatre is limited.

Two-dimensional shadows As the three-dimensional puppet cannot be

99

Figure 7 *Shadow puppets at the Little Angel Marionette Theatre, London*

Figure 8 *Varying shapes and expressions are obtained with this wire shadow puppet, made by the author*

held flat against the screen, a strong, single source of light, such as a projector, is needed.

Three-dimensional shadows Two lights are required, one with a green filter, the other with a red filter.

Cut glasses frames from card. Tape to the inside of the frames two pieces of coloured acetate, one green, one red, for the lenses. Arrange the lights behind the screen on the left and right to correspond with the lenses in the glasses. The positioning of the lights will require careful adjustment to produce a good three-dimensional image.

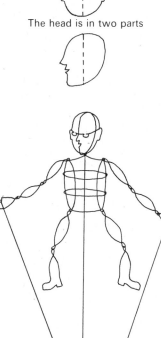

The head is in two parts

Figure 9   A three-dimensional wire-sculpture shadow puppet

Weighting the shadow puppet

Shadow figures made of fairly stiff card do not as a rule need any special weighting. On the other hand, the puppeteer who is developing his skill may find that he can improve the control of his figures by gluing a thin strip of lead to certain parts. These will vary depending on the particular needs of the situation but will usually be the feet, the forearm and, or, the hand.

Control

It is common practice to attach control wires to the body and one arm (and to the head if it moves). The other arm and the legs are allowed to swing freely. In fact, considerable control can be exercised indirectly over the puppet's legs from the one main control rod.

Many of the control techniques described use galvanised wire. A medium gauge wire (eg 14 gauge) is suitable in most cases as it is strong but easily bent to the required shape.

To attach a wire to a shadow puppet either use tape, or make a small loop in the end of the wire and attach it with thread. Tie one end of the thread to the loop and push the other end through a small hole made in the card. Knot the thread on the other side of the card. Tape is generally used for the main supporting wire and thread for moving parts.

To hold a wire it is useful either to make a large loop in the end or, preferably, to glue the end into a dowel rod or a piece of bamboo cane.

Control from below

Figures controlled from below the screen level are usually supported by a control wire taped to the body.

To control an acetate puppet, leave an extension of the figure below one of the feet (*figure 14*).

One hand is used to hold the main control and to support any head control; the other hand moves the head control and any controls for the limbs.

Arm control

Three arm controls are described: the first is the most common.
1   Join a wire to one hand with thread (*figure 15/1*). With acetate puppets, use a strip of strong clear acetate instead of wire; join it to the hand by thread knotted at each end, as for arm and leg joints (*figure 15/2*).
2   Extend the top of the arm to give a little leverage and attach a string (*figure 16*). Pull the string to raise the arm. Attach a piece of elastic to the arm and the body to provide a counter pull to the string for better arm control.
3   Make the arm in two parts, with an elbow joint. Two strings control its movement. Attach one to the top of the arm and the other to the forearm. The latter string passes through a loop of thin wire fixed in the upper arm (*figure 17*) and is used to raise and lower the forearm.

101

Figure 10   (Right) Hatziavatis who contends with Karaghiosis in the traditional Greek shadow show (here by E. Spatharis)

Figure 11   (Below, left) Mr Punch, designed and cut by Lotte Reiniger in less than two and a half minutes

Figures 12 and 13   (Below, right) The Eagle and the Owl, and Butterflies from Black Fantasy, *by the author*

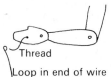

Thread

Loop in end of wire

Figure 15/1   Arm control for a
cardboard puppet

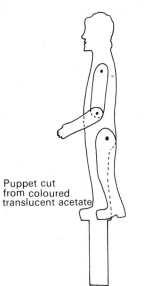

Puppet cut
from coloured
translucent acetate

Extension for holding the puppet

Figure 14   Controlling an acetate
puppet

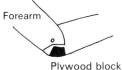

Thread

Strong clear acetate

Figure 15/2   Arm control for an
acetate puppet

Elastic

Figure 16   A string control for arm
movement

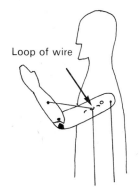

Loop of wire

Figure 17   A string control for an
arm with an elbow joint

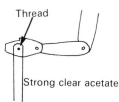

Forearm

Plywood block

Figure 18/1   Restricting arm
movement using a plywood block

Thread

Figure 18/2   Using thread to
restrict arm movement

Figure 19/1   Galvanised wire leg
control

Figure 19/2   Leg control of strong,
clear acetate

Restricting arm movement

To prevent a joint bending the wrong way or the arm sections snapping together and sticking, it may be necessary to do one of the following.
1   Glue a small piece of plywood on to the arm at the elbow. Cut away part of the elbow to accommodate this block which restricts the movement (*figure 18/1*).
2   Tie thread to the two sections (*figure 18/2*).

Leg control

The best advice on leg controls is: do not use any. Movement is invariably better when the legs hang and move freely. The Chinese and Turkish method involves only slight pressure downwards with the main control rod.

103

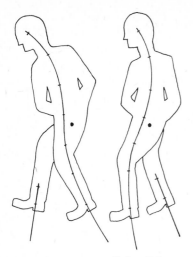

If it is essential to move a leg in a particular way, attach a piece of galvanised wire (*figure 19/1*) or a strip of strong, clear acetate (*figure 19/2*), joined to the foot with string.

If a controlled walking action is required, cut out the figure with one leg articulated as shown in *figure 20*. Attach the main control wire to the figure and an extra wire to the articulated leg. The puppet stoops forward slightly and then straightens up as he walks along.

The palette control

The 'palette' control is an old method of both supporting and moving the puppet (*figure 21*). It is simply an extension of the figure. All strings controlling the figure are attached to the palette and pulled to move the limbs. It is limiting in that the figure cannot leave the ground, for the palette would show on the screen.

Figure 20   A controlled walking action

Moving heads

The two most convenient methods for controlling an articulated head are *either* by a wire (14 or 16 gauge) attached to the back of the head (*figure 22/1*), *or* by two threads tied to a bell-bottomed neck and moved by a length of dowelling (*figure 22/2*).

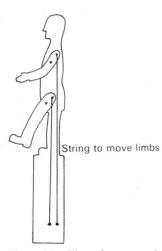

String to move limbs

Wire

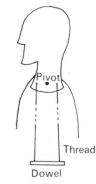

Pivot

Thread

Dowel

Figure 21   The palette control

Figure 22/1   Head controlled by a wire

Figure 22/2   Head controlled by threads

Moving mouths

Two types of moving mouth are described. The first lends itself best to comic use. The technique can be extended to include opening and closing eyes (*figures 23/1* and *23/2*). The second type of mouth action is used for profile views.

1   Cut out the eyes and mouth, both wide open, from a figure viewed full face (*figure 23/3*).

Cut a strip of card so that it can be used to cover part of the eyes whilst uncovering part of the mouth (*figure 23/4*).

Attach the card to the head with cardboard strips (about 1 in wide) glued at the ends and further secured with rivet-type paper fasteners (*figure 23/5*).

Figure 23/1 and 23/2   A moving mouth (full-face view)

Figure 23/3   The shapes cut from the head

Figure 23/4   The cardboard shape which produces the effect

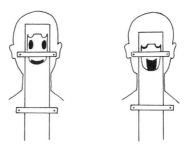

Figure 23/5   The strip of card attached: eyes open, mouth closed

Figure 23/6   The strip of card attached: eyes closed, mouth open

Figure 24   A moving mouth (profile view)

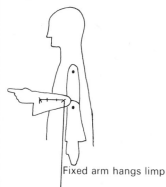

Fixed arm hangs limp

Galvanised wire

Figure 25   A substitute hand

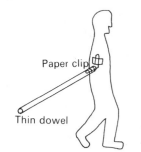

Paper clip

Thin dowel

Figure 26   A simple control from behind

Raise and lower the strip of card to effect eye and mouth movement (*figures 23/5* and *23/6*).

2   Cut out the figure with the upper part of the head separate and the lower jaw attached to the body.

Join the separate piece to the main figure so that, by pulling a wire or string at the back of the head, the mouth appears to open (*figure 24*).

Substitute hands

You may wish your shadow figure to have a variety of positions for his hand. To achieve this, cut out substitute hands and arms and mount them on a wire or strip of strong acetate (*figure 25*). The arm that is attached to the puppet must hang completely out of sight.

Control from behind

Manipulation from behind is the most common method used by puppeteers today. With each of the methods described, head and body controls are usually held in one hand (*figure 27*) and hand controls in the other.

A simple control

Make the control from a thin dowel or cane. Bend a paper clip into an L shape and tape it to the dowel and to the puppet (*figure 26*).

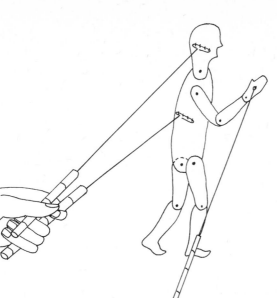

Figure 27   *The standard control*

Figure 28   *A control wire clipped onto the card*

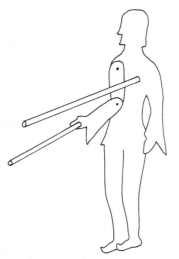

Figure 29/1   *A control for acetate puppets*

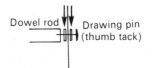

Figure 29/2   *Securing the control*

The standard control

The control is a length of galvanised wire glued into a bamboo or dowel handle. With this type of control the puppet must always face in the same direction; it cannot be turned round. However, this is not really a problem as a duplicate, facing in the opposite direction, can easily be made.

Bend the end of the wire into a long loop and fasten it to the puppet with strong thread (*figure 27*) so that the control may be lowered to hold the figure 'in repose' (ie when it is in view but not moving).

Additional control wires may be attached as required.

A control with a clip fixture

A 'clip' fastening is a much stronger fixture than thread and is recommended for children to use. The only disadvantage is that the control cannot be lowered to hold the puppet in repose.

Glue on to the body a piece of cardboard, 'stepped' as shown in *figure 28* (and another to the head if an articulated head is required).

Bend the end of the control wire into a clip shape to hold the cardboard.

Attach hand controls by thread, as usual.

A control for acetate puppets

Use two thin dowel rods for the body and hand controls as shown in *figure 29/1* (and another for the head if necessary). Attach the rods to the puppet with drawing pins (thumb tacks).

It is important that the puppet should not turn on the main rod; to prevent this happening, cut two small washers from thin rubber and place them on each side of the acetate so that they cling to the dowel, the acetate and the head of the pin (*figure 29/2*).

106

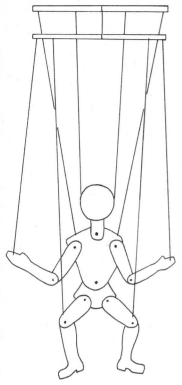

Figure 30   Control from above

Control from above

Shadow puppets can be hung on threads like a marionette and suspended from one or two control bars (*figure 30*). (Nylon threads will be scarcely visible on the screen.) The control bar is simply a length of dowelling.

If one bar is used, hold it in one hand and move individual strings with the other. If the limbs are attached to a separate bar, join the head and limb bars with string. Hold the head bar with one hand and use the other hand for the limb bar and for moving individual strings.

In order to obtain the sharpest possible image the puppet must hang flat against the screen.

Extending shadow puppets

The following methods can be used to make bodies extend and contract.

The concertina body

Cut out a figure in cardboard, making the body from arm to waist level about twice the normal length.

Pleat the cardboard.

If the body is to be manipulated from behind, attach one control wire to the lower part of the body and another to the top (*figure 31/1*).

If it is to be manipulated from below, attach one wire to the lower part of the body and another as a vertical rod running through the folds and attached to the head (*figure 31/2*).

The scissor control

Cut strips of strong card and join them to form a trellis using rivet-type paper fasteners (*figure 32*).

Cut out a cardboard figure but make the body from arm to waist level from a long strip of material glued to the card.

Attach the 'scissor' control to the top and bottom of the body only.

Operate the control like scissors to extend and contract the body.

Figure 31/1   A 'concertina' body: operation from behind

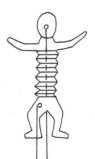

Figure 31/2   Operation from below

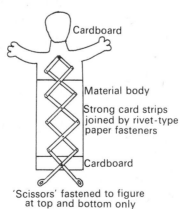

Cardboard

Material body

Strong card strips joined by rivet-type paper fasteners

Cardboard

'Scissors' fastened to figure at top and bottom only

Figure 32   A scissor control for an extending body

107

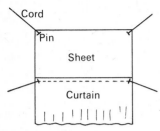

Figure 33 A simple screen

Figure 34/1 The theatre assembled

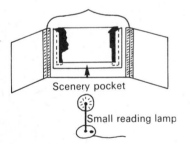

Figure 34/2 The theatre viewed from back-stage

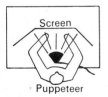

Figure 34/3 The performance

108

Presentation

The screen may be made from any semi-opaque material. A piece of sheeting is the most common and is quite satisfactory.

Paper may be used, greaseproof paper being especially suitable. Lotte Reiniger* recommends the use of a Cinemoid acetate called *Frost*, used with the matt surface towards the audience. Some professional shadow-play performers use architects' tracing linen for their screens.

Whichever material is used, the screen must be taut; if it sags or wrinkles it will spoil the performance.

For the *shape* of the screen, see *Scenery* (page 111).

A simple screen

How a simple screen is set up depends on the situation. A few examples suitable for operating puppets from any position are described.

1 Pin, or tape, the screen in an open doorway. Shield the space below the screen with coloured paper or a curtain.

2 If there is some fixture in the room (eg metal beams in a classroom) from which the screen can be suspended, fasten safety pins at the top corners and tie cords to these. Stitch, or pin, a masking curtain to the bottom of the screen to hide the operators.

Further cords attached to the sides of the screen can be tied to tables or other heavy furniture or fixtures to keep the screen taut (*figure 33*).

3 Fasten the screen in the centre section of a clothes-horse and cover the other sections with curtains.

A small cardboard table-top screen

This fitup (*figure 34/1*) may be used with figures operated from *behind* and, if the controls are very short, may also be used with figures worked from *below* the screen. It is intended for very small audiences in a confined space, for example when entertaining in the home.

Cut the three parts of the main framework from strong card (*figure 34/2*).

Join the parts by gluing on linen hinges.

Carefully glue the screen to the inside of the centre section. The screen must not become wrinkled.

Fold the bottoms of the wing pieces outwards and stand a weight on each flap to hold the fitup steady. (The weight may be disguised as some form of ornament.)

Items of scenery can be held between cardboard strips and the screen (*figure 34/2*). These cardboard scenery pockets are glued to the inside of the fitup, one at the bottom of the screen and one at each side.

Light may be provided by a candle, a bicycle lamp, or a small reading lamp. Sit at the table upon which the screen stands and manipulate the figures with one arm on each side of the lamp (*figure 34/3*). Take care not to let your hands cast shadows on the screen.

* *Shadow theatres and shadow films:* Batsford, 1970.

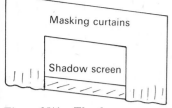

Masking curtains

Shadow screen

Figure 35/1   The theatre

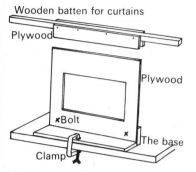

Wooden batten for curtains

Plywood

Plywood

×Bolt

The base

Clamp

Figure 35/2   The basic framework

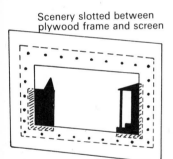

Scenery slotted between
plywood frame and screen

Screen on audience-side of frame

*Figure 35/3   Holding scenery
between the frame and the screen*

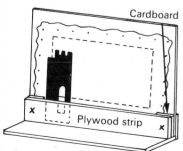

Cardboard

×   Plywood strip   ×

Screen on operator's side of frame

Figure 35/4   A scenery pocket

A table-top screen

This fitup (*figure 35/1*) is intended for use with shadow figures that are operated from behind. The dimensions depend upon individual requirements but there should always be sufficient draped space on either side of the screen to allow long objects to be brought on to the stage.

The framework

Make a support for the screen by screwing a length of plywood to an equal length of fairly thick (eg $\frac{3}{4}$ in) wood (*figure 35/2*).

Make a frame for the screen by cutting out the centre of a piece of plywood.

Bolt the frame to the support.

Carefully glue, or pin, the material for the screen over the hole. Which side of the frame you attach the screen depends on which method you are going to use for holding scenery (see below). Do not fasten the screen too close to the edge of the hole.

Hang an inverted U-shaped masking drape (which must be thick enough to exclude light) from a batten (*figure 35/1*). Nail, or screw, a plywood strip to each side of the batten, forming a groove that fits over the top of the plywood frame (*figure 35/2*). This must be a snug, secure fit or it will need to be bolted to the frame.

A light may be attached to the batten by a fixed, or adjustable, arm, or it may stand separately.

Hold the base firmly on a table top by one or two 'G' clamps ('C' clamps in America).

Holding scenery

Scenery can be *either* slipped between the frame and the screen as in *figure 35/3* (in which case the screen must be fastened to the frame on the audience side), *or* slipped into a scenery pocket as in *figure 35/4* (in which case the screen must be fastened to the frame on the operator's side). The latter method is recommended as the scenery does not interfere with the screen.

To make the scenery pocket, take a piece of plywood the same length as the width of the frame and the same depth as the bottom of the frame and glue to either end a piece of card of the same thickness as the scenery. Fasten this to the screen frame with the same bolts used to fasten the screen frame to its support.

A large fitup

The construction of this fitup varies slightly, depending on whether it is used for operation from below or from behind. When dismantled, it packs neatly to become a bundle of sticks which can be tied or strapped together for carrying.

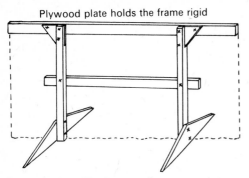

Plywood plate holds the frame rigid

Figure 36/1 *The framework*

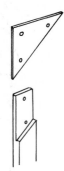

Figure 36/2 *The upright support cut away to accommodate the plywood plate*

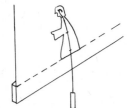

Screen on operator's side of frame

Figure 36/3 *Figures operated from below: screen on operator's side of frame*

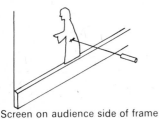

Screen on audience side of frame

Figure 36/4 *Figures operated from behind: screen on audience-side of frame*

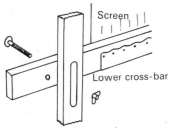

Screen

Lower cross-bar

Hole made into slot

Figure 36/5 *An adjustable screen*

The frame

The parts bolt together as illustrated (*figure 36/1*). Large, triangular, supporting 'feet' bolt on to the vertical posts to keep the frame upright.

Cut away the top of each vertical post to accommodate the small plywood plates which hold the frame secure (*figure 36/2*).

If the puppets are to be operated from below, attach the screen to the operator's side of the framework so that the puppets and scenery may be held flat against the screen (*figure 36/3*). If they are to be operated from behind, attach the screen to the audience side of the frame so that the lower cross bar provides a ledge upon which the puppets can walk (*figure 36/4*).

Attach drapes in the same way as for glove- and rod-puppet booths (see page 74).

Adjusting the tension of the screen

This small modification is not essential but may be desirable. It involves making the lower cross bar adjustable.

Make the hole in the vertical post into a slot to allow the bolt in the lower cross bar to slide (*figure 36/5*).

To increase the tension of the screen, lower the cross bar and tighten the bolts.

A ledge for characters in repose

If the puppets are operated from behind, the fitup may have a ledge on which to rest the controls of the characters 'in repose' on the screen whilst the others are manipulated.

Make the ledge from a strip of plywood, to each end of which are screwed two short dowels (*figure 37/1*).

The ledge rests on two triangular blocks of wood which are hinged to the vertical posts below screen level. Drill two holes in the top of each block to accommodate the dowels (*figure 37/1*).

Cover the ledge with thick felt, foam rubber, or a comparable material, so that the controls do not slide about. In order to prevent the control

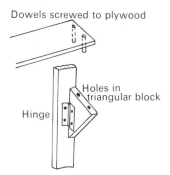

Dowels screwed to plywood

Holes in triangular block

Hinge

Figure 37/1   Construction of the ledge

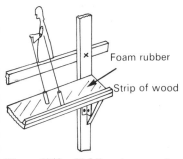

Foam rubber

Strip of wood

Figure 37/2   Holding the controls securely

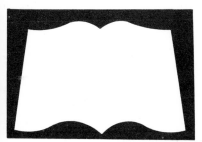

Figure 38   A screen in the shape of an open book

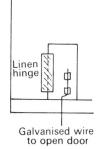

Linen hinge

Galvanised wire to open door

Figure 39   Hinged scenery

rods slipping off the ledge, glue and nail a narrow wooden batten to the outside edge of the ledge (*figure 37/2*).

Scenery

Scenery for the shadow theatre need not be elaborate: beautiful scenes can be achieved by simple means. Often, as with other aspects of puppet theatre, a mere suggestion will evoke an idea. Something simple can be just as effective as, or even more effective than, elaborate scenery.

Remember that (unless the scenery is acetate) figures cannot cast a shadow if they are held in front of scenery, and that every piece of scenery cuts down the acting area.

The screen

The shape of the screen is the first consideration when setting the scene. With the basic shape of a large rectangle, a masking shape can be fastened against the screen to establish any other shape required (*figure 38*). It may be a material drape, a cardboard cutout, a thin sheet of plywood or even a coloured sheet of translucent acetate. Some authorities suggest the use of movable shutters to adjust the screen dimensions, but these would seem unnecessarily elaborate as the above methods are quite satisfactory.

Constructing scenery

The scenery is best made from stiff card or, for special effects, coloured translucent acetate. It can be made as individual pieces or a complete unit cut from one large sheet of card or acetate.
Cardboard   Cut out the scenery with a sharp craft knife.

Some parts of the scenery, such as doors, may be fixed with linen hinges (glued on) so that it is possible to open and close them. Tape a small piece of galvanised wire to the moving part so that it can be opened and closed easily (*figure 39*).

If the puppet is required to walk on parts of the scenery, it is useful to glue and tack wooden blocks on to the back of the cut-out scene to provide a surface (*figure 40*).

To create a greater feeling of depth in the scene, a horizon piece may be used (*figure 41*). Most of the action will take place below this line although smaller figures may be used above it for action in the distance.
Acetate   Either cut out coloured acetate shapes, *or* paint the scene on a sheet of coloured acetate with quick-drying, black enamel paint. On plain acetate use black enamel, glass painting colours or Letrafilm.

Figure 40   Blocks of wood glued on to scenery for puppets to walk on

111

Figure 41   A scene from The Wooden Soldier *by the author, which makes use of an horizon piece*

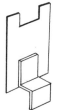

Slot for scenery

Screw

Aluminium

Figure 42/1   Operation from behind: The slot for scenery

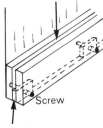

Stepped strip of aluminium glued to scenery

Figure 42/2   Stepped strip of aluminium glued to scenery

Supporting the scenery in a large fitup

With figures operated horizontally   Make a groove to hold the scenery by attaching a length of wood to the lower cross bar, with a few small strips of aluminium between them (*figure 42/1*).

Glue a stepped strip of aluminium to the back of the scenery (*figure 42/2*); the aluminium fits neatly into the slot and the scenery is held firmly against the screen.

For large pieces of scenery it is advisable to make a second groove at the top of the screen so that the scenery is held more securely.

With figures operated vertically   The arrangement described above is not satisfactory with figures operated from below as it prevents the puppets from being held against the screen.

Glue button magnets into holes drilled in the lower cross bar.

Fix the screen on the operator's side of the framework with the screen stretched across the magnets.

Screw a series of hooks into the top cross bar.

Sew small curtain rings to the top of the scenery; these hang from the hooks. Glue strips of metal (eg tin) to the bottom of the scenery; these are held by the magnets (*figure 43*).

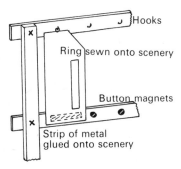

Hooks

Ring sewn onto scenery

Button magnets

Strip of metal glued onto scenery

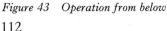

Figure 43   Operation from below

8 The marionette

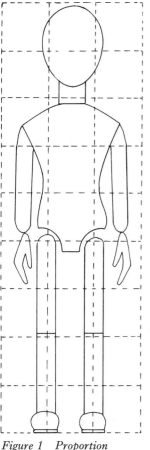

Figure 1   Proportion

Cardboard disc

Figure 2/1   The shoulders

Figure 2/2   Card overlapped and glued

Construction

Proportions for a marionette

A marionette usually looks unnatural if given human proportions and so often the head, hands and feet are made slightly larger than human proportions and the legs slightly shorter. A satisfactory size for the hands is usually approximately the length from the chin to the middle of the forehead, the feet a little longer.

It must be emphasised that these are not rules for puppet proportions: any part of the puppet may be exaggerated (either larger, smaller, bonier, fatter, etc) but there must always be a theatrical reason for the proportions chosen and it is often the variations from the norm which are important.

Checking the puppets from a distance and, if possible, under stage lighting will help to make clear any exaggerations or changes that may be necessary.

The body

The body of a marionette is usually constructed in two parts with a joint at the waist. A body in one piece restricts the way a puppet moves, particularly its walk.

Usually the neck is built on to the head but if it is to be built on to the body and jointed inside the head, the body should be made from plastic wood or carved from a wooden block.

A cloth body

(Normally used with a sock head.)

To make a shoulder piece cut a hole in the centre of a cardboard disc. Make one cut from the perimeter to the centre (*figure 2/1*), then overlap and glue together the edges (*figure 2/2*).

Attach the head to the shoulder piece by pushing the loose end of the sock through the disc and sewing it to the cardboard, both near the centre and at the edge of the disc (*figure 2/3*).

Glue or stitch the edges of a piece of fabric together to make a tube for the body. Glue and stitch one end of the tube on to the cardboard shoulder piece.

113

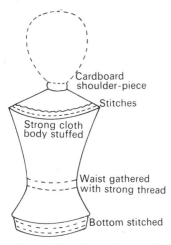

Cardboard shoulder-piece

Stitches

Strong cloth body stuffed

Waist gathered with strong thread

Bottom stitched

Figure 2/3   The body assembled

Figure 3/1   Plywood shape for thorax

Figure 3/2   Foam rubber glued to plywood

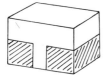

Figure 3/3   The shaded parts are cut from the block to form the pelvis

Figure 3/4   Two pieces joined for the pelvis

Run two strong threads round the centre of the body and draw up to form a waist (*figure 2/3*).

Stuff the body with fabric, or foam rubber, and stitch across the bottom.

Stitch cloth arms and legs to the body.

A wood and foam rubber body

Make the thorax by gluing foam rubber to a piece of plywood, or hardboard, cut to the shape illustrated in *figure 3/1*.

With scissors, snip the foam rubber into the required three-dimensional form (*figure 3/2*).

To make the pelvis, saw two sections from a block of wood (*figure 3/3*), leaving a T shape. Round off the sharp corners and pad with foam rubber. Alternatively, glue and screw together two pieces of wood in the T shape (*figure 3/4*) and pad.

A rubber body

Model the two parts of the body in plasticine on dowels and take a plaster cast as described on page 61. *Figure 4/1* shows how to place the metal strips in the plasticine model when making the plaster cast. When the dowels in the body are removed from the casts, they will leave holes in the plaster through which the latex rubber can be poured and this will also leave holes in the rubber body parts that can later be used for joining them.

Cast the body in rubber (see page 62).

When dry, cut open the thorax and glue into the centre a hardboard or thin plywood shape (as used for a wood and foam rubber body) with four holes drilled in it (*figure 4/2*) for attaching neck, arms and pelvis.

Stuff the body with foam rubber and seal the slit with glue.

A plastic wood body

Model the body in plastic wood over a rough shape of balsa wood. When dry, smooth the surface with glasspaper.

A wooden body

Carve the body from two blocks of wood. The thorax may be cut open and hollowed out to reduce the weight of the puppet.

Plastic wood and carved bodies are both suitable for being left unclothed.

Waist joints

Screw-eye joints

This joint can be used with wooden bodies.

Fasten a screw-eye in each section. Open up one of the screw-eyes with a pair of pliers, interlock it in the other and close the link again (*figure 5*).

Alternatively, join the screw-eyes with string.

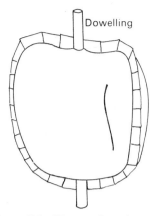

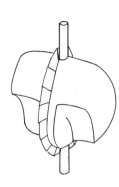

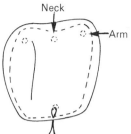

Figure 4/1   How to place the metal
strips in the plasticine models

Figure 4/1   How to place the metal strips in the plasticine models

Figure 4/2   A hardboard or plywood shape glued into the rubber body

Cord to join thorax to pelvis

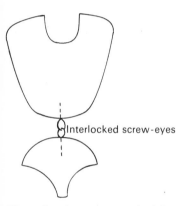

Figure 5   A screw-eye waist joint

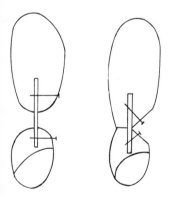

Figure 6/1   Leather waist joint prevents turning at waist

Figure 6/2   This restricted joint allows forward movement only

Leather joints

Leather may be used with plastic wood bodies built on balsa wood or with solid wooden bodies.

Cut slots in each section. Glue the ends of the strip of leather and insert them in the slots. Secure the leather further with nails (*figure 6/1*).

If you want a restricted joint, permitting movement in only one direction, make the joint so that the thorax and pelvis are in contact. Cut away part of the thorax and pelvis (*figure 6/2*) to facilitate movement in the direction required.

Cord joints

These joints can be used with wood and foam rubber or moulded rubber bodies.

For the former, drill a hole in the plywood base of the thorax, insert a screw-eye in the top of the pelvis, and thread through cord (*figure 7/1*).

To join rubber body parts, tie a strong cord to the hardboard or plywood in the thorax and push the ends through the hole in the top of the rubber pelvis (*figure 7/2*). Pour plaster of Paris into the pelvis. This secures the cord and weights the body. (It is wise to join the legs to the pelvis at the same time. See pages 120, 121.)

Joints for unclothed bodies

A ball joint

This joint allows movement in all directions.

Make the body with hollows in the pelvis and thorax to accommodate a wooden ball (*figure 8*).

Drill a hole through the centre of the ball and through the thorax and pelvis.

Thread a string through all three sections and knot it at each end where it emerges from the body. Sink the knots in the body and cover them with plastic wood.

115

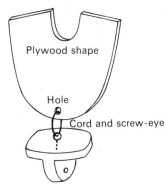

Figure 7/1   *Cord joint for a wooden body*

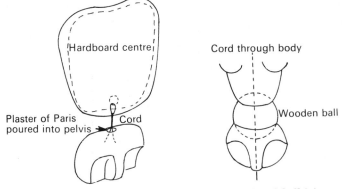

Figure 7/2   *Cord joint for a rubber body*

Figure 8   *A ball joint*

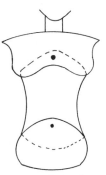

Figure 9   *A body in three sections*

A body in three parts

This joint allows only sideways movement.

Make the body in three sections, leaving the chest and pelvis hollow to take the shaped centre piece (*figure 9*).

Insert the ends of the centre piece into the chest and pelvis and join the three sections with two large nails so that they are free to pivot sideways.

Neck joints

Joints used when the neck is built onto the head

How to join a sock head to a cloth body is described on page 113. All other types of body and head can be joined by using any one of the following:

1   interlocked screw-eyes (*figure 10/1*);
2   screw-eyes joined by string (*figure 10/2*);
3   a string through a hole in the body and a screw-eye in the neck (*figure 10/3*).

All these methods presuppose a dowel built into the neck.

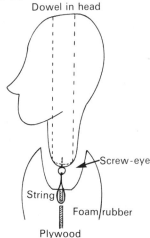

Figure 10/1   *Interlocked screw-eyes*

Figure 10/2   *Two screw-eyes joined by string*

Figure 10/3   *A screw-eye and string*

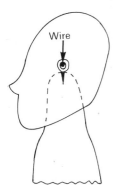

Figure 11/1   Screw-eye in neck and wire through the head

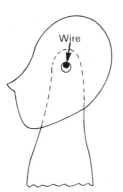

Figure 11/2   Hole through neck and wire through the head

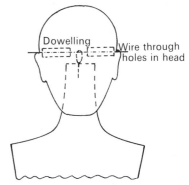

Figure 11/3   Full-face view of the screw-eye method

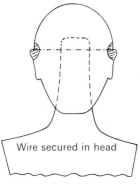

Figure 11/4   Full-face view of the wire through the neck, secured in the head

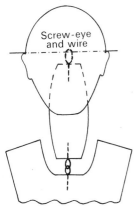

Figure 12   Two joints for a separate neck

Joints used when the neck is built onto the body

Fasten a screw-eye in the top of the neck (*figure 11/1*) or drill a hole from side to side through the neck (*figure 11/2*).

Drill a hole in either side of the head, just behind the ears.

Take a length of strong galvanised wire and pass it through the screw-eye or the hole in the neck and through the holes in the head (*figure 11/3*). With the screw-eye method, to prevent the screw-eye sliding too far on the wire, it might be necessary to drill holes through two short dowels and slip these on to the wire on each side of the screw-eye (*figure 11/3*).

Cut off the ends of the wire and secure the wire in the head with glue and more of the material used for the head (applied inside and outside the head as shown in *figure 11/4*).

Using a screw-eye allows the head to turn and nod, whereas the hole drilled through the neck restricts head movement to nodding.

Joints used when the neck is a separate piece

The neck piece is usually carved from a thick dowel or built up around a dowel (*figure 12*). Any of the appropriate joints described above may be used to join it to the head and body.

Hands

The shape of the hands is important in helping to create character. Characterless hands may spoil an otherwise exciting puppet. They can be simply shaped—detailed modelling is quite unnecessary—or indeed stylised, but the fingers should be held in an expressive manner.

Cloth hands

Cloth hands may be used with any sort of marionette. They are described on page 67.

Carved hands

Hands may be carved from wood but this requires considerable skill.

117

Figure 13   A pipe-cleaner base for a plastic wood hand

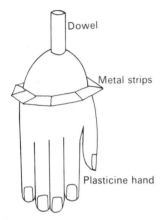

Figure 14   Preparing to make a cast for a rubber hand

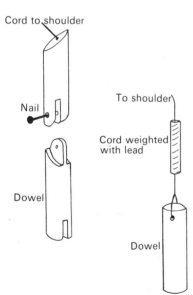

Figure 15   A dowelling arm with an open mortise and tenon elbow joint

Figure 16   A dowelling and cord arm

Plastic wood hands

Plastic wood is an ideal material for modelling hands. When it is hard it can be cut away, carved, filed, sanded or built up with more plastic wood until the required shape is obtained.

To model the hand, intertwine three pipe cleaners and bend them into the required position (*figure 13*).

Cover the pipe cleaners with glue (Bostik No. 1, Sobo or another suitable, all-purpose adhesive) and add plastic wood in fairly large pieces. Do not try to attach it to the fingers individually. Snip between the fingers with a pair of scissors and model the shape of the fingers.

When hard, build up or cut away the plastic wood as necessary, sand the hands smooth and attach a screw-eye for the wrist joint.

Rubber hands

Rubber hands are moulded in the same way as rubber heads. *Figure 14* shows where to place the metal strips in the plasticine model to make the plaster cast.

When the hand is made, glue a dowel into it. This provides a strong fixture for a screw-eye for the wrist joint and for attaching a hand string later.

Arms and wrist joints

Cloth arms

Make cloth arms from tubes of material stuffed with stockings or foam rubber.

Stitch across the arms at the elbows to help them bend and sew cloth hands on to the arms.

Dowelling arms

Arms may be made from two pieces of dowelling with interlocked screw-eyes for the elbow joint. For more restricted movement, use one of the open mortise and tenon joints (*figure 15*) described for the legs.

For greater freedom of movement, it is common to use string for the upper arm, sometimes weighted with lead. Make the lower arm from dowelling (*figure 16*).

The following joints are suitable for the wrist:
1   interlocked screw-eyes;
2   string threaded through a hole in the arm and through a screw-eye in the hand (*figure 17*).

To restrict hand movement, first cut a slot in the end of the arm. Fix a screw-eye in the hand, insert the screw-eye in the slot and secure it with a small nail (*figure 18*).

Legs and knee joints

Legs may be made from cloth, rubber, dowelling or plywood. Take care that they are in correct proportion with the puppet's body. Legs that are too thin not only look odd but affect the way trousers hang.

118

Figure 17   A screw-eye and string wrist joint

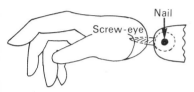

Figure 18   A restricted wrist joint

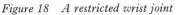

Figure 20/1   The shaded parts are cut away

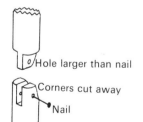

Figure 20/2   The rear corners are cut away to allow bending

Cloth legs

Cloth legs are made from stuffed tubes of material, in the same way as cloth arms. They are sewn on to the cloth body.

Rubber legs

Rubber legs are moulded in one piece so no knee joint is necessary. The procedure is the same as for the rubber head. *Figure 19* shows the shape of the plasticine model.

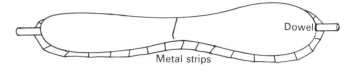

Figure 19   A plasticine model for rubber legs

Dowelling legs

Dowelling is a suitable material for making legs. If necessary, shape it with a knife or build it up with plastic wood. To make the knee joint use one of the following two open mortise and tenon joints or the leather joint.

1   Saw away the sides of the top leg section as shown in *figure 20/1*, leaving a 'tongue'.

With a saw, cut a slot (the 'groove') in the lower leg section.

To allow the leg to bend cut off the rear corners where the parts join (*figure 20/2*).

Put the leg together with the tongue in the groove and drill one hole through both parts (*figure 20/2*).

Insert a nail in the hole to hold the two parts together. The hole in the tongue must be large enough to allow it to pivot freely on the nail.

Secure the nail with glue and plastic wood.

2   Use a screw-eye in the top of the lower leg instead of a wooden 'tongue' (*figure 21*).

3   Cut away the back of each part of the leg to allow it to bend.

Saw a slot in each section (*figure 22/1*).

Insert the ends of a strip of leather in the slots and secure with glue and/or nails (*figure 22/2*).

Plywood legs

These legs are each built up of six plywood shapes, which give an open mortise and tenon knee joint.

With a coping saw, cut out the six leg shapes as illustrated in *figure 23/1*.

Either cut off the bottom of section C to accommodate a 'tongue' attached to the foot (for the ankle joint), *or* leave an extra piece on

119

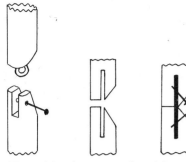

Figure 21   A screw-eye knee joint

Figure 22/1   A leather knee joint: the slot cut for the leather and the rear corners cut away

Figure 22/2   Securing the leather

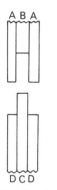

Figure 23/2   Joining the six parts to form the leg

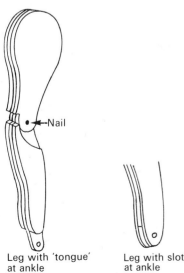

Leg with 'tongue' at ankle   Leg with slot at ankle

Figure 23/3   Securing the knee joint

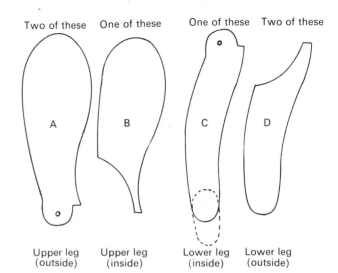

Two of these   One of these   One of these   Two of these

A   B   C   D

Upper leg   Upper leg   Lower leg   Lower leg
(outside)   (inside)   (inside)   (outside)

Figure 23/1   The plywood shapes

section C to form a projection to fit into a slot in the foot. The former method may be used with modelled or carved feet, the latter with carved feet.

Glue one section A to each side of section B and one D to each side of C (*figure 23/2*).

Sand down the top surface of section C so that it moves freely in the groove in the upper leg.

Join the upper and lower leg with a nail (*figure 23/3*) as described above.

Hip joints

For a wooden leg and body use either a strip of leather (1) *or* a piece of galvanised wire (*c* 12 gauge) (2).

1   Glue and nail one end of the leather into a slot in the top of the leg and the other end into a slot in the pelvis (*figure 24*).

2   Drill a hole through (or fix a screw-eye in) the top of the leg (*figure 25*).

Drill a hole through the part of the pelvis that divides the legs.

Push the wire through this dividing section and through the tops of the legs.

Drill a hole in each side of the pelvis, near the top. With pliers, bend each end of the wire upwards and then bend the tips again so that they fit into the holes drilled in the pelvis.

Secure the wire with glue and a small staple.

To join rubber legs and body use a strip of rubber. (Pour a little liquid latex into a tin or tin lid and allow to dry; then peel off the rubber and cut out the shape required.)

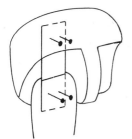

Figure 24   A leather hip joint

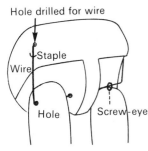

Figure 25   A wire hip joint, showing two methods for attaching the legs

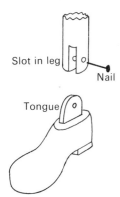

Slot in leg

Nail

Tongue

Figure 26   An ankle joint for a modelled or carved foot

Tongue on leg fits into slot in foot

Nail

Figure 27   An alternative ankle joint for a carved foot

Make a slit in the top of the leg and glue the strip of rubber into it. Slot the other end of the strip into the pelvis and pour in liquid plaster of Paris. When this sets it will hold the strip securely. (This should be done at the same time as making the waist joint, described on page 115.)

Feet and ankle joints

Modelled feet and carved feet

Feet may be carved or made from plastic wood or some similar material, modelled on a plasticine base (see page 59). To remove the plasticine, cut off the sole.

Build a piece of plywood into the foot to project above the foot as a 'tongue'. Fit this tongue into a slot in the leg and secure it with a nail (*figure 26*).

With a carved foot the tongue is carved as part of the foot. Alternatively, make a slot (by drilling a series of holes) in the foot to accommodate a projection from the leg. Secure with a nail as before (*figure 27*).

Glue pieces of felt on to the bottoms of the feet to prevent them making a noise on the stage floor.

Rubber feet

Rubber feet are moulded in the same way as a rubber head (page 61). When making the plaster cast, insert the metal strips around the sole.

If the bottom of the leg is moulded with the foot (*figure 28/1*), this may be glued over the actual leg when attaching the foot. Otherwise, glue a rubber strip into a slot cut in the leg and insert the other end of the strip into the foot. Pour liquid plaster of Paris into the heel to hold the strip and weight the foot (*figure 28/2*).

Weighting the marionette

To give really precise control it may be necessary to weight a puppet, although with a really well-made figure it should not be. *Figure 29* shows points at which weight may be added. It is especially important that the pelvis is not too light as it will affect the puppet's walking action.

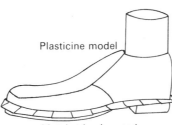

Plasticine model

Metal strips inserted above the sole of the shoe

Figure 28/1   Preparing to make the plaster cast

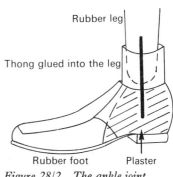

Rubber leg

Thong glued into the leg

Rubber foot   Plaster

Figure 28/2   The ankle joint

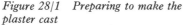

121

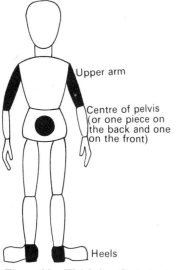

Upper arm

Centre of pelvis (or one piece on the back and one on the front)

Heels

Figure 29   Weighting the puppet

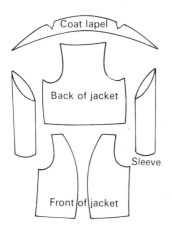

Coat lapel

Back of jacket

Sleeve

Front of jacket

Glue or stitch the edges together.

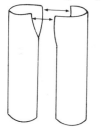

Trousers

Figure 30   Dressing the marionette

If it is necessary to weight the foot, avoid making the toe too heavy or it will drag when the puppet walks.

The usual method for adding weight is to glue and, or, nail on a piece of lead. With moulded rubber parts, pour liquid plaster into the part to be weighted.

Dressing the marionette

The marionette must be dressed before you start to string it.

The material used should be soft and fairly lightweight. If it is too heavy it will restrict movement; if too thin, light will shine through it. Select materials under artificial lighting or, preferably, stage lighting.

Glue or stitch the clothes together. I prefer gluing as it is quicker and leaves no seam edges inside the clothes to restrict movement. The glue used depends on the material. Bostik No. 1 or Sobo glues are suitable for most materials.

To make a hem, smear glue sparingly but evenly along the edge, turn it up and press firmly. To make a seam, glue one edge and press it on top of the other. The use of glue prevents the outer edge fraying.

Make trousers from two tubes of cloth fastened together at the top (*figure 30*).

When making a jacket, first glue together the front and back panels, then add the sleeves, collar and lapels. For a shirt under a jacket, glue a wide strip of material down the front of the body for the shirt front and a narrower strip around the neck for the collar.

Felt is excellent for trimmings such as ties, coat lapels and buttons.

Take care not to make sleeves, trouser legs and collars too tight or movement will be hindered.

The same methods are used for dresses, skirts etc, which are somewhat simpler to make than men's clothes.

Animal puppets

The head can be made in any of the ways described in Chapter 4. Most leg shapes required cannot be carved from dowelling so they are usually made from plywood with open mortise and tenon joints (see *figure 38* and *Plywood legs*, page 119). Occasionally rubber is used. Methods for making bodies are described below.

A cardboard body

A cardboard body is made in the same way as a cardboard head (see page 57).

Cut a basic shape from strong card.

Make a hole in the neck for a cord from the head (for the neck joint).

Make two holes in the card to accommodate $\frac{3}{4}$ in dia dowels (for attaching the legs later) and glue the dowels into the holes.

Glue 'ribs' and strengthening pieces to the basic shape then cover it with card (*figure 39*). Over the end of each dowel glue a circle of smooth card on which the legs may turn.

Screw the legs to the ends of the dowels.

Figure 31 A Day at the Seaside: *marionettes by John Thirtle*

Figure 32 Professor Ozgood, by *the author*

Figure 33 Charles Henry, the *author's compère, with Sammy, by Julie Gosling*

Figures 34 and 35   Clown Percy, and the Chauffeur, by John Thirtle

Figure 36   Charlemagne from the Hogarth Puppets' production of Master Peter's Puppet Show

Figure 37   The King from Derek Francis' production of The Light Princess

Cover the cardboard body with plastic wood, nylon 'hair', fur, thick knitting wool fluffed up, or cloth. If necessary, a plain cloth may be coloured with dye or even paints. Polymer colours mixed thinly with water can be used to paint on special markings.

Cover the neck joint with material and then colour it or cover it with fur, etc.

A plywood body

Cut out a plywood body shape with a coping saw.

Drill two holes in the shape and glue dowels into them for attaching the legs (as described for a cardboard body).

Cut out plywood 'ribs' and cut slots in the ribs and the body shape so that they slide together (*figure 40*). Glue the ribs in place; fill any gaps and strengthen the joints with plastic wood.

Cover the body with cardboard and material as described above.

As an alternative to this method, having cut out the plywood body shape and secured dowels for attaching legs, as before, glue layers or blocks of foam rubber to each side of the plywood and trim the foam rubber to the shape of the body.

Cover the body with material, wool, fur, etc.

A 'junk' body

Junk bodies can be made successfully from a variety of scrap materials. For example, a large tin might be used for the centre of the body. Glue and nail a block of wood to the bottom and another to the lid (which is itself then glued to the tin) to attach the neck and legs (*figure 41*). Cover the tin with foam rubber, trim to shape and cover as described above.

Junk-box marionettes

Any type of marionette can be made by the junk-box method. A few examples are illustrated (*figures 46-49*).

Controlling the marionette

Strings attached to the puppet are joined to a wooden control which is constructed in such a way as to produce movement of a particular part of the puppet when appropriately moved.

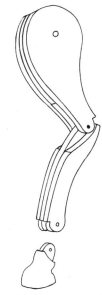

Figure 38   Plywood legs for an animal marionette

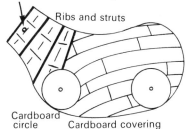

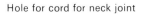

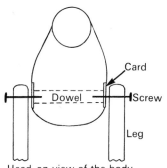

Head-on view of the body

Figure 39   A cardboard body for an animal

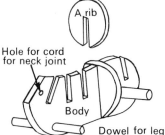

Figure 40   A plywood body

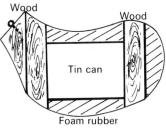

Figure 41   A 'junk' body

125

Figure 42   The Elephant from
the Mejandes Marionettes'
Children's Show

Figure 43   The Stork, by
Albrecht Roser

Figure 44   The Lion from the
Lanchester Marionette Circus

Figure 45   Gigi, a giraffe with
an extending neck, by the author

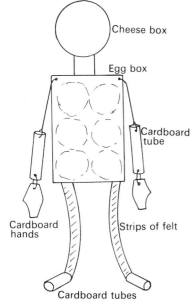

Figure 46   A scarf marionette

Ball

Knot

Scarf

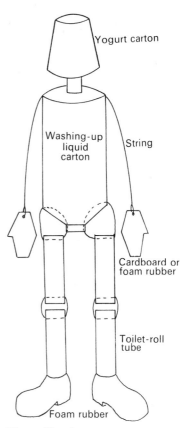

Figure 47   A carton marionette

Yogurt carton

Washing-up liquid carton

String

Cardboard or foam rubber

Toilet-roll tube

Foam rubber

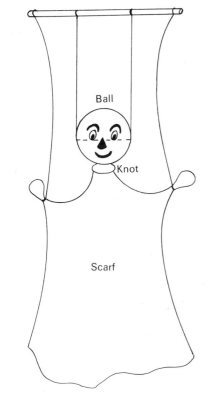

Figure 48   A cardboard marionette

Cheese box

Egg box

Cardboard tube

Cardboard hands

Strips of felt

Cardboard tubes

Figure 49   A watering can marionette. Legs and arms: rope. Feet and hands: foam rubber

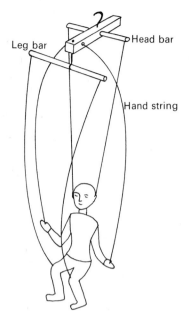

Figure 50   *A simple aeroplane control*

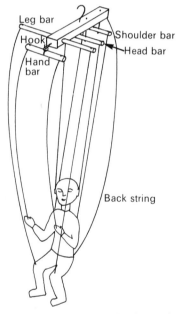

Figure 51/1   *The standard aeroplane control and stringing*

Figure 51/2   *An alternative joint for the leg bar*

The control

Two kinds of marionette control are in common use: the upright control and the 'aeroplane', or 'paddle', control. The tendency in Britain is to use the upright control for human puppets and the aeroplane control for animals but in America the aeroplane control is used extensively for both. The determining factor must be the requirements of the individual puppet. For children's use, a simple aeroplane control is recommended.

As a rule small holes are drilled in the control for the strings, the strings being threaded through and tied. (Some puppeteers prefer to fasten screw-eyes for the strings but this is not recommended as the screw-eyes tend to catch in the strings of other puppets.)

All controls should have a large hook at the top (*figure 50*) for hanging up the puppet.

A simple aeroplane control

The control consists of a main wooden bar (1×1 in and 6 in long) to which are attached the hand strings and dowels for the head bar and leg bar (*figure 50*).

To attach the head bar, drill a hole through the main bar and glue the dowel into the hole.

To attach the leg bar, drill a hole down through the front of the main bar. Thread a strong cord through the hole and knot the top; tie the other end to the leg bar.

To attach the hand strings, drill a hole across the main bar just behind the leg bar. The hands are controlled by one long running string threaded through the hole.

The standard aeroplane control

This aeroplane control consists of an 8 in main bar (of 1×1 in wood) from which are suspended dowelling head and shoulder bars and a removable hand bar. A leg bar is firmly secured to the control, forming a T shape (*figure 51*). All dowels are approximately $\frac{1}{4}$ in dia.

To attach the head bar, drill a hole down through the main bar, approximately in the middle, and another through the centre of the dowel rod. Thread a cord through the holes and knot the ends (*figure 51/1*).

The shoulder bar is suspended from the back of the control in the same manner.

To attach the leg bar to the front of the control, *either* glue the dowel into a hole drilled across the main bar (*figure 51/1*), *or* glue and screw the dowel on to the top of the main bar (*figure 51/2*).

To attach the hand bar, tie a small curtain ring to the dowel. Screw a small hook into the front end of the main bar and hang the hand bar from it (*figure 51/1*).

To attach a back string, drill a hole down through the rear end of the control.

If the puppet is to have a moving mouth (or eyes), the string for operating these is controlled by a wire lever attached to the main control.

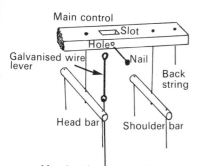

Main control
Slot
Hole
Nail
Galvanised wire lever
Back string
Head bar
Shoulder bar
Mouth string or eye strings

Figure 51/3 Controlling eye or mouth movements

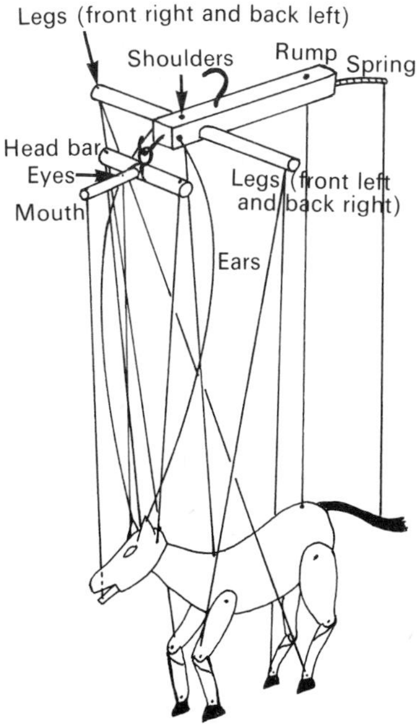

Legs (front right and back left)
Shoulders
Rump
Spring
Head bar
Eyes
Legs (front left and back right)
Mouth
Ears

Figure 52 An aeroplane control for animal puppets

Make the lever from a piece of 12 or 14 gauge galvanised wire with each end bent into a loop. Cut a slot in the control just behind the head bar (an easy way is to drill a series of touching holes,) and fix the lever in the slot by a nail through one of the loops (*figure 51/3*). The mouth or eye string(s) is tied to the other loop.

An aeroplane control for animals

This control consists of a (1×1 in) main wooden bar of about the same length as the puppet, with a dowelling leg bar attached at the front as described for the previous control. A removable T-shaped head bar is suspended from the front of the main bar and a spring to control the tail is attached to the rear of the control. Back strings are attached directly to the main control bar (*figure 52*).

To make the head bar, drill a hole in the centre of a $\frac{1}{2}$ in dia dowel and glue into the hole a $\frac{1}{4}$ or $\frac{3}{16}$ in dia dowel. The main head strings are attached to the ends of the larger dowel. A string to the nose, or to a moving mouth, is attached to the end of the smaller dowel.

To attach the head bar to the control, screw a hook into the front of the main control and suspend the head bar from it by means of a small curtain ring tied to the bar.

To attach back strings, drill a small hole down through each end of the main bar. Thread the strings directly through these holes and knot them on the top.

To attach the tail control, drill a hole into the end of the main bar and glue the spring into the hole.

Add ear and eye strings if required. *Either* thread them through holes drilled in the head bar and knot them, *or* thread them through holes drilled across the front of the main control bar. If either of the strings is attached to the main bar, the ears will be raised or the eyes closed whenever the head bar is unhooked and lowered.

Note For most animals each front leg is connected to the control at the same point as the opposite back leg, so that the puppet lifts these two legs together (ie front right and back left; front left and back right). Some animals, however, (eg giraffes and camels) move their near and offside legs together, which produces a rather rolling gait.

The upright control

The upright control consists of a vertical 8 in rod into which is fixed a head bar, forming an inverted T shape. To the back of the control is secured a shoulder bar. A detachable leg bar is suspended near the top of the control and wires to control the hands are attached to the main dowel rod just below the leg bar (*figure 53/1*). The control is made entirely of dowelling (*c* $\frac{3}{4}$ in dia for the main rod and $\frac{1}{4}$ or $\frac{5}{16}$ in dia for all attachments, and galvanised wire (*c* 14 gauge).

To attach the dowelling head bar (which should be a little longer than the width of the puppet's head), drill a hole across the bottom of the main rod. Glue the head bar into the hole and secure with a nail (*figure 53/1*).

To attach the dowelling shoulder bar, drill a hole at an angle in the

129

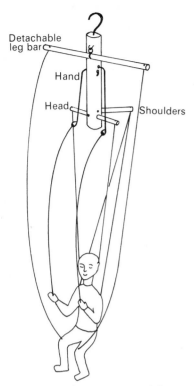

Figure 53/1   The basic upright control and stringing

rear of the control. Glue the end of the shoulder bar into the hole and secure with a nail (*figure 53/1*). The bar must be long enough to hold the shoulder strings away from the head so that its movement is not restricted.

As an alternative to making the shoulder bar of wood it can be made of galvanised wire, which has the advantage that it can be folded for packing. To attach the wire to the control, first drill a hole through the main bar just above the head bar. Loop the wire through the hole, bend the ends together and glue and bind together the two halves of the wire with strong thread (*figure 53/2*). Bend the ends of the wire into a loop for attaching the shoulder strings. Preferably, to keep the shoulder strings well clear of the head, attach them to the ends of a separate dowel and suspend the dowel by a curtain ring from the loop in the end of the wire (*figure 53/3*).

To attach the dowelling leg bar, screw a small hook into the front of the control, near the top. Tie a small curtain ring to the centre of the dowel and hang it from the hook (*figure 53/1*).

To attach the wires for the hand controls, drill two holes from side to side through the control, one above the other with a small gap in between. Bend the top of each wire into an inverted L shape; push the top of each piece through one of the holes and bend over the wire at the other side to prevent it coming out (*figure 53/1*). Make a loop in the lower end of each wire for attaching the hand strings. The wires must be long enough to rest on the head bar.

If fixtures are required for mouth and eye strings, attach them to the ends of short dowels. To attach the dowels to the control, drill two holes in the front of the control above the head bar and glue the dowels into the holes (*figure 53/4*).

Any back string may be attached to some part of the shoulder bar (*figures 53/2* and *53/3*).

Stringing

To string the puppet use No. 18 carpet thread (dark green or black), or a comparable substitute. Rub the thread with beeswax from time to time to prevent it becoming brittle and fraying. Nylon thread is not recommended as it has a tendency to stretch, glistens under stage lighting, and retains crinkles after being wound up for packing.

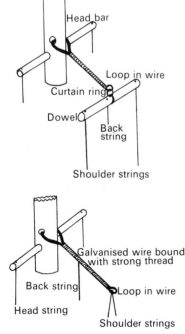

Figure 53/2 and 53/3   Shoulder bars that fold up for packing

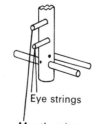

Figure 53/4   Fixing mouth and eye strings to the control

130

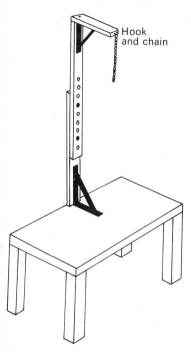

Hook
and chain

Figure 54/1   Securing the gallows

Figure 54/2   A more secure fixture

The strings should be long enough to allow the control to be held comfortably over the back cloth (usually about elbow height) when the puppet is standing on the stage. If the stage has a bridge, the strings must, of course, be longer.

With any removable control bars, such as a leg bar, make the strings just long enough to allow the bar to be unhooked without moving the puppet.

It is easiest to string a puppet when it is supported in a standing position. The best way of achieving this is to stand the puppet on a table or a work bench and suspend it from a gallows.

To make a gallows

Screw a 12 in length of wood to a length of about 5 or 6 ft to form a right angle. Strengthen the joint with a shelf bracket. Attach the upright to the table or work bench with another bracket (*figure 54/1*) or, for added firmness, three brackets (*figure 54/2*). Screw a hook into the horizontal bar and from this hang a length of chain for hooking on the control.

Attaching the strings

All strings must be attached securely to the puppet, not to the costume or body padding. When attaching the strings to the control, knot them loosely at first so that adjustments can be made.

The procedure for stringing the puppet is as follows.

1   Attach the head strings (with an animal, the back strings) so that the control is the required height.

To attach the head strings *either* drill holes for the strings through the tops of the ears if they are strong enough, *or* fasten screw-eyes into a dowel built into the head just behind the ears, as described in Chapter 4.

2   Attach the shoulder strings and back strings *either* to screw-eyes fastened in solid bodies, *or* thread the strings directly through holes drilled in the plywood centre piece of padded bodies. (With an animal, attach the head strings.)

Adjust the tension of the head and shoulder strings so that it is approximately the same for each but with the shoulder strings just taking the weight.

3   Attach hand and leg strings. To do this, drill holes in the hands (usually the thumb) and in the legs just above the knees. Thread the strings directly through the holes and knot the ends of the strings. (Countersink the holes in the hands so that the knots do not show.)

4   Having attached the main strings, attach any other strings that may be required and seal all knots with Bostik No. 1 glue, Elmer's Glue All or some other all-purpose glue.

Note   When stringing a cloth marionette it will be sufficient to sew securely on to the material any strings that bear little weight.

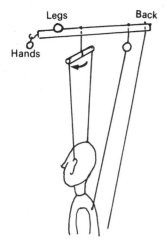

Figure 55/1 To turn the head: tilt control slightly and turn head bar

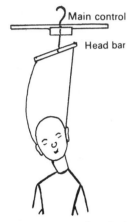

Figure 55/2 To incline the head: rock the head bar sideways

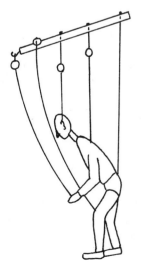

Figure 55/4 To bow the head and body: tilt the control

Manipulation

The simple aeroplane control

Hold the main control bar with one hand.
   To move the head, turn or tilt the control appropriately.
   To move the hands, lift the strings with your free hand.
   To walk the puppet, rock the leg bar in a paddling motion.

The standard aeroplane control

Hold the control with one hand.
   To turn the head, tilt the control very slightly forwards to take the weight on the shoulders, and turn the head bar with your free hand (*figure 55/1*).
   To incline the head to one side, tilt the head bar sideways (*figure 55/2*).
   To nod or bow the head, lift the shoulder bar with your free hand, or pull the string by which it is suspended with one of the fingers with which you are holding the control. At the same time lower the control slightly, taking care to keep it level (*figure 55/3*).
   To bow the body and the head, tilt the control forwards (*figure 55/4*).
   To bow the body, keeping the head upright, tilt the control and lift the head bar (*figure 55/5*).
· To move the hands, hold the hand bar in your free hand. Lift the whole bar to move both arms together or, to move just one, tilt the bar or lift individual strings (*figure 55/6*).

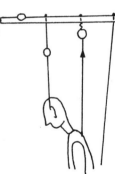

Figure 55/3 To nod or bow the head: lift the shoulder bar

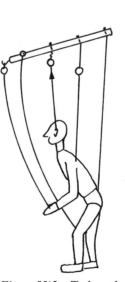

Figure 55/5 To bow the body, keeping the head upright; tilt the control and lift the head bar

Figure 55/6 Hand movements

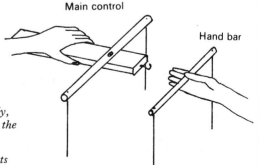

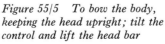

132

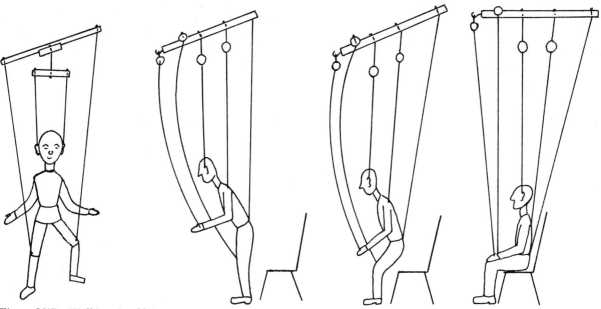

Figure 55/7   Walking: 'paddle' the control

Figure 55/8   To seat the puppet: tilt the control; bend the knees and lower the control; straighten up

To walk the puppet, rock the main control from side to side in a paddling motion (*figure 55/7*). The head and shoulders will remain level as they are suspended from the control.

To make the puppet sit, first tilt the control so that it leans forward. Then bend the knees and lower the puppet to the chair. Finally, straighten the control so that the puppet sits up (*figure 55/8*). It is poor technique to stand the puppet and then simply lower the control so that he has a straight back throughout.

The aeroplane control for animals

Hold the control with one hand.

To move the head, unhook the head bar and move it with your free hand (*figure 56/1*).

To effect movements of the body, tilt and turn the main control.

To walk the puppet, rock the control from side to side (*figure 56/2*).

The upright control

Hold the main control with one hand. Take the weight of the control with the second, third and fourth fingers wrapped around the centre of the control (*figures 57/1* and *57/2*).

To nod or bow the head, tilt the main control forwards (*figure 57/3*). The shoulder strings take the weight.

To incline the head to one side, tilt the control sideways (*figure 57/4*). This will not affect the movement of the shoulders.

To turn the head, tilt the control very slightly forward to take the weight on the shoulder strings, at the same time turning the control in the appropriate direction (*figure 57/5*).

To close the eyes or open the mouth, pull the strings with your free

Figure 56/1   To lower the head: unhook and lower the head-bar. To turn the head: turn the head bar

133

Figure 56/2   To walk the puppet:
'paddle' the control

Figure 57/1   The author
manipulating an upright control

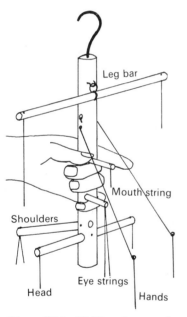

Leg bar

Mouth string

Shoulders

Head

Eye strings

Hands

Figure 57/2   Holding the control to
effect head/body, hand, mouth and
eye movements

Figure 57/3   To bow or nod the
head: tilt the control forwards

Figure 57/4   To incline the head:
tilt the control sideways

Figure 57/5   To turn the head: tilt
and turn the control

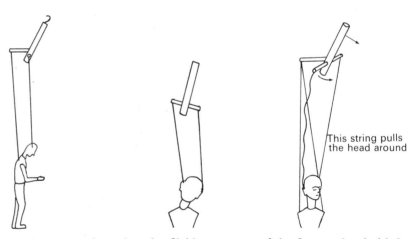

This string pulls
the head around

hand or move the strings by flicking out one of the fingers that hold the control.

To bow the body and head, pull the back string taut to take the weight and tilt and lower the control (*figure 57/6*).

To bow the body whilst keeping the head upright, pull the back string taut and lower the control, keeping it upright so that the head strings are taut and the shoulder strings loose (*figure 57/7*).

To move the hand wires, use your index finger and thumb of the hand holding the control (*figures 57/1* and *57/2*). You can also lift the individual strings with your free hand.

To walk the puppet, unhook the leg bar and move it in a paddling motion with your free hand (*figure 57/8*).

134

Figure 57/6   To bow the body: tilt the control and pull the back-string

Figure 57/7   To bow the body, keeping the head upright: pull the back-string and lower the control slightly

Figure 57/8   To walk the puppet: 'paddle' the leg bar

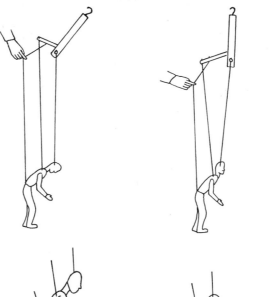

Leg bar

Tilt the control forwards and pull the back string

Bend the knees and lower the puppet with the control still tilted

Straighten up

Figure 57/9   Sitting the puppet

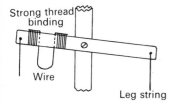

Strong thread binding

Wire

Leg string

Figure 58/1   Rocking bars for upright controls: a wooden bar with a wire thumb loop

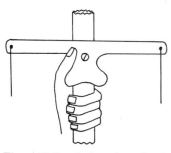

Figure 58/2   A shaped wooden bar

To make the marionette sit convincingly, first tilt the control slightly forward. If the puppet has a back string, pull this taut and lower the control a little, as well as tilting it. Keeping the body bent forwards, bend the knees and lower the body on to the chair. Finally, straighten up the control (*figure 57/9*).

Variations on controls

Rocking bars

A rocking bar is a wooden leg bar which is screwed to the main control. It permits the control to be held and the puppet walked with one hand, leaving the other hand free. The disadvantage is that the leg action is not usually as good as when a separate leg bar is used, except in the hands of a very skilled operator.

1   *The upright control*   Drill two holes through the leg bar and push the ends of a loop of wire through the holes (*figure 58/1*). Bend over the ends of the wire, then glue and bind them with strong thread. Slip your thumb into this wire loop to move the bar. Alternatively, use an all-wooden leg bar (cut from strong plywood) with two large notches cut out for your thumb (*figure 58/2*).

135

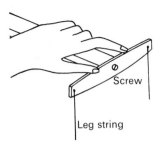

Figure 59 A rocking bar for the aeroplane control

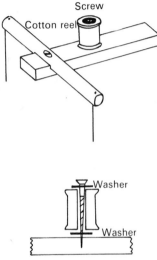

Figure 60 A rotating control

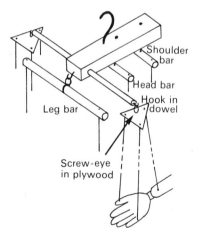

Figure 61 A control for elaborate hand movements

Figure 62 The control may be designed to perform a specific function, as with this control used by Daniel Llords

2 *The aeroplane control* Screw the rocking bar onto the front end of the control and move it with your thumb and index finger whilst holding the control with your other fingers (*figure 59*).

Rotating controls

A rotating control allows the puppet to be spun round. Screw a cotton reel (empty spool of thread) to the top of the control (*figure 60*). Use washers on top of, and underneath, the cotton reel and ensure that the screw is secure, or it will unscrew when you turn the control. Hold the reel with one hand whilst turning the control with the other.

A control for more elaborate hand movements

The unusual feature of this control is the incorporation of two triangular plywood plates to which the hand strings are attached (*figure* 61). There are three strings to each hand. One string is attached to the wrist to facilitate a greater degree of arm and hand movement, and of control. The positions of the other strings depend upon the performer's requirements, but it is suggested that one is attached approximately at the knuckle of the little finger and the other to the thumb.

Drill small holes in the corners of the triangular plates, thread the strings through them and knot the ends. Suspend the plywood plates from the control by a screw-eye in the top of each plate hanging from hooks screwed in the control.

This hand control may be used with any type of main control, usually with little, if any, modification of the control. (*Figure 61* shows a slight modification of the standard aeroplane control: the leg bar and hand bar have been interchanged and the new hand controls are suspended from the ends of what was the leg bar.)

Care of the marionettes

To prevent tangling when transporting marionettes, it is advisable to wind the strings round 'winders', ie pieces of hardboard or plywood in which two slots have been cut to take the string (*figure 63*).

It is also a good idea to keep puppets when not in use in polythene bags (large enough to allow them to stand upright). Fasten the bag with a pipe cleaner.

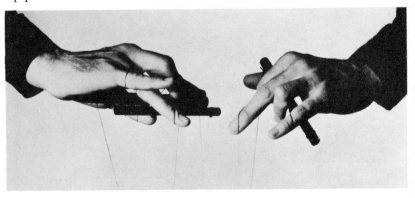

Figure 63 A 'winder'

To the control

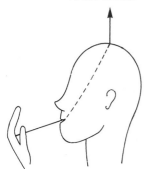

Figure 64   Raising a hand to the mouth

Head strings pass
through brim of hat

Extra string to hand
through brim

Figure 65   Raising a hat

Figure 66/1   Using an extra string to pick up an object

Figure 66/2   Using an extra string to bring the hands together

Specialised marionettes

The term 'specialised' is used to cover a wide variety of techniques from the simple addition of a few carefully positioned strings to something far more complex. The techniques described illustrate the basic principles involved and show the sort of effects that may be achieved without special tools or facilities. Most of them can be used in situations other than those described.

For the best results, keep mechanisms and stringing as simple as possible.

Raising an object to the mouth

Attach a string to the object; thread the string through a hole drilled in the mouth and out through another in the top of the head. (It is helpful to glue a plastic drinking straw in the head for the string to run through.) Pull the string to raise the object (eg a bottle) to the mouth (*figure 64*).

Raising a hat

Thread the head strings through holes drilled in the brim of the hat. Attach an extra string to one hand and thread it through another hole drilled in the brim (*figure 65*). Pull the string to raise the hand to the hat; continue to pull it to lift the hat.

Picking up an object

Attach a string to the object. Drill a hole through the hand, thread the string through the hole and then attach it to the control (*figure 66/1*). To pick up the object, first rest the hand on it then pull the string taut. As the object is lifted the hand will be lifted with it. The same technique is used to bring the hands together (*figure 66/2*).

It is not always feasible to pick up an object in the way described as the puppet may then be required to put it down and leave it. In such a case a wire hook or button-magnet built into the hand is useful (*figures 66/3* and *66/4*). If a magnet is used, it is necessary to put the object down on a stronger magnet than the one used to pick it up. (With non-metallic objects, glue a strip of tin to the surface.) If the object does not need to be put down on the stage but extra stringing is impractical, glue strips of 'Velcro' into the hand and on to the object (*figure 66/5*) so that they cling together when the hand is placed on the object.

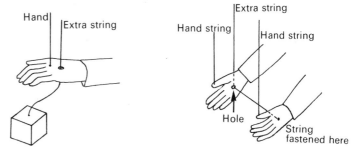

Figure 66/3   Hook in palm of hand

Figure 66/4   Button magnet

Figure 66/5   'Velcro' fastening

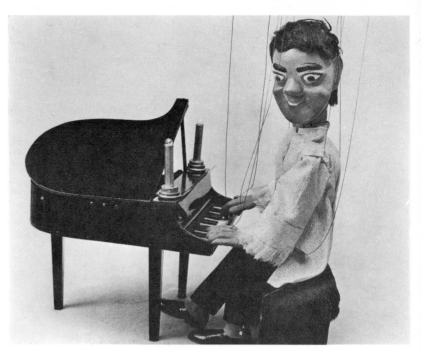

Figure 67   Toski, the author's pianist

Stringing for a pianist's hands

Fasten a string to the back of each hand and another to each forearm.

Make the hand control from three pieces of dowelling fixed in an H shape. Attach the strings to the corners of the H (*figure 68*).

Rock and tilt the bar to produce a simulation of a pianist's hand action. Tie a small curtain ring to the centre of this control and hang it from a hook screwed into the main control.

Stringing for dual control

Dual control (*figure 69*) is used when two or more marionettes are required to perform the same actions side by side.

Glue and nail the shoulder bar into a hole drilled in the head bar; this allows the heads to be tilted forward. Alternatively, attach the shoulder strings to the head bar on either side of the head strings.

Join the head and leg bars with a length of string tied to the centre of each bar.

Fix the right hand and right leg strings of both puppets together on the right-hand side of the leg bar and the left hand and left leg strings on to the left of the bar.

Now the puppets will move or dance together.

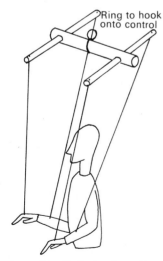

Ring to hook onto control

Figure 68   Stringing for a pianist's hands

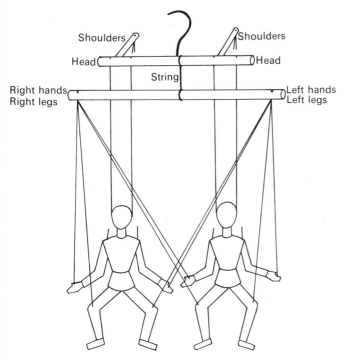

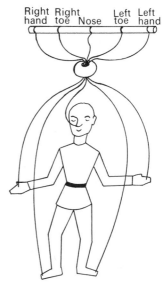

Figure 69   Dual control

Figure 70   A juggler puppet

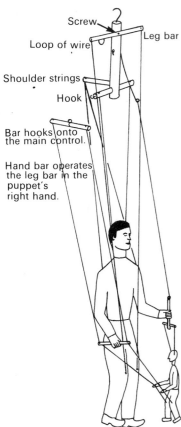

Figure 71/1   The control and stringing

Extra stringing for a juggler

The extra strings are attached to a special bar. They have nothing to do with the puppet's support or any of its movements apart from those involved in juggling.

Attach a string to each part of the body to be involved. Thread these strings through a hole in the object to be juggled and attach them to the juggling bar (*figure 70*).

To juggle the object, simply take the tension on each of the strings in turn. Pulling the string to the end of the nose, *whilst leaving all the others slack*, takes the object to the nose. Releasing the nose string and pulling a hand string transfers the object to the hand. Each of the strings must be long enough to let the object bounce to any part of the puppet (if, for example the nose string is too short, the object will not be able to drop to the toe).

A puppet puppeteer

The two puppets are made by any of the methods described earlier. Only the stringing differs from the usual (*figure 71/1*).

Attach the head and shoulder strings of the large puppet to the upright control as usual and use a rocking bar for the leg control. Only one hand wire is needed on the control of the larger puppet; use this to raise and lower the small control, held in the puppet's left hand.

In one end of the head bar fix a small hook and from it hang another dowel rod. This rod controls the hand/leg bar held in the large puppet's right hand. Attach the hand and knee on each side of the small puppet by a short cord, so that when a hand is raised the corresponding leg is raised too.

Figure 71/2 Jerome, the author's puppet-puppeteer, manipulating Frederick

Figure 71/3 Gordon Staight's Uncle Gordon operates Herbert Jnr watched by Mr. Herbert

Figure 72 Scrooge from Derek Francis' production of A Christmas Carol

Creating a stoop

Tension on a back string attached to the pelvis will create a stoop, but the effect will be much enhanced if the puppet is made with the head set lower on the body than usual ((*figure 72*).

A tight-rope walker

This requires no special features except a slot cut along each foot (*figure 73/1*).

Make the tight-rope (*figure 73/2*) as follows.

Screw two pieces of wood at right angles to the bottom of two uprights (dowelling) to make bases.

Cut a slot in the top of each upright to accommodate the tight-rope.

Fasten metal angle brackets to the bases and fit them into slots in the stage. To help to hold them securely, screw blocks of wood under the stage on each side of the slots.

Fasten the tight-rope between the upright posts. Secure the ends to screw-eyes in the bases. To maintain the tension of the cord, attach a strong rubber band (such as a Meccano 'driving band') between one end of the cord and the screw-eye.

Figure 73/1   The feet

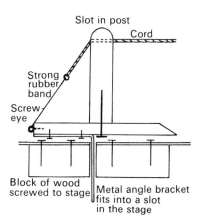

Slot in post

Cord

Strong
rubber
band

Screw
eye

Block of wood
screwed to stage

Metal angle bracket
fits into a slot
in the stage

*Figure 73/2   Supporting the
tightrope*

Weights

Figure 74   A tumbler puppet

Figure 75/1   Heads inside the body

*Figure 75/2   Heads 'nested' inside
each other*

A tumbler puppet

This can be an extremely effective transformation. The puppet consists of two heads and two bodies joined together at the waist. The lower body is hidden by a large 'full' skirt, which may need to be weighted around the hem (*figure 74*). Make the skirt from a reversible material which looks attractive when turned inside-out or use two pieces of material joined at waist and hem.

Raise the strings attached to the lower head, whilst releasing the tension of the upper head strings, to make the puppet 'tumble', or turn over, and reveal the hidden puppet. The skirt drops to cover the other puppet.

The two heads must face in opposite directions, so that when it tumbles, the hidden puppet will rise facing the same way as the other.

Scaramouche

There is more than one version of this type of puppet. One has a number of heads which are hidden in a hollow body and which emerge one above the other (*figure 75/1*). Another has hollow heads which fit inside each other (*figure 75/2*).

A collapsible (or extending) puppet

Make the body from three pieces of hardboard joined by thread at the front, rear and sides (*figure 76/1*). Make the legs from a series of wooden discs cut from a large dowel rod and joined in the same way as the body (*figures 76/1* and *76/2*).

On each side of the legs and body pieces drill small holes. The strings which raise and lower the legs and body pass through these holes (*figure 76/1*). The strings run freely through the whole puppet, being attached only to the feet and to the control.

Figure 76/3 shows the stringing for the extending puppet. The legs and body are contracted when normal; to lower them, tilt the control forward.

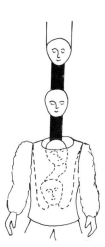

These strings run through holes in the body and in the legs

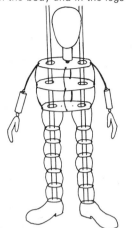

A string is also fixed at the back and front of each leg section

Figure 76/1   Construction of the puppet

Four strings hold the legs

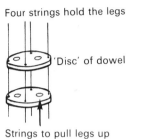

'Disc' of dowel

Strings to pull legs up run through these holes

Figure 76/2   The leg sections

Figure 76/3   The control for an extending puppet

Figure 76/4   The control for a collapsible puppet

Figure 76/4 shows the collapsible puppet. When the control is held upright, the legs and body are at their maximum length; to raise them, tilt the control, raising the bottom.

The dissecting skeleton

Construction

Figure 77/1 shows the skeleton complete.
The head   Make this from plastic wood or a similar material. Fasten a dowel across the head with Bostik No. 1 glue and plastic wood. Screw a screw-eye into each end of the dowel, through the sides of the head (*figure 77/2*).
The body   Make the ribs, breast bone, shoulder blades and pelvis from plastic wood over a cardboard shape smeared with Bostik No. 1 glue. It is best to have eight ribs. (If the proper number is used, the body will appear too long and thin.)
   The first five ribs are made as a closed loop and the bottom three open in the front (*figure 77/3*) to join on to the breast bone which is glued on to the top five ribs.
   File, or carve, grooves in small pieces of dowelling for the vertebrae.
   The body is assembled on a length of strong galvanised wire which is glued in the pelvis and runs through the whole backbone.
   When all the parts are glued together (*figure 77/4*), cover and strengthen the joints with plastic wood.
The limbs   Model the hands and feet with plastic wood on pipe cleaners smeared with Bostik No. 1 glue, as described on page 118.
   Roughly carve the arms and legs from dowelling and build up details in plastic wood.

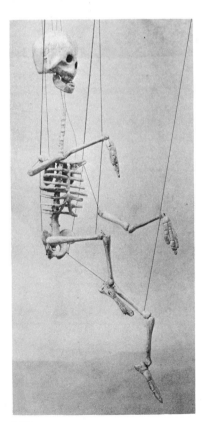

Figure 77/1   Georgina, the author's dissecting skeleton

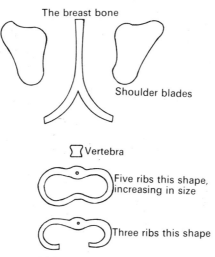

The breast bone

Shoulder blades

Vertebra

Five ribs this shape, increasing in size

Three ribs this shape

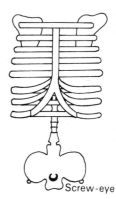

Screw-eye

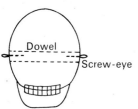

Dowel

Screw-eye

Figure 77/2   The head, showing the dowel and screw-eyes fastened in place

Figure 77/3   The parts of the rib-cage

Figure 77/4   The body assembled

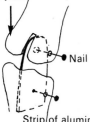

For the elbow, ankle and knee, one side is built up to restrict the joint.

Nail

Strip of aluminium glued and nailed in leg

Figure 77/5   The wrist, elbow, knee and ankle joint (an open mortise and tenon joint)

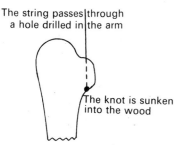

The string passes through a hole drilled in the arm

The knot is sunken into the wood

Figure 77/6   Fastening a string to the top of the arm

The wrist, elbow, knee and ankle joints are open mortise and tenon joints (see page 119). The 'tongue' is a strip of aluminium, glued and nailed in one part, and pivoted on a nail in the other part (*figure 77/5*).

The head, arms and legs are joined to the body by strings which form part of the control (see below). *Figure 77/6* shows how to attach the strings to the arms and legs.

Stringing

String the puppet so that when the control is held upright with the leg bar hooked on to it, the parts are all close together and not dissected (*figure 77/7*).

The puppet is supported by the body strings, L and M, and the centre string J. Attach strings L and M to each side of the top pair of ribs; they run through the screw-eyes in the head to the control and *must be parallel*. Attach J to the top of the neck; thread the other end through a hole in the dowel fixed in the head, and through the top of the skull to the control.

Fasten another string, K, to the dowel in the head; this runs through a screw-eye in the centre of the control to the centre of the arm-and-leg bar. Pull this bar forward to raise the head. (The head returns to its normal position when the bar is replaced.).

Attach the hand strings, E and G, to the arm-and-leg bar. F and H join the wrists to the knees. By paddling the bar the arms and legs are moved together.

Fasten the strings, A and C, which support the arms, and B and D, which support the legs, to the top cross bar of the control. A and C run through the shoulder blades; B and D run through screw-eyes on each side of the pelvis, up through the rib cage and through a hole in the top rib. The arms and legs are detached from the body by tilting the control forwards.

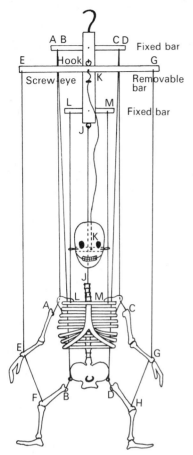

A B   C D   Fixed bar
E   Hook   G
Screw-eye   K   Removable bar
L   M   Fixed bar
J

K

J
L   M
A   C
E   G
F   B   D   H

Figure 77/7   *Control and stringing*

Figure 77/8   *Twonky Feathers,
a dissecting marionette by Gordon
Staight*

Figure 78   *John Thirtle's
unicyclist*

Figure 79 Gipsy Violinist from Eric Bramall's Marionette Cabaret
Figure 80 Willie, an extending puppet who blows up a balloon and goes cross-eyed, by the author
Figure 81 Trippy, by Gordon Staight

Presenting marionettes

The construction of any stage depends on the particular needs of the puppeteer and his facilities for transporting it. The performer will find that copying somebody else's design is never as satisfactory as designing his own stage to meet his own needs.

With any method of presentation it is desirable to have a stage floor covering such as thin carpet, hessian (burlap) or felt to provide a good surface for puppets to walk on.

An open stage

In general open stages are suitable for variety performances but not for plays. Some variety puppeteers perform without stage or back drop, but they usually require some sort of rostrum or raised platform.

Open-stage back drops are usually waist high.

An apron back cloth

This is the simplest form of back drop for open-stage performances. To make one, suspend a curtain from a dowel rod and attach a long loop of cord to the rod. Hang this around your neck so that the curtain just touches the ground (*figure 82*).

A free-standing back cloth

A free-standing frame to hold a back cloth (*figure 83*) consists of a cross bar (known as a *leaning bar*) bolted to two upright supports which are themselves bolted to supporting 'feet'.

For ease of transportation, make the leaning bar in two parts, joined together with two bolts.

Screw a strong plywood triangle to the upright supports. Bolt the ends of the leaning bar to the triangles, using two bolts at each end.

Make each foot about 24 in long and screw on to it a metal angle bracket. Bolt the uprights to the brackets. (If the holes in the brackets will not accommodate a bolt, enlarge them with a drill or a file.) For greater rigidity, use a bracket on each side of the uprights.

Use one of the following methods to suspend the curtain.

Sew loops of tape on to the top of the back cloth, take them over the top of the leaning bar and fasten them on hooks screwed under the leaning bar.

Screw a few small hooks into the leaning bar, to hold a curtain wire.

Fasten the curtain to the leaning bar by means of 'Velcro'. (Velcro consists of two nylon strips; the surface of one is covered with tiny hooks, that of the other with loops. They grip securely when pressed together but may be pulled apart and pressed together again like press fasteners.) Glue an inch length of Velcro at intervals along the leaning bar and stitch the matching pieces on to the back cloth at corresponding points.

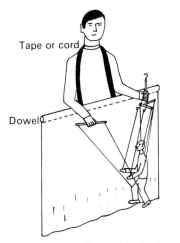

Figure 82 An 'apron' back-cloth

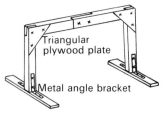

Figure 83 A free-standing back-drop

Figure 84/1 The stage

Figure 84/2 A back-stage view

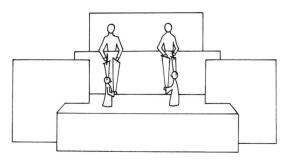

Figure 84/3 The centre joint in the perchery or back-curtain rail

An elaborate open fitup

The stage (*figures 84/1* and *84/2*) consists of two raised platforms (for the stage floor and operating area); a back cloth; wings to hide back-stage activity and puppets about to enter; a perchery (hanging rack) for the marionettes; and a drape suspended behind the puppeteers to concentrate attention on the stage (and give it a neater appearance).

For the platforms, use trestle tables or home-made, collapsible 'bridges' of a similar type. It may be desirable that the operating area should be higher than the stage floor, if, for example, the puppets are large, or if the puppeteers wish to be further removed from their puppets.

Bolt all upright supports for the leaning bar, perchery and back drape on to the legs of the platforms. The horizontal rods for the back drape and perchery are supported by the same uprights. For each rod use two strong dowels joined in the centre. For the centre joint screw or nail half of a length of metal tubing to one dowel and insert the other dowel into the other half of the tube (*figure 84/3*). This dowel is secured by a metal pin or bolt. (To dismantle the rods for packing, remove the pin.)

Cut away the back of the operating area to allow the puppets to hang freely from the perchery.

The back cloth is attached to the leaning bar as described for a free-standing back cloth.

To suspend the back drape, stitch a hem at the top to accommodate the dowel rod.

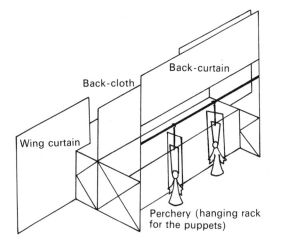

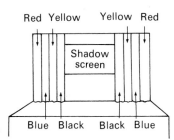

Red Yellow   Yellow Red

Shadow
screen

Blue Black   Black Blue

Figure 84/4   Different colour back-drops and a shadow screen incorporated in the open stage

Black drapes serve most purposes well but pale green, grey, blue or maroon are also suitable colours. Not all puppets are shown to their best advantage against the same colour and it is possible to have three or four sets of plain coloured back cloths on the stage (*figure 84/4*). Divide each set in the middle. (If they are gathered into folds, the central join will be disguised.) Suspend each set from a separate wire and draw back, or close, the various sets as necessary. Behind the last set of curtains some puppeteers have a scenic back cloth, or a shadow puppet screen (*figure 84/4*).

A portable proscenium stage

Five types of proscenium stage are illustrated (*figure 85*). The most elaborate will make great demands in terms of construction, weight,

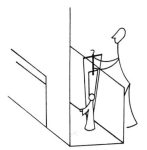

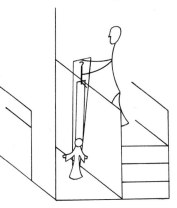

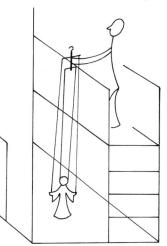

Figure 85/1   A stage with no bridge

Figure 85/2   A stage with a higher back-cloth and a small bridge

Figure 85/3   A stage with a high bridge over the stage floor

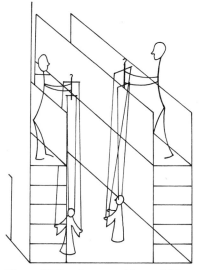

Figure 85/4   A stage with two high bridges over the stage floor: one over the proscenium opening and one over the back-cloth

Figure 85/5   An elevated proscenium stage

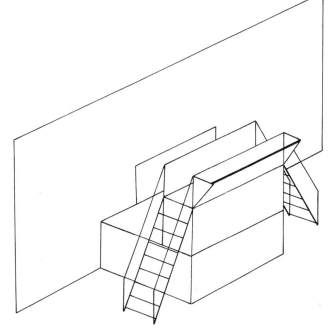

transport and setting-up time. The simplest stage (*figure 85/1*) has a proscenium, stage floor and back cloth.

Although a bridge is not essential, it is certainly desirable. A bridge behind the back drop (*figure 85/2*) raises the puppeteers and is essential in situations where the puppeteers would otherwise be visible to the audience through the proscenium opening. A deeper stage floor with a bridge, or bridges, over part of it (*figures 85/3* and *85/4*) is desirable; it creates a greater sense of depth than the previously mentioned stages as the puppets no longer perform close to the back cloth.

These stages need to be set up on a platform, or elevated by legs incorporated in their structure (*figure 85/5*). (The 'platform' for a simple stage can be contrived by lashing two trestle tables together. A curtain should be hung round them to prevent the audience seeing back stage).

In the following examples of construction techniques, the dimensions given are only suggestions. (Much depends on the size of the puppets.)

A stage without a bridge

Make the stage floor from two sheets of hardboard, or plywood, each measuring 3×2 ft. Screw each sheet on to a framework of $2 \times \frac{3}{4}$ in timber. Bolt the two frames together (underneath) to make a 6×2 ft acting area (*figure 86/1*). Fasten clasps to the sides of the frames so that they can be held together, thus forming a box to hold the stage curtains (*figure 86/2*). Attach a handle to one section.

Hinge the leaning bar in the centre for packing and hold it firm with an 8 in joining piece. Screw it to one half of the leaning bar and bolt it to the other half (*figure 86/3*). Bolt the leaning bar to two uprights which in turn bolt on to the frame of the stage floor.

Bolt together (using another 8 in joining piece) two 3 ft lengths of wood and screw the ends to the back drop supports, making a bar along the back of the stage floor. (This stops the uprights swaying and prevents the back cloth from swinging back off the stage.)

The front curtain frame (*figure 86/4*) consists of an upper cross bar (three 4 ft pieces); a lower cross bar (two 4 ft pieces); two upright supports (each made up of one 30 in and one 42 in piece); and four angle struts (two 36 in long and two 28 in long) to hold the framework steady. The joints in the uprights and cross bars should be constructed in the same way as that in the leaning bar, using a hinge, joining piece and bolts.

Bolt the uprights to the stage floor frame. Bolt the cross bars on to the insides of the uprights (sawing away part of the joining piece on the upright so that the lower cross bar can be attached at the same point, as shown in *figure 86/5*).

Screw one of the 28 in angle struts to the side of each upright and bolt the other ends of the struts to the frame of the stage (*figure 86/4*). Use the 36 in angle struts to join the upper and lower cross bars and hold the frame steady. Bolt the struts to one cross bar and screw them to the other.

Wing curtains help to conceal back stage activity from the audience. They may be supported in one of the following ways.

1 Suspend each curtain by means of a short curtain wire and two

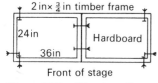

Figure 86/1   The stage floor

Figure 86/2   The stage floor made into a box for carrying the curtains

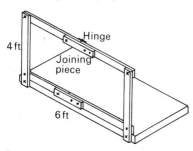

Figure 86/3   The leaning bar

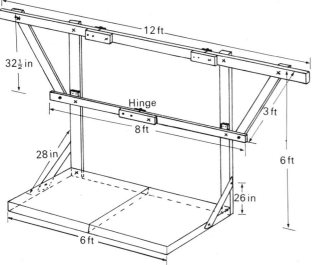

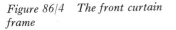

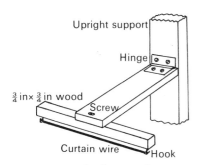

Figure 86/4   The front curtain frame

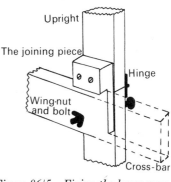

Figure 86/5   Fixing the lower cross-bar

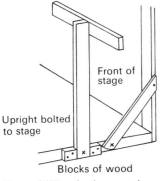

Figure 86/6   A wing curtain support attached to the front curtain frame

Figure 86/7   A wing curtain support bolted to the stage

hooks under a 2 ft length of $\frac{3}{4} \times \frac{3}{4}$ in timber. Pivot this bar by a screw under one end of a 12 in length of $2 \times \frac{1}{2}$ in timber. Hinge the 12 in bar to the front upright of the stage, above the lower cross bar, so that the wing supports rest horizontally (*figure 86/6*). (This folds up easily for packing but does not permit puppets to make an entrance in front of the wings.)

2   Screw together in a T shape two pieces of $2 \times \frac{1}{2}$ in timber. Hang the wing curtain from the cross bar of the T by a curtain wire or Velcro. Bolt the support on to the side of the stage and screw a block of wood to the stage on each side of the support to hold it steady (*figure 86/7*). Alternatively, three blocks of wood screwed to the stage floor as shown in *figure 86/8* produces a slot for the wing support; no bolt is needed provided it is a tight fit.

A stage with a bridge

When a stage has a bridge it is essential that the construction of the whole framework is very strong. For this purpose 'Dexion' slotted metal angle strips are ideal. Dexion packs neatly and is lighter and no more expensive than the comparable strength of timber. The Dexion may be cut and joined at any point to facilitate packing for transportation.

Use Dexion also for the stage floor surround as the bridge is bolted to it. Support the bridge by four vertical lengths of Dexion. Two horizontal lengths joined at 3 ft intervals by cross pieces form the frame for the bridge floor, which is strong plywood bolted on to the Dexion. Two more horizontal lengths form the leaning bar and back rail of the bridge (*figure 87/1*).

Strengthen the frame by using triangular plates, or angle struts, at the main joints.

Attach a small set of steps to each end of the bridge. (It will usually be necessary to buy these or have them made.)

149

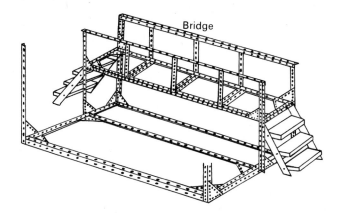

Bridge

No bolt needed

Figure 86/8   Securing a wing support without a bolt

Figure 87/1   The stage floor and bridge framework built from Dexion slotted metal angle

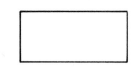

Removable bolt

Rear uprights of bridge

Figure 87/2   A perchery

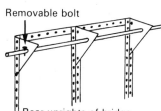

Figure 88/1   Pageant (or processional) opening

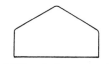

Figure 88/2   Archway opening

Figure 88/3   Lunette opening

150

It is wise to have a number of boards or metal strips bolted between the bridge floor and the upper rails to prevent anybody falling through.

To make a perchery for hanging up the puppets, bolt three triangular plywood plates to the rear uprights of the bridge, one at each end and one in the centre. In each plate drill a large hole to take a strong dowel or aluminium rod, and secure the rod by a bolt at each end (*figure 87/2*).

Drapes for a proscenium stage

The methods described for fastening a back cloth on an open stage may be used for proscenium stages, but for a heavy front curtain a stronger method may be required. Sew Rufflette tape to the curtain, gather in the drapes and then hang the loops in the tape over hooks screwed into the top cross bar.

The proscenium opening in the front curtain may be any size or shape required. The most popular shape for marionettes is the 'pageant' (or 'processional') opening which is approximately twice as wide as it is high (*figure 88/1*). This is the best all-purpose shape.

'Lunette' (*figure 88/2*) and 'archway' (*figure 88/3*) openings are not common, but, when necessary, a drape with one of these openings may be suspended on a rod to mask the pageant opening. Usually the masking drape is suspended just inside the proscenium opening (*figure 88/4*) but it may be fixed to the wing supports, so dividing the stage area (*figure 88/5*). This latter method restricts movement on the stage but may be desirable for a particular effect.

Whichever of the following curtains is used for the proscenium opening, attach the curtains to a batten. With all except the pull-up curtain, bolt the batten on to the lower cross bar of the front curtain frame.

The straight curtain   Hang two curtains from a curtain wire or rail attached to a batten. They are opened and closed by two cords (nylon cord is excellent). Thread the cords through the curtain rings and over hooks in the batten, as illustrated (*figure 89*). Tie the cords to the innermost ring on each curtain. Fasten small weights on the ends of the cords to keep them taut. Pull one cord to open the curtains and the other to close them.

The pull-up curtain   Tack the top of the curtain to a wooden batten.

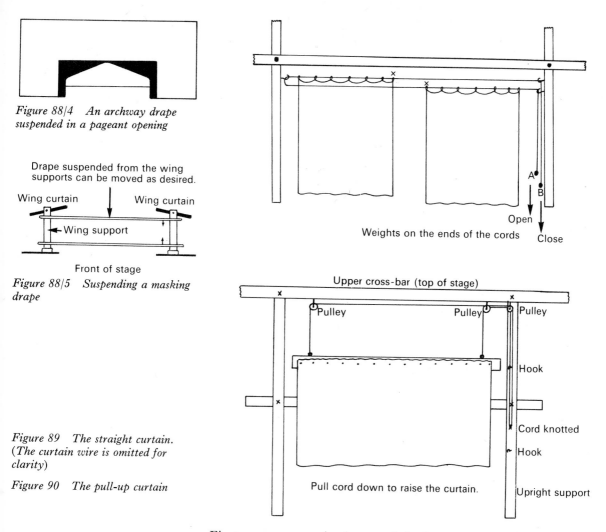

Figure 88/4   An archway drape suspended in a pageant opening

Drape suspended from the wing supports can be moved as desired.

Wing curtain   Wing curtain

←Wing support

Front of stage

Figure 88/5   Suspending a masking drape

Weights on the ends of the cords

Open   Close

Figure 89   The straight curtain. (The curtain wire is omitted for clarity)

Figure 90   The pull-up curtain

Upper cross-bar (top of stage)

Pulley   Pulley   Pulley

Hook

Cord knotted

Hook

Pull cord down to raise the curtain.

Upright support

Fix two screw-eyes in the top of the batten, one at each end, and tie a cord to each screw-eye. Screw two pulleys into the upper cross bar directly above the screw-eyes in the batten and screw a third pulley into the cross bar just inside the upright support. Thread the cords over the three pulleys (*figure 90*) and knot the ends of the cords together. Pulling the cords down raises the curtain. Screw hooks into the upright support and loop the cord around the appropriate hook to keep the curtain open or closed. This type of curtain may also be used to reduce the height of the opening.

The draped curtain   This curtain is not recommended for general use as it considerably reduces the size of the proscenium opening.

Tack the tops of the curtains to a batten so that they overlap slightly in the centre. Sew curtain rings diagonally across each drape; thread cords through the rings and tie them to the lowest ring on each drape. Thread the cords through screw-eyes at each end of the batten and take one of the cords along the batten and through the other screw-eye so that both cords can be pulled together (*figure 91*). If necessary, weight the corners of the drapes so that they drop smoothly and quickly when the cords are released.

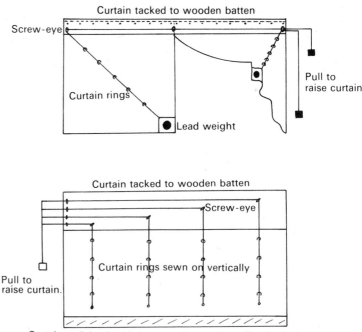

Figure 91   *The draped curtain*

Curtain tacked to wooden batten
Screw-eye
Pull to raise curtain
Curtain rings
Lead weight

Figure 92   *The drop-curtain*

Curtain tacked to wooden batten
Screw-eye
Curtain rings sewn on vertically
Pull to raise curtain.
Curtain weighted with batten or heavy dowelling in the hem

The drop curtain   Tack the top of the curtain to a batten. Sew about four sets of curtain rings to the curtain in vertical rows. Thread cords through the rings and tie them to the lowest ring in each row. Screw four screw-eyes in the batten, thread the cords through these screw-eyes and then through a fifth at one end of the batten. Tie the cords together so that when they are pulled they raise the curtain (*figure 92*). Weight the bottom of the curtain with a thin batten or fairly heavy dowel stitched into the hem.

Scenery

A scenic back cloth

Scenery may be painted with poster colours on unbleached calico, but dyes usually produce better colours. (The batik method on cotton material is particularly suitable for puppet theatre back cloths.) It is also possible to paint, or sponge, dyes on to the fabric, either allowing them to run into each other or picking out fine outlines with hot wax to keep them apart.

Either tack the top and bottom of the back cloth to two wooden battens *or* slip the battens into wide hems.

In a simple theatre, suspend the back cloth from the leaning bar. When a bridge overhangs the stage floor, for greater depth on stage, suspend the back cloth between the vertical supports at the back of the bridge. If necessary, attach extra wing flats to the front supports of the bridge.

It is possible to suspend a number of sets of plain curtains under the bridge and open or close them as desired.

Figure 93 Raising and lowering a back-cloth under a bridge

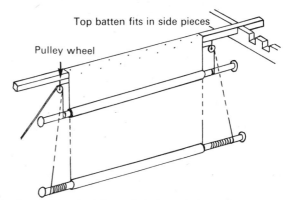

Top batten fits in side pieces

Pulley wheel

As the cord is raised, it unwinds, but winds up the scenery.
As the roll unwinds, the cord winds around the dowel

The following technique is useful for raising or lowering scenes fixed to battens under the bridge.

Tack the bottom of the back cloth to a thick dowel which is used as a roller. Roll up the scene around the dowel, then attach a strong cord to each end of the roller. Thread the cords over pulleys screwed into the batten. When the cords are released, the roller is lowered and the cords wind around each end of it (*figure 93*). Pulling the cords causes them to unwind and the roller to roll up.

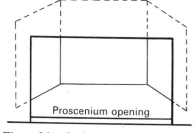

Proscenium opening

Figure 94 An inset

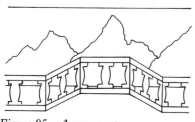

Figure 95 A screen set

Scenery sets

An inset is used to screen off part of the stage (*figure 94*). Make the screen from sheets of hardboard, or strong card, joined by strips of linen glued along the edges. (It can be folded up for packing.)

Screen sets are more elaborate than insets. They are flat, cut-out shapes made into a three-dimensional background (*figure 95*). Hang a back cloth behind the screen set. It is usually convenient to have this painted with some fairly generalised scene of sky, distant hills, etc.

Three-dimensional scenery is usually too troublesome for the travelling entertainer but it is ideal for a school show, a group established in a hall, a club, or permanent theatre. Corrugated card is a particularly suitable material from which to make it.

Build the shape around a box, or hold the card in the required shape by lengths of galvanised wire. For a smooth surface, cover the corrugations with paste and paper. Attach the scenery to a board so that it cannot be knocked over by a puppet.

Gauze

Theatrical gauze suspended across the stage is used for special effects. If it is illuminated from the front with the lights to the sides, not shining directly on to the gauze, any scene painted on it is visible to the audience whilst objects and scenery behind are invisible. If lighting is introduced behind the gauze instead of in front, the scene previously invisible becomes visible and the scene on the gauze will disappear. This technique is particularly effective for taking the audience within a building, or for a dream sequence.

153

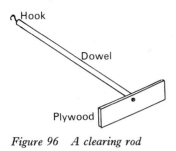

Figure 96   A clearing rod

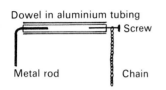

Figure 97/1   Constructing the gallows

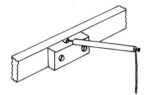

Figure 97/2   Supporting the gallows

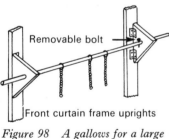

Figure 98   A gallows for a large stage

A clearing rod

This is a wooden 'rake' used to reach props on the stage during scene changes. It is simply a strip of plywood screwed on to one end of a dowel rod (*figure 96*).

A gallows for the stage

Gallows are used to suspend a puppet on the stage, either if two free hands are needed to manipulate it for a special effect or if the puppet is required to be on stage but not moving.

Any form of projection with a length of chain or loop of cord will serve the purpose, but a hinged gallows is often preferred as it can be pushed out of the way when it is not needed. Two methods for constructing gallows are described; the second is better for a large 'stage.

1   Bend a metal rod into a right angle. Drill a hole in the end of a dowel rod, then glue one end of the metal rod and jam it tightly into the hole. To strengthen the dowel, a 'sleeve' of aluminium tubing may be glued over it. Use a screw or screw-eye to fasten a chain or cord to the other end of the dowel (*figure 97/1*).

Make a groove in a block of wood and screw the block to the upper cross bar of the front curtain frame. The metal rod fits into, and turns in, the groove (*figure 97/2*). Hook the puppet's control into a link in the chain or a loop in the cord.

2   Drill a hole in each of two triangular blocks of wood. Hinge the blocks to the vertical supports of the front curtain frame. Fit the ends of a strong dowel into the holes in the blocks (*figure 98*). In each end of the dowel drill a hole to accommodate a bolt (to prevent the dowel coming out of the blocks). Suspend lengths of cord or chains from the rod.

A perchery

This is a rack used for hanging up the puppets during a show. A perchery attached to a stage with a bridge has been described on page 150, but often a free-standing rack is needed.

For each support, bolt together two lengths of fairly thick wood. Tie a length of string to each upright to prevent them opening too far.

Make cross bars from 1 in dia dowelling. Drill holes in the supports to accommodate the dowels (*figure 99/1*). (They should be a tight fit.) Through each support and dowel drill a hole to take a bolt with a wing nut for securing the rack (*figure 99/2*).

Glue and nail smaller dowels into holes drilled in the cross bars. These act as 'stops' and help to line up the holes in the cross bars with those in the uprights (*figure 99/2*).

If necessary, add a few bracing strips of wood to prevent the perchery from wobbling.

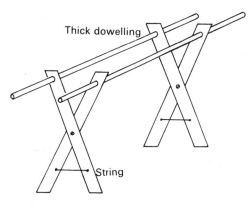

Thick dowelling

String

Figure 99/1 The perchery assembled

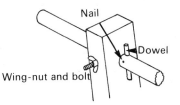

Nail

Dowel

Wing-nut and bolt

Figure 99/2 Securing the cross-bars

Figure 100 An open-stage sketch by Fred Tickner

Figure 101 A scene from Ali Baba and the Forty Thieves *by the Eric Bramall Marionettes at the Harlequin Theatre*

Figure 102   The Hogarth Puppets' production of Master Peter's Puppet Show

Figure 103   Maria pleads with William Corder in Maria Marten or the Murder in the Red Barn, *presented by the Eric Bramall Marionettes*

9 Related puppetry techniques

The toy theatre

The term 'toy theatre' refers to a small table-top theatre in which cut-out figures are moved on 'slides' projecting from the sides of the stage. The terms 'toy theatre' and 'model theatre' have become almost synonymous but, strictly, a model theatre is a scale model of a real theatre. Toy theatre performances, known as the Juvenile Drama, date from the early nineteenth century and are thought to have their origin in the contemporary fashion for caricatures. Not only caricatures of the famous and infamous were published, but also portraits of actors and actresses in poses from their plays. These became extremely popular as souvenirs and to supply the demand they were soon printed not as large single figures but in sets of sheets with six figures on each. Soon it was possible to buy all the characters of a play in all their different costumes *and* in a variety of attitudes. By 1812 scenery was being published too, then prosceniums and orchestra strips.

These souvenir prints were sold for a penny a sheet or for twopence, hand coloured. (Hence the famous term 'penny plain, twopence coloured'.) It was the young boys of the day who were the great enthusiasts for these theatrical souvenirs and they were soon animating the figures cut from the sheets and performing their favourite scenes or plays. This was the start of the Juvenile Drama, a young man's pastime rather than a child's toy.

The characters and scenery were cut from the sheets and mounted on card. To manipulate the figures they were held in slots cut in wooden 'slides' which were moved in grooves in the stage floor. Between 1830 and 1840, tin slides with long wires attached were introduced, which allowed considerably more movement.

Originally home made, the earliest manufactured toy theatre was advertised in 1829, probably by the shop that sold it rather than the publishers of the figures.

The Juvenile Drama was essentially drawing-room entertainment, taking its life and inspiration from the theatre of the day.

In America the toy theatre never really became popular although some of the English toy theatre sheets and plays were published there about 1825.

The toy theatre suffered a decline in the second half of the century. One of the publishers who continued in business was the firm of J. K. Green which in 1860 was taken over by John Redington. Redington

157

Figure 1 Aladdin, *performed in a toy theatre by the author*

Figures 2, 3 and 4 Characters *from* The Miller and His Men

Banditti Carousing.

was himself succeeded by his son-in-law, Benjamin Pollock, whose last new sheet was published in 1883. After this he contented himself with reprinting old sheets. Pollock managed the business from 1876 until his death in 1937. The business subsequently changed hands and premises a number of times and at one stage was forced to close down. However,

Claudine.　　　*Ravina.*　　　*Count Friberg*

the demands of the enthusiasts led to Pollock's being bought and re-opened by Mrs Marguerite Fawdry as a toy theatre shop and toy museum, which is now situated in Scala Street in the heart of London under the name of 'Pollock's Toy Museum'.

Although the toy theatre trade was declining, there was formed in 1925 an organisation known as the British Model Theatre Guild, later called the British Puppet and Model Theatre Guild. The Guild was formed by H. W. Whanslaw ('Whanny') and Gerald Morice, following the considerable interest that had been aroused by the publication of Whanny's book, *Everybody's Theatre*. They originally aimed at reviving interest in the Juvenile Drama and developing model theatre technique. Through exhibitions the Guild played a part in promoting the interests of the toy theatre makers and various Guild publications on the toy theatre are of particular interest. Although its scope has widened and other types of puppetry are now the main interest of most Guild members, the toy theatre enthusiasts continue to play an active part, exhibitions still contain toy theatres, and toy theatre performances draw good audiences at the Guild meetings.

The theatre and the characters

Theatres may still be purchased from Pollock's Toy Museum (see Appendices) but suggestions are offered for those who wish to construct their own. It is advisable to limit the size of the theatre so that a solo manipulator can operate the figures from both sides of the stage at once and see from above what he is doing.

Constructing a toy theatre from a cardboard box

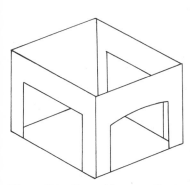

Figure 5/1   Box with proscenium arch cut out and sides partly cut away

Remove the top of the cardboard box and cut a proscenium opening in one side (*figure 5/1*).

159

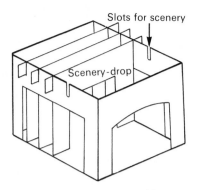

Slots for scenery

Scenery-drop

Figure 5/2   The theatre with scenery drops

Partly cut away two sides to allow the figures to be operated from the wings.

Cut slits in the sides to hold the scenery (*figure 5/2*).

Make scenery drops and a back drop from cardboard.

A plywood theatre

Figure 6/1 shows the completed theatre.

Make the stage floor from plywood with four pieces cut out to accommodate the uprights. Tack, or screw, strips of wood to three sides of the plywood (*figure 6/2*).

Screw the four corner uprights to these strips of wood. Secure the back corner posts by triangular plywood plates (*figure 6/3*).

Screw two other side pieces to the tops of the uprights with angle halved joints (*figure 6/3*). These side strips may be slotted or not, depending on the type of scenery grid to be used (see below).

Fix a batten between the back corner posts, near the top, to hold them firm (*figure 6/3*).

To make back drops and wings: *either* tack cardboard scenery drops to cross-battens which fit into slots in the side pieces (*figure 6/4*), *or* make a scenery grid with small strips of wood tacked to the side pieces (not slotted). The scenes, mounted on card, stand between the cross bars (*figure 6/5*).

The proscenium arch is made of plywood. Glue and screw or nail it to the front uprights.

Mask the front of the stage with three strips of plywood tacked to the wooden battens under the stage floor. The plywood tacked to the sides helps to secure the front uprights.

The 'front curtain' is made of plywood. It is held in place by double

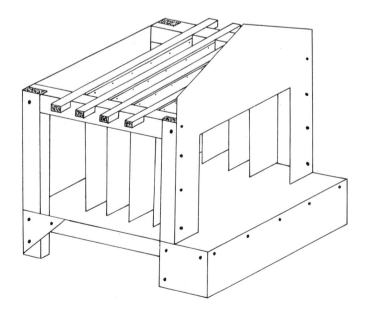

Figure 6/1   The theatre assembled

160

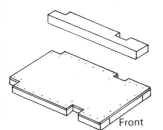

Figure 6/2   The stage floor

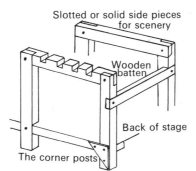

Slotted or solid side pieces for scenery

Wooden batten

Back of stage

The corner posts

Figure 6/3   The framework attached to the stage floor

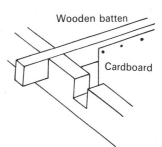

Wooden batten

Cardboard

Figure 6/4   Supporting the scenery: scenery battens fit into slots in the framework

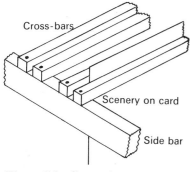

Cross-bars

Scenery on card

Side bar

Figure 6/5   Supporting scenery: scenes on card stand between cross-bars fixed to the framework

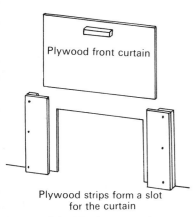

Plywood front curtain

Plywood strips form a slot for the curtain

Figure 6/6   The front curtain

strips of plywood, glued, screwed or tacked to the inside of the pro-scenium arch (*figure 6/6*). Glue and screw a small block of wood to the inside of the 'curtain' so that it may be lifted easily and removed for the performance.

Note   It is best to paint the stage floor matt black to help to show up the characters and scenery. They are not so clear against a light floor colour.

Lighting for the theatre

The following are the two most useful types of light in the toy theatre.
1   A striplight attached to a small wooden batten and connected to the electricity supply.
2   Flashlight bulbs (or coloured lights) screwed into bulb-holders and fastened to small wooden battens. The bulbs are connected in parallel in a circuit with a battery and switch (*figure 7/1*).

The batten is fastened to the wooden strips which form the slots for the front curtain (*figure 7/2*).

For extra illumination of the back drop, another batten may be held above the stage by *either* slotting it into the side strips that hold the scenery *or* attaching the batten to the scenery grid. The method used depends upon the type of scenery construction employed.

Footlights will impede the audience's view unless a small section is cut from the front of the stage floor to make a well to accommodate them. All lights must be adequately shielded so that they do not shine in the eyes of the audience.

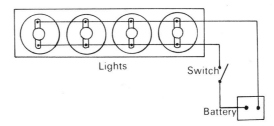

Lights

Switch

Battery

Figure 7/1   Connecting the lights, switch and battery

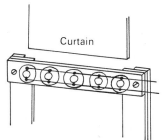

Curtain

Plywood strips to hold curtain

Figure 7/2   Mounting the lights in the theatre

Wire

Figure 8/1   Traditional tin slide

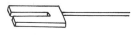

Figure 8/2   Wood and wire slide

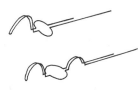

Figure 8/3   Wire slides

The characters

Making the characters   For the toy theatre proper, the 'Penny Plain, Twopence Coloured' type of sheet is still supplied by Pollock's with the printed plays. The characters printed on these are mounted on card and cut out.

For the sort of original performances that children might engage in, the characters may be drawn on card, then coloured or painted, and cut out.

Slides for the figures   The slide performs two functions: holding the cut-out figure so that it can stand without being held, and moving the figure. The following types of slide are in general use.

1   The traditional tin slide has been replaced by a plastic one but the tin version may still be made by the performer himself if he has the facilities (*figure 8/1*).

2   A wooden strip with an end slit to hold the cardboard figure (*figure 8/2*).

3   The slide made entirely of wire, bent to shape, went through a popular period but was never as popular as the tin slide. It is, however, the easiest type to make, galvanised wire being used (*figure 8/3*).

Note   It is advisable to paint the slides matt black.

The performance

The first consideration is the manipulation of the figures. The Juvenile Drama requires swift action so there is no time during a performance to change the characters in the slides. It is therefore necessary to have a slide for each character.

The obvious difficulty in the toy theatre is in showing clearly which character is speaking. This can be achieved by moving the slide with a slight shaking motion, more accentuated movement accompanying stronger speech.

The Juvenile Drama seems to benefit from having a solo operator as this brings greater unity to the performance, but this is not a hard and fast rule. When considering the number of manipulators, one must also consider the number of speakers. A solo performer may be able to provide all the voices himself or he may rely upon a number of speakers back stage. It is preferable that the manipulator(s) speaks for the characters so that movement and speech are synchronised, but if the manipulator is to speak, he must know his play by heart. It is impossible to read the play and operate the figures successfully.

Three other factors help to keep the play moving at a steady pace and minimise the length of scene changes. The first is to have only the bare essentials in terms of effects as these divert the attention of the manipulator from the main business of speaking and operating the characters. Secondly, he should be able to recognise each character from the back, by its attitude or outline shape. The characters stand beside the theatre on each side, ready to be used, so they must be immediately recognisable in a restricted light. Finally, to speed up scene changes it is advisable to arrange the scenery systematically. As far as possible, place all the scenery drops in order on the stage, the first at the front. Then, as each scene ends, remove the scenery to reveal the next. Alternatively, insert

them as required, working from the back to the front of the stage.

Music aids the performance but great care should be exercised in selecting the piece or pieces to be used. Old musical boxes are ideal, the quality of the music being in keeping with the atmosphere of the performance.

The operator may be screened so that he is not visible to the audience, but for many it is part of the enjoyment of the performance to see the manipulator furiously at work back stage. Remember that the toy theatre was a drawing-room entertainment and is not suited to large audiences. Between twenty and thirty people is a workable proposition, being enough to make a good atmosphere but not to preclude anyone seeing.

There are two further essential elements in a toy theatre performance if it is to be played in the conventional manner: there must *always* be

Figure 10 The Adventures of
Prince Achmed, *a Lotte Reiniger*
silhouette film.

movement on stage and the audience must be involved in the performance. As George Speaight* writes: 'They must co-operate; they must
applaud the heroic and moral passages, and they must hiss the villain'.

Puppet films

Apart from a straightforward recording on film of a puppet performance
there are three types of puppet film, each of which involve special
techniques of filming and performance.

Silhouette, or shadow, films

The art of making this type of film owes an immeasurable debt to Lotte
Reiniger who began her career in Germany but now lives in Britain.
One of her films, *The Adventures of Prince Achmed*, was the first animated
full-length feature film in the history of the cinema.

For silhouette films, the usual technique is to lay the articulated
figures on a transparent glass surface, illuminated from below, then take
a picture of it with an overhead camera. The figure is then moved very
slightly and another picture taken; in this way a series of 'frames' is
built up which, when projected at the correct speed on to a screen,
results in animation. Apart from the design and construction of figures
and sets, Lotte Reiniger's unique talent is evident in her ability to
analyse and visualise the components of each movement. Without her
appreciation of this aspect of the art her films would undoubtedly lack
the charm and grace that help to make them the masterpieces that they
are.

* *The History of the English Toy
Theatre,* Studio Vista, London/Plays
Inc, Boston, 1969.

Figure 11 A scene from the phase puppet series Trumpton *by Gordon Murray*

Phase puppet films

These films use three-dimensional figures and sets. The technique is related to that of silhouette films in that it uses the 'stop motion' method of putting separate frames together to make an animated or 'phased' film. The puppets are sometimes made of wood, sometimes like the rubber 'Bendy' toys that stay in whatever shape they are put.

Phase puppet films are now made in many countries for young children's television programmes. The leading figure in this field was Jiří Trnka, a Czechoslovak puppeteer and artist whose work has been internationally acclaimed. He died in 1969. In Britain, Gordon Murray and Oliver Postgate excel, each of them making series of stop-action films for television.

Both phase puppetry filming and silhouette filming require considerable patience, as can be seen from the fact that twenty-four frames are needed to make one second of film time.

Supermarionation

This term was coined to describe the elaborate marionette films made for television by Gerry and Sylvia Anderson. The series which paved the way for the development of this technique was *Four Feather Falls*. Within three and a half years of this series starting, its successor, *Supercar*, the first of the 'space-age' puppet programmes, was being viewed in a dozen countries, and in Britain yet another series, *Fireball XL5*, had made its impact and was drawing four million viewers every week. More series, such as *Stingray*, *Thunderbirds*, *Captain Scarlet and the Mysterons* and *Joe 90* were to follow, each one a technical advance on its predecessor.

The characters have interchangeable eyes for blinking and swivelling movements, and an electric solenoid in the neck to synchronise lip

165

Figure 12 Mr and Mrs Pogle from Oliver Postgate's Pogle's Wood

Figure 13 On the set of a Clangers *television film. The* Clangers *are knitted puppets with friction-tight, jointed skeletons*

movements with pre-recorded speech. Some critics argue that the techniques involved are more closely allied to film making than to puppetry. It is true that the figures do not have the characteristic puppet movement which can convey character and moods so expressively but it must be realised that this is not puppet *theatre*: it is puppet *film*, so we may expect it to rely upon film technique.

Whether or not supermarionation is puppetry in the strictest sense, it must be recognised that the general public regards it as such and its tremendous popularity has helped considerably to revive interest in puppetry.

Figure 14   Kyrano servant to
Jeff Tracy from a Thunderbirds
supermarionation television film

Figure 15   The Dragon Who
Loved Music, *a 'black art'*
production by the Caricature
Theatre

'Black art'

'Black art' is a form of presentation which has been developed with great success by the Black Theatre of Prague and in Britain by Jane Phillips with her Caricature Theatre which has its own studio in Cardiff.

Basically, black theatre involves holding puppets in carefully directed beams of light, whilst the rest of the stage remains completely dark. The operators, usually dressed in black clothes (or leotards) and hoods, are not visible as long as they do not step into the light. The figures may be painted with fluorescent paint and used with ultra-violet lighting for added effect.

Very often 'black art' presentations involve interaction between animated objects and human actors, a controversial puppetry trend but a fascinating form of theatre.

Finger puppets

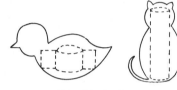

The simplest form of finger puppet is the type which fits over one finger. These may be used to particularly good effect in telling stories to young children. The characters in the story can be made very quickly and slipped on to fingers to show the characters speaking. One quick method of construction is to use two strips of card (or one small cylinder of card) for the piece into which the finger fits and to build a felt body around this (*figure 16/1*). This may be stuffed with foam rubber if required.

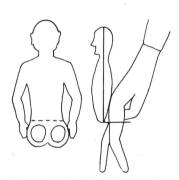

Figure 16/1   Single-finger puppets

The more usual type of finger puppet is a small figure with loose arms, the puppeteer's own fingers forming the legs. It may be just a cut-out cardboard shape with features, costume, etc, painted on, or it may be a figure modelled and dressed over a central piece of cardboard. The end of the card is folded backwards just below the waist and at right angles to the body. Two holes for the puppeteer's fingers are cut in this part of the card (*figure 16/2*). The fingers both support the puppet and form the legs. Small boots can be slipped over the tips of the two fingers and it is also possible to have loose trouser-legs attached to the body so that the fingers are covered. It is usual for operators to wear black gloves with the first two fingers cut off for manipulating the figure.

Another variant of finger puppet has strings to the arms, manipulated by the puppeteer's free hand, which of course precludes using more than one puppet at a time.

Figure 16/2   Two-finger puppets

Fist puppets

This type of puppet is used most frequently by ventriloquists. It may be formed by simply painting the features on the hand with lipstick and other make-up. Alternatively a white glove or mitten may be used with felt features glued, or stitched, on and hair (wool) added. In each case, the thumb becomes the lower jaw (*figure 17*).

Note   Some American authors have used the term 'fist puppet' as a synonym for 'glove puppet'.

Figure 17   A fist puppet

Figure 18   A humanette

Figures 19/1, 19/2   A Jumping Jack made by the author's pupils

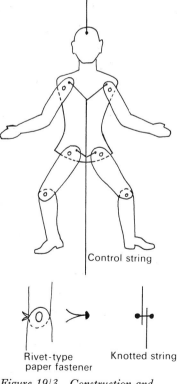

Control string

Rivet-type   Knotted string
paper fastener

Figure 19/3   Construction and control

Humanettes

A humanette is a figure that is part human (head and hands) and part puppet (body and legs). Strictly speaking, it is not a puppet but it is included here because it is closely associated with puppetry, and puppeteers occasionally include an act using a figure of this type in their shows.

There are many variations on the humanette: it may be used in 'black art' presentations (see opposite) with the operator's body remaining in the darkness, or on a table top with the operator hidden under a dark cape. *Figure 18* shows a humanette performed on a table with the operator's head and arms through a hole in the back cloth.

The stuffed puppet body either hangs from the operator's neck or is attached to the back cloth. Sometimes, particularly when used in black theatre with the operator kneeling on the floor, the legs are moved by the operator's own hands. Alternatively, a large curtain ring may be fastened to a cord running from each shoulder to the knee. By slipping a finger into the ring and raising the hand, the leg can be moved.

The humanette can be extremely funny, even intriguing, but if it is not designed with care it may appear rather grotesque.

Jumping Jacks

The jumping jack (or *Pantin*) is a simple type of puppet that became popular in the eighteenth century. It is a flat cut-out figure which is best made from stiff cardboard, although thin plywood can be used. The costume and features are painted on the figure, or the card may be decorated with other materials—such as gold paper shapes (*figures 19/1* and *19/2*). It was once possible to buy printed paper sheets of the parts and mount them on card but these are rarely found today.

To fasten the separate parts use knotted string or rivet-type paper fasteners (*figure 19/3*). Suspend the figure by a string attached to the head.

Attach a control string to a string connecting the arms and to another connecting the legs. A downward pull induces movement of the limbs. Alternatively, use two control strings, one for the arms and another for the legs.

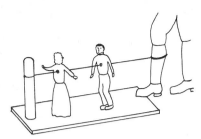

Figure 20/1   One-man version

Figure 20/2   Two-man variation

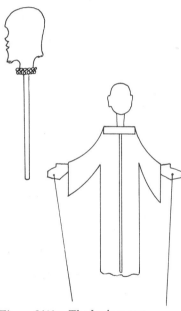

Figure 21/1   The basic marot

Figure 21/2   The rod puppet that developed from the marot

Figure 22   Puppets and a masked actor in I Am Travelling From Krakow *by the Theatre Groteska, Poland*

'Marionnettes à la planchette'

This type of puppet was common in Western Europe by the end of the fifteenth century. Little painted wooden figures with dangling limbs are suspended on a horizontal string which passes through a hole in each body. (The hole must be fairly high in the body or the figures will turn over and hang upside down.) Originally the supporting string was attached to a small post fastened to a plank hence the name.

One end of the string is fastened to a post, a chair, a table leg or any other suitable fixture, whilst the other end is tied around the operator's leg, below the knee (*figure 20/1*). Slight movements of the leg make the puppets dance. Alternatively, one or two operators may hold the ends of the string to make the figures dance (*figure 20/2*). Originally the leg was used to leave the operator's hands free to play a musical instrument, such as bagpipes.

A slight variation is to have two strings, each one passing through both figures. These are operated by two people.

The marot (or marotte)

In medieval times the *marot* was the 'Fool's stick' carried by a jester. It is really a simple form of rod puppet, consisting of a head on a rod (*figure 21/1*).

The type of rod puppet which consists of a shoulder piece and flowing robes but no body or legs (*figure 21/2*) is said to be a development of the marot.

Masks for puppeteers

George Speaight* refers to the puppet as 'the complete mask—the mask from which the human actor has withdrawn'. There is, indeed, a close relationship between the puppet and the mask. When human actors are introduced into puppet performances, masks are often used as a bridge between actors and puppets, helping to make the combination more acceptable to the audience.

The mask may take on many forms, ranging from a thin cardboard mask that covers or partly covers the face to an elaborate figure or costume that covers the perfomer. It may also take advantage of modern materials, such as fibreglass. This can be made into a mask in the same way as a puppet head.

* *The History of the English Puppet Theatre*, Harrap, London 1955.

10 Lighting and sound

Figure 1 A Photax Interfit reflector with a non-focusing lamp-holder and clip-on frame

Figure 2 An Attralux spotlight (sealed beam reflector) with the fitment adapted to fit onto an aluminium tube

Most puppeteers use some form of artificial lighting as it helps enormously to focus the audience's attention. Home-made lighting is not generally recommended for reasons of safety but it can be both satisfactory and safe. (Instructions are given here on how to make a light box for spotlight or floodlight, a flood batten and a lighting unit for shadow play or projected scenery.)

Equipment bought from stage lighting firms is not necessarily expensive and it is possible to buy exactly what is suited to the needs of the puppeteer. In general, spotlights are more useful than floodlights. The lighting equipment most useful for puppeteers is described below (prices include 10%V.A.T.).

The Lights

Spotlights

100 watt reflector spotlights   (Price: c 75p)

These lamps are the type commonly used in shop window displays and now generally available for use in the home. They are not photographic lamps and they last for a considerable time.

Reflector spotlights are ideal for clear, inexpensive lighting on a small stage and can be used with colour filters if required.

Each lamp may be mounted in a home-made box (see page 177) or a cheap photographic reflector (*figure 1*). Reflectors may be purchased with a PVC-covered clamp which can be attached safely to any part of the stage, a telescopic stand, a chair or any other suitable object. (Price of reflector with clamp £3·20.) They may also be purchased mounted on a lightweight, telescopic, photographic stand (Price: c £6).

Sealed beam reflector spotlights (150 watt)   (Price incl fitments from £3·60 each)

These are small but powerful spotlights with very efficient built-in reflectors. The lamp screws into a fitment which can be rotated and adjusted to many different positions. The fitment may be screwed to part of the stage or adapted to fit on to a stand (*figure 2*). The lamps and fitments are available from most electrical shops.

These lights are sturdy and, as they need no separate reflectors, they are particularly useful for the small, portable show. Because of their size

172

they may be placed fairly close to the stage without obscuring view. Because of the heat generated, these lamps are not recommended for use with colour filters.

Profile (Ellipsoidal) spotlight (250/500 watt)   (Price: £19·90 incl lamp)

This is a professional lamp with built-in adjustable shutters for shaping the beam (*figure 3*). The light has a hard edge which permits a sharper delineation of the beam. It weighs 6¾ lb.

The profile spotlight is excellent for all types of open stage performance, for a front-of-house spotlight (ie one placed in the auditorium) with proscenium theatres, and for shadow play. It may also be used for side lighting within very large marionette theatres, provided that the lamp is not too powerful.

Among the accessories that can be used with the spotlight are colour filters, a colour wheel and an iris diaphragm mask which gives a variable circular beam.

The spotlight has a tilting fork which allows the lantern to be adjusted to any position, and there are a variety of mounting devices which allow it to be attached to a ceiling, wall, metal pipe, telescopic stand or part of the stage. A handle (80p) may be attached for adjusting the direction of the lantern when it is hot.

Figure 3   The Rank Strand Electric profile spotlight (Patt. 23II)

Figure 4/1   Rank Strand Electric Minispot Fresnel shown with a ceiling mounting (Patt. 103)

4/2   A Minispot Fresnel shown with an integral transformer on a Lytespan track

Fresnel spotlights

Fresnel spotlights have a soft-edge circular beam the spread of which may be varied (by means of a sliding knob) from a near-parallel beam to a medium angle flood. Thus, they are versatile lights which can be used with colour filters and are recommended for side lighting within a fitup as the light is easier than that of a profile spotlight to blend on the stage. There are three useful Fresnel spotlights (the larger the lens diameter, the greater the light).

2 in Mini-Fresnel (12 volt 100 watt) (Price incl lamp but no transformer from £13·90. Price incl lamp and integral transformer from £19·30). This lamp is specially made for puppet theatres. It weighs only 1¾ lb and is being used increasingly by professional puppeteers. About eight of these lights would provide a versatile lighting scheme for quite a large stage. Each light is available either with or without an integral transformer (*figures 4/1 and 4/2*).

It is completely adjustable on its own fitment which may be screwed to the stage, the wall or the ceiling.

4½ in Junior Fresnel (250/500 watt)   (Price incl lamp £10·70)   This is a 'junior' spotlight (*figure 5*), designed for modest budgets but providing more light than the Minispot, than which it is much heavier (8¼ lb).

6 in Fresnel (250/500 watt) (Price incl lamp £18·40) This lamp (*figure 6*) may prove too powerful for all but the largest theatres. It weighs 5¾ lb. With this model, stray light can be controlled by means of a rotatable, four-door, 'barn-door' attachment.

Note   The 4½ in and 6 in Fresnel spotlights may be mounted by any of the methods described for the profile spotlight.

Floodlights

Reflector floodlights (150 watt)   (Price: *c* £0·85)

Reflector floodlights (*figure 7*) are the flood equivalent of reflector spot-lights. They are not generally used for open-stage performances as they give too great a spread of light but they may be used for floodlighting within a fitup and for shadow play.

The lights may be mounted in home-made light boxes with colour filters, in photographic reflectors or, if they have a screw fitting, in fitments available from most electrical shops.

Figure 5   The Rank Strand Electric 4½ in Junior Fresnel (Patt.45)

Floodlight (150/200 watt)   (Price incl lamp £6·06)

This professional floodlight (*figure 8*) has a wide-angle (105°) evenly distributed beam and can be used with or without colour filters. The light is useful within larger proscenium stages: two or three floodlights provide an ideal wash of light over the acting area to consolidate the spotlighting. In this respect they are preferable to batten lights as each lamp can be directed individually.

A 'masking hood' (77p) can be inserted into the internal colour frame runners to direct light.

A hook clamp (with a safety chain) is generally the most useful method for mounting floodlights; the hook clamps on to a metal pipe. However, most of the mounting fixtures for spotlights can be used with this lantern too.

Figure 6   The Rank Strand Electric 6 in Fresnel (Patt. 123)

Compartment floodlighting   (Price incl lamps: 4-light batten: £19·40; 8-light batten: £28·60)

These are battens of floodlights for overhead lighting (*figure 9*); they are obtainable in 3 ft (4 compartment) and 6 ft (8 compartment) lengths. Each compartment has a 150 watt bulb and a separate colour filter.

These battens may be used over the proscenium arch in a large marionette theatre or for overhead lighting (where possible) with open-stage glove or rod puppet performances. However, the battens tend to be rather large and heavy for puppet theatres and individual floodlights are generally more satisfactory.

Each batten has two hangers for attaching to a $1\frac{7}{8}$ in dia metal pipe.

Figure 7   A reflector floodlight

Striplights (60/70 watt)   (Price incl fitments: *c* £2 each)

These are tubular lights, about 12 in long (*figure 10*) and intended for household use, generally as wall lights. They are useful to the puppeteer as footlights and for special effects, such as the illumination of a sky cloth.

Striplights have special fitments which may be screwed into any type of home-made light box, a well in the stage floor or on to any part of the stage. Often it will be found desirable to have runners on the box for colour filters.

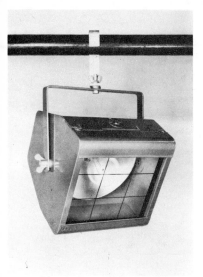

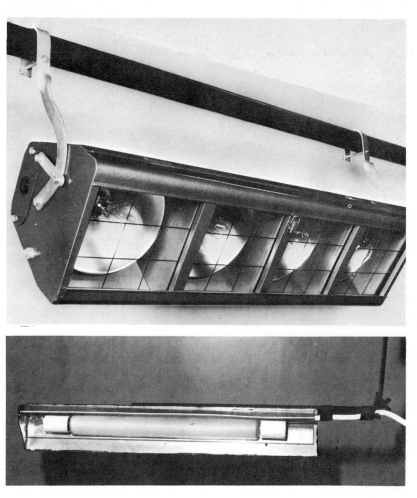

Figure 8   The Rank Strand Electric reflector floodlight (Patt. 137)

Figure 9   The Rank Strand Electric compartment floodlighting unit (Patt. S Batten)

Figure 10   A striplight held in a fitment made to fit onto the side of a stage

Telescopic stands

When lights have to be stood outside a booth they are—unless it is a permanent theatre—mounted on adjustable telescopic stands. When professional stands are used, a spigot adaptor screws over the lamp's suspension bolt; the adaptor fits into the top of the stand.

Aluminium stands   (Price from £3·75)

Photographic shops generally supply these lightweight telescopic stands (*figure 11*) sometimes complete with a reflector mounted on top (*c* £6). Those without reflectors usually have some kind of wing nut and bolt which can be used to secure a home-made light box. The base of the stand folds up for transportation.

This type of stand is suitable only for very lightweight units. Any professional light would be far too heavy for the stand.

Junior telescopic stand   (Price £9·13)

This is a sturdy stand, reasonably light (14½ lb) for transporting but capable of holding the professional lights (*figure 12*). It adjusts from

175

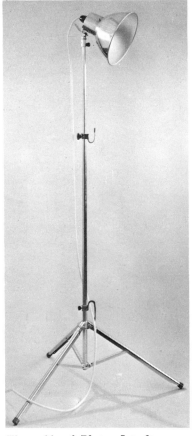

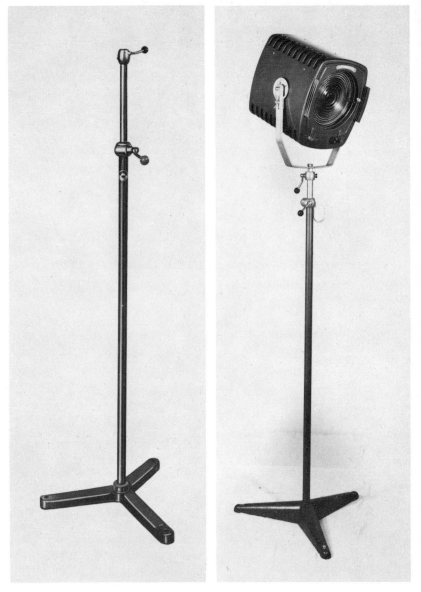

Figure 11   A Photax Interfit lighting stand with a reflector mounted on top

Figure 12   The Rank Strand Electric Junior Telescopic Stand (Ref. 627)

Figure 13   The Rank Strand Electric Telescopic Stand (Ref. 626) with a light attached by means of a spigot adaptor

43 in to 77 in high. The stem unscrews from the base but the thread on the stem is delicate.

Telescopic stand   (Price £13·75)

This stand is heavy (20 lb) but very secure and recommended for all professional lights described above (*figure 13*). It adjusts from 52 in to 89 in high. The stem unscrews from the base and the thread is strong and well protected.

Home-made lights

A single spotlight or floodlight

This is a simple light made from a large tin can (*figure 14*).

Cut a hole in the bottom of the can and fasten a light bulb holder in the hole. Drill three holes in a strip of aluminium, one at each end and one in the centre. The holes must be large enough to take bolts. Bend the strip into a 'U' shape. This forms a 'suspension fork' which is bolted to the sides of the can. Use wing nuts to permit adjustment. A bolt through the hole in the centre of the strip can be used to attach the light to any part of the stage.

Bolt three small metal angle brackets (eg Meccano brackets) around the top of the can to form runners for colour filters.

A spotlight or a floodlight can be used in this lantern.

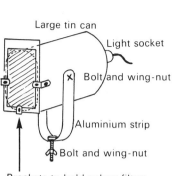

Large tin can

Light socket

Bolt and wing-nut

Aluminium strip

Bolt and wing-nut

Brackets to hold colour filters bolted onto can

Figure 14   A home-made light-box

A floodlight batten

Fasten light bulb holders in holes drilled in the bottom of large tin cans. Screw the bottoms of the cans to a wooden batten (*figure 15*) This may be suspended inside the fitup, and floodlights fitted in the sockets, or spotlights if desired.

Use metal angle brackets to hold colour filters, as detailed above.

The lights may be wired up individually or they may be grouped so that some of them are switched on and off together for economy in lighting control.

Note   When tin cans are used for lanterns, it is advisable to paint the insides of the cans with white, heat-resistant paint.

A lighting unit for projected scenery and shadow play

This unit provides excellent lighting for shadow play and for projecting scenery for all types of puppet show. It is not recommended for general stage lighting as the light is too harsh.

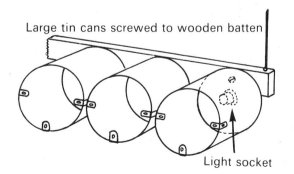

Large tin cans screwed to wooden batten

Light socket

Figure 15   A home-made floodlight batten

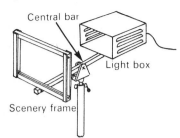

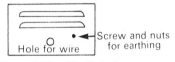

Figure 16/1　The lighting unit mounted on a stand

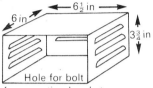

Figure 16/2　The light box

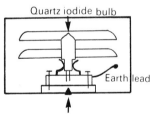

Figure 16/3　Mounting the bulb

The unit (*figure 16/1*) consists of a bulb in a light box which is mounted on one end of a wooden bar. On the other end of the bar is fastened a scenery frame, a rectangular wooden frame with grooves to take cut-out cardboard silhouette scenes or large home-made transparencies of scenery. The light projects the images on to a shadow screen, or a back screen for other puppets. Large colour filters may be inserted into the frame too. The central wooden bar fastens on to a telescopic stand.

The box　This is made of aluminium. It has one open end and ventilation slots across the back and along the sides (*figure 16/2*). Paint the inside matt black, using heat-resistant paint, to prevent reflection. (If a really sharp image is to be obtained, the light must not be diffused in any way.)

The light　A small quartz iodide bulb (24 volt/150 watt) is most suitable. This is inserted into a bulb holder which is screwed to a piece of plywood (to insulate the bulb holder from the light box). The plywood is screwed in position near the back of the box by a screw through the base of the box (*figure 16/3*).

Wiring the light　The light is connected to the mains via a small transformer which converts the current to 24 volts. A fairly heavy three-core wire is used to connect the bulb to the transformer. Drill a hole ($c\ \frac{1}{2}$ in dia) through the back of the light box to accommodate the wire. Insert a rubber 'grommet' into the hole to grip the wire and insulate it. (Grommets are obtainable from motor accessory shops for car wiring.)

Connect the 'live' and 'neutral' leads to the bulb holder and the 'earth' lead to the inside of the light box by a small screw, held by two nuts. The other ends of the lead are connected to the appropriate terminals of the transformer, the 'earth' lead being attached to its casing. (If the transformer is attached to a base board, the earth lead may be attached to one of the screws.) The transformer is plugged into the mains, again by means of a three-core lead with the 'earth' attached to the casing of the transformer.

Note　It is a good idea to incorporate a plug and socket between the transformer and the light box to allow them to be separated for packing. (It is wise to use a different type of plug from the one connecting the transformer to the mains so that the light box cannot be plugged straight into the mains by mistake.)

The scenery frame　This consists of two lengths of wood with two grooves in each (it can be bought already grooved) and four connecting strips which are glued to the grooved pieces and further secured with veneer pins (*figure 16/4*). The grooved strips form the horizontal runners which hold the scenes to be projected. It is important to have two grooves for a number of reasons.

1　One scene can be inserted as another is removed.

2　A title (painted on acetate) can be projected above a scene.

3　A masking card, giving a particular shape to the screen, can be retained in one runner whilst scenery within the shape can be changed in the other runner.

4　Colour filters can be used in one runner and scenery in the other.

The central bar　Use a 15 in ($\frac{3}{4} \times \frac{3}{4}$ in) length of wood for this supporting bar. The light box is attached to one end of the bar. Cut a slot in the bar

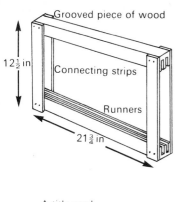

Grooved piece of wood

12½ in

Connecting strips

Runners

21¾ in

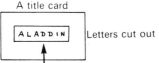

A title card

ALADDIN · · · Letters cut out

Sellotape, Scotch Tape, Takibak or *Contact* to hold in place loose centres of letters

Figure 16/4   The scenery frame

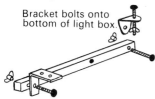

Bracket bolts onto bottom of light box

Bracket screws onto scenery frame.

Figure 16/5   The central bar

9 in   8 in

Figure 16/6   The distance between the light box and the frame alters as the central bar is angled to permit the light to shine through the frame.

to accommodate a metal 'L' shaped bracket; fasten the bracket to the bottom of the light box and to the central bar by means of bolts with wing nuts, so permitting adjustment (*figure 16/5*).

A smaller bracket is used to attach the scenery frame to the other end of the bar. Screw the bracket to the bottom of the frame and bolt it to the central bar (*figure 16/6*). This is also adjustable.

A form of 'U' bracket permits the unit to be mounted on a stand or other fitment. Make the sides of the 'U' from two pieces of strong plywood. Glue and screw them to each side of a piece of wood the same thickness as the central bar. Drill a hole in each piece of plywood to accommodate a bolt upon which the central bar pivots (*figure 16/7*). Drill the hole through the central bar at the point of balance when the light box and scenery frame are attached. Washers used between the central bar and the plywood help to tighten the joint. Use of a wing nut on the bolt allows adjustment of the bar.

Drill another hole downwards through the bottom of the 'U' bracket; this accommodates a bolt which is used to secure the whole unit to a suitable fitment. A spigot adaptor (see page 175) may be screwed on to the bolt so that the unit can be mounted on a telescopic stand.

Note   The dimensions given have been used successfully but are only a guide. (No light should spill over the outside of the frame: arrange the dimensions so that the edges of the beam fall on to the frame itself.) For screens of different size, simply alter the distance between the light and the screen.

The scenery   Scenery for projection can be made in the following ways:

by cutting out silhouettes from cardboard (leave the edge of the sheet of card as a frame as shown in *figure 16/8*);

by painting or drawing on clear acetate with glass-painting colours or felt pens;

by cutting out shapes from Letrafilm and sticking them on to clear acetate;

by painting on coloured acetate with quick-drying black enamel.

Mount the acetate sheets in cardboard frames, like coloured filters (see page 181).

Lighting control

For nearly all puppet presentations the individual lights are carefully directed before the performance and remain in the same position throughout. Occasionally, in a very large open-stage show, it may be desirable to use a 'follow spot'—that is, a spotlight which is moved to follow a character around the stage—but not often. Therefore, in terms of lighting control, the puppeteer is concerned simply with 'raising' and 'dimming' different lights.

A useful dimming manoeuvre, satisfactory for use with a small amateur fitup, is simply to slide a piece of card over the light. (It will fit into the runners for colour filters.)

Ideally, each light should have its own dimmer control. Small, lightweight dimmers taking loads up to 2 amps are now available (of the type increasingly used for lighting in the home). For larger loads,

179

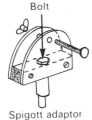

Bolt

Spigott adaptor
screwed onto bolt

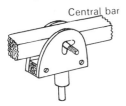

Central bar

Figure 16/7   The 'U' bracket

*Figure 16/8   A cardboard silhouette
for scenery*

Rank Strand Electric produce dimmers which can be used with single lights or, to economise, more than one light can be connected to each dimmer, although the control of the lighting is not so efficient.

Junior 8 dimmer   (Price £79; Weight 55 lb)

A versatile unit with eight 5 amp control channels sharing four 500/1000 watt slider dimmers (*figure 17*). An extension unit known as a 'Slave 8' may be added at any time; each unit gives another eight channels and costs £79.

The Rank Strand 'Mini-2' range of dimmers   (Price of control desk and dimmer pack *from* £212)

This is an excellent, lightweight range which gives finger-tip control over the whole lighting system (*figure 18*). The Mini-2 six channel 'control desk' which is only $7\frac{1}{2} \times 5\frac{3}{4} \times 3\frac{1}{8}$ in, weighs 6 lb and controls six 2000 watt dimmers. The control unit is complemented by a compact dimmer pack, weighing 25 lb, which can be positioned as desired.

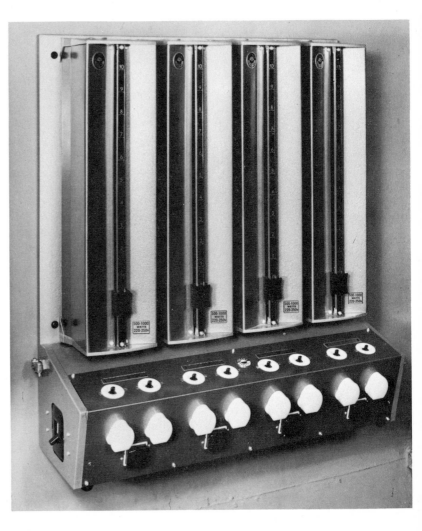

*Figure 17   The Rank Strand
Electric Junior 8 Dimmer*

Figure 18 One of the Rank Strand Electric 'Mini-2' range of dimmers: a 12-way control desk complete with dimmer packs

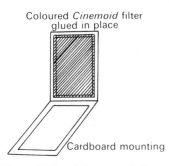

Coloured *Cinemoid* filter glued in place

Cardboard mounting

Figure 19/1 A home-made frame for colour filters: the cardboard mounting and the filter

Mounting card fastened with tape

Figure 19/2 Fastening the mounting

There are also units for twelve, eighteen or twenty-four dimmers with 'pre-set' controls (ie during one scene, the next scene's lighting can be pre-set and the changeover effected simply by moving the master control).

Colour lighting

Like all forms of lighting, coloured lighting should be used with caution. If carefully used it can do much to produce or enhance atmosphere but equally it can have a very destructive effect if used carelessly.

Any light may be coloured by covering its source with a colour filter. Cinemoid (coloured transparent acetate) is the best material for the filters; it may be purchased in sheets or pre-cut sizes and then mounted in home-made cardboard frames (*figure 19*) or, preferably, in metal frames which can be bought in sizes suitable for use with spotlights or floodlights.

In a fairly large-scale production where a number of lights are in use, changing colour is a comparatively simple matter: one set of lights is dimmed and another is raised. In a smaller show, with perhaps only a

181

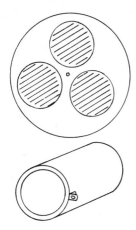

Figure 20/1   The wheel and the light box

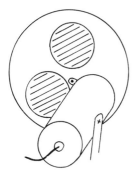

Figure 20/2   The wheel attached to the light box

couple of lights, filters may have to be changed during the performance. This may be done simply by removing one filter and replacing it with another or by using a colour wheel which may be bought with or without remote control or may be home-made. A colour wheel is desirable as the light blends smoothly from one colour to the next.

A home-made colour wheel

This consists of two pieces of strong card with three, four or five corresponding circular holes cut in them. Between these pieces of card are placed pieces of coloured acetate, each covering a hole. The diameter of the holes is slightly larger than that of the light they are to cover (*figure 20/1*).

The acetate and the two enclosing pieces of card are stapled in position. The wheel is fastened to a bracket (by a nut and bolt through its centre) and the bracket is bolted to the side of the light box (*figure 20/2*).

The attributes of colour

Of the primary colours, red, green and blue, red is the strongest and blue the weakest, which should be borne in mind when planning lighting effects.

The primary colours may be combined to give the secondary colours thus:

red and green	give	yellow
red and blue	give	magenta
blue and green	give	cyan (blue-green)

Of the primary colours, red and green are said to be 'complementary'; that is, they kill one another if superimposed and enhance one another if placed side by side. This attribute is shared by all the colours of the spectrum in a lesser degree. Red and green are the 'true complementaries' but all the 'warm' colours have their complementary amongst the 'cool' colours. (Thus with four lights it is possible to produce complementary secondary colours.)

Colour lighting effects

Cinemoid can be bought in a wide range of colours (a sample book can be purchased from Rank Strand Electric). The following are recommended to produce, or enhance, certain 'standard' effects:

Candlelight	No. 3	Straw
For a 'murky' scene	No. 55	Chocolate Tint
To cool the light	No. 17	Steel Blue
To warm the light	No. 52	Pale Gold
To 'boudoir' the light	No. 54	Pale Rose
To sharpen the light	No. 50	Pale Yellow
	or No. 1	Yellow
Sunlight	No. 50 or No. 1 may be used but it is often better left as plain white	

Blue sky	No 18	Light Blue
	or No. 32	Medium Blue
		With strong 'sunlight' on the acting area and on some scenery to show it is a warm day
Cold Sky	No. 18	Light Blue
	or No. 40	Pale Blue
		with No. 17 Steel Blue on the rest of the scene
Moonlight	No. 17	Steel Blue
	or No. 40	Pale Blue
Sunset or Firelight	No. 34	Golden Amber
	or No. 35	Deep Golden Amber

Never use Primary Red (No. 6) or Ruby Red (No. 14) for firelight.

Black light and fluorescent colours

'Black light' is the term commonly used for ultra-violet lighting. The ultra-violet rays are invisible but they cause certain materials to emit cold light or to 'fluoresce'. This shows most clearly when the room or hall is totally blacked out. For this reason, the puppeteer should not rely too heavily upon ultra-violet lighting for his show as he may have to perform in places that cannot be blacked out.

There are different kinds of fluorescent colours: some are visible only under black light and invisible under any other type of lighting; others are visible under all kinds of lighting but much stronger under ultra-violet lights. To produce a stronger glow, it is best to have a light-coloured base upon which to paint the fluorescent colours. The colours can be mixed but they do not produce the same colours as ordinary paints. To illustrate the point, blue and yellow, which would normally produce green, give an off-white glow with fluorescent paints. It is therefore wise to experiment with the fluorescent colours under ultra-violet lighting. It is useful to see how the colours look under ordinary lighting too.

There are also a number of materials that will glow under black lighting, such as corn-starch, mentholatum and petroleum jelly. These transmit a bluish-white light and may be used if fluorescent paint is not available.

Some interesting effects can be achieved with black light. For example, paint a figure or piece of scenery with an ordinary—but not dark—paint and then paint over it with invisible, transparent, fluorescent colours. By changing from ordinary lighting to ultra-violet lighting, the paint underneath 'disappears' and the fluorescent paint glows, and vice versa. It is essential to test both the ordinary and fluorescent paints under both types of lighting to ensure that they all fulfil the requirements to produce the desired effect.

Lighting for different types of performance

Apart from lights for shadow play and special effects, lighting may be categorised into: side lights, front-of-house spotlights, overhead lights and footlights.

Sidelights

These provide much of the illumination for most puppet presentations. They may consist simply of two spotlights cross-lighting the stage, but for more elaborate productions it will generally be necessary to have a mixture of floodlights and spotlights, or all Fresnel spotlights. These are placed either on each side of a proscenium opening, within the fitup; or to the sides, well clear of the stage, with an open presentation. Side lighting may also be placed behind the wings to illuminate the back cloth. This will usually be provided by floodlights but in a small fitup striplights may be used.

The number of lights will depend on the size of the stage but, as a guide, a fitup with an acting area about ten feet wide might have three floodlights and one spotlight on each side. When lighting an open stage, two spotlights are the minimum necessary to highlight modelling, eliminate heavy shadows and prevent the 'flatness' unavoidable when only one light is used.

A front-of-house spotlight

This is a spotlight placed in the auditorium. It aids illumination and helps to balance the lighting. One 250 watt or 500 watt profile spotlight is usually the most satisfactory as it is important that light does not spill on to the stage curtains.

Overhead lighting

This is generally by floodlights (individual lights or a batten) placed over a proscenium arch or suspended above, and just in front of, an open booth. Such lighting enhances modelling and scenery and blends with the side lighting for the overall effect. Care must be taken however to avoid lighting the tops of the puppets' heads, casting heavy shadows on their faces. For this reason, overhead lighting is often omitted, especially in small proscenium booths.

Footlights

Footlights help to achieve clear illumination but usually their main purpose is to balance overhead lighting. Thus, in the puppet theatre with little overhead lighting, footlights may not be necessary. If they are required, striplights are probably the most suitable as larger lights might block the audience's view. They are most frequently used with marionettes, marionette productions often being more elaborate, but are occasionally used under the top edge of an open booth for glove or rod puppets (*figure 21*), sometimes as the main lighting for a small fitup.

Lighting for glove and rod puppets

Glove and rod puppets are often presented without special lighting but stage lighting does much to enhance a performance.

Open booths

A good way of lighting a small booth is to use reflector spotlights or sealed beam reflector spotlights (see page 172) mounted on plywood extension arms attached to the two front corners of the stage.

For larger booths, profile spotlights (see page 173), mounted on telescopic stands on either side of the stage and just in front of it, are efficient. If conditions and expenditure permit, coloured floodlighting and a front-of-house profile spotlight are also desirable.

Proscenium booths

It is difficult to illuminate a small proscenium booth with lighting in the auditorium, and lighting within the booth itself may be too close to the puppets. The most successful arrangement is to mount Attralux spotlights and their fitments or 2 in Mini-Fresnel lamps to the top corners of the booth, outside the proscenium arch. Alternatively strip-lights can be placed around the inside of the proscenium arch but, although they provide reasonable illumination, this form of lighting is by no means exciting.

With a large proscenium booth a front-of-house profile spotlight can be used but it is usually preferable to mount the main lighting inside the booth, often a mixture of spot and flood coloured side lighting. Some of the smaller lights such as the Mini-Fresnel may be used inside the booth.

In a large booth overhead lighting may be possible. This might be one home-made flood batten (see page 177) suspended above the proscenium arch or, preferably, a wooden projection may be constructed to bolt on to the outside of the booth, above the arch, to hold individual light boxes. Thus, light may be shone *into* the booth rather than *down on to* the acting area and may be more precisely directed. In addition a batten to highlight scenery and back cloth may be supported by the plywood plates that hold the scenery drapes.

Lighting for shadow puppets

In principle it is possible to use any source of light for shadow play. There should be only one source of light: two lights may produce a blurred shadow.

Daylight

Position the screen so that the light from a window falls on it. Position the audience so that they are not sitting with the light in their eyes.

'Live' light

A candle, or oil lamp is ideal for shadows. This type of light is in keeping with the nature of the shadow puppet and, more important, the flickering light gives added movement to the figures, which is not possible with any other kind of lighting.

Electric light

The most satisfactory source is any type of floodlight usually mounted on a stand or, preferably, a specially made light box (see *figure 16*). Both provide a considerable spread of light at a comparatively short distance from the screen. With the home-made box, scenery can be projected too.

Slide projectors

These provide a sharp, satisfactory light and make it possible to project scenery on to the screen. Photographic slides can be used or plain slides upon which scenes have been drawn (see page 111).

Overhead projectors

Like other types of projector, these give a crisp light and allow scenes drawn on transparencies to be projected on to the screen. However, if instead of single transparencies the scenery is drawn on a long acetate roll, the roll can be wound on so that the scenery moves across the screen. By simulating a walking movement, the puppet appears to be walking some distance whereas, in fact, the action remains in the centre of the screen. It is also possible to lay small shadow figures horizontally on an overhead projector and project the shadows and scenery together.

Lighting for marionettes

Open stages

For smaller open-stage performances use two reflector spotlights or sealed beam reflector spotlights, one on either side of the stage, cross-lighting the acting area.

For larger shows profile spotlights are ideal: for economy, one light placed behind the audience may be used alone but one on either side of the stage is the minimum recommended for effective lighting. Professional floodlights at each side in addition to the spotlights are desirable for elaborate productions.

Proscenium stages

Marionette proscenium stages are generally illuminated by sidelights, overhead lights (if conditions permit), at least one front-of-house profile spotlight and, occasionally, footlights.

Sound

Sound equipment can be a very expensive outlay for the puppeteer, but reasonable equipment is necessary if the show is to be enhanced by music and sound effects. For the professional, there is every justification for allocating a generous proportion of his budget to this, but even the amateur should bear in mind that the art of presentation is as important to puppetry as the art of construction.

Live voices are always preferable to recorded or amplified voices but, in large and elaborate productions, recordings are often needed and amplification is often made necessary by poor acoustic conditions.

When recording and amplifying equipment is used, it should be the best. If an amplifier with two inputs (one for the tape recorder and one for a microphone) is used, it will be possible to amplify recorded sound, live sound or both and to balance the volumes of the two. Although many tape recorders can be used as amplifiers for the live voice they are not suitable for shows. They are not sufficiently powerful, and they cannot play back recordings whilst the tape recorder is being used as an amplifier.

It is suggested that separate loudspeakers are always used: this is essential when an amplifier is used but is also recommended for use with a tape recorder alone. A small cassette recorder without an amplifier may be adequate for small, intimate shows. Most other recorders give sufficient volume for all but very large shows; however, their built-in loudspeakers are usually small and cannot cope with high volume without much distortion. The use of larger (eg 10 or 12 in) extension loudspeakers permits greater volume with better tone and less distortion.

Any of the following portable sound systems may be suitable, depending on requirements.

1 *A small cassette tape recorder with a compact amplifier and one or two extension loudspeakers* (Total price from c £65)
Small tape recorders cannot be used for a show without an amplifier but up-to-date amplifying equipment is now moderately priced and ideal for the small portable show.

2 *A portable tape recorder with two extension loudspeakers* (Price from c £55)
Most tape recorders in common use at home or in schools would be suitable with extension loudspeakers for providing background or introductory music for a show with an audience of 100 to 150 people.

3 *A portable tape recorder with an amplifier and two loudspeakers* (Price from c £85)
This is the previous system, incorporating a small amplifier. It is necessary for larger audiences or when the puppeteer wishes to amplify his voice.

4 *A Stereophonic tape recorder with two loudspeakers* (Price between £80 and £200)
Stereophonic recording may be used to very good effect for all shows and often these tape recorders have sufficient power for large shows.

When loudspeakers are used, they should be carefully positioned so that the voices appear to come from the puppets. It is advisable to place one loudspeaker on each side of the stage, turned slightly towards the stage. A third speaker may be placed either above or below the stage and is often kept just for sound effects, to obtain added realism.

11 The show

Plays

Selecting a play

Puppetry lends itself ideally to fantasy and simple comedy and is unsuited to most serious drama, and very complex plots. Folk tales and fairy stories offer endless sources of suitable material.

There is very little written especially for puppets: individual tastes and requirements vary greatly and often puppets are created without any thought as to what they might perform and are literally 'characters in search of an author'.

Good stories do not always make good plays so possible stories must always be considered from the point of view of their dramatic content. How much of the story can be translated directly into action? Action, not dialogue, is the key to a successful puppet play. Puppets that stand still and talk are not interesting to watch: dialogue should complement the action, not vice versa.

Any material that you may think of using should be considered from the point of view of copyright (see Appendices). There is much that is not copyright but it pays to make certain.

Writing a script

Script writing is a creative process and no hard and fast rules can be laid down as to how it should be tackled but it does pay to set about it systematically.

The scenario

Having decided what to make into a play, the first requirement is a brief outline of the story. This can then be developed into an account of 'who does what and where'. The number of characters and changes of scene that is going to be possible is limited, so it may be necessary as part of this process to do away with, or combine, some of the characters and places of action.

From the outset it is most important to keep in mind the shape of the play. Each development vital to the plot should be noted and the whole series of actions arranged in the most telling order. At the same time it should be decided which are the characters essential to the development of the plot so that the stage can be kept clear of those that are not important (and the number of manipulators required in any scene kept to a minimum).

Decide where the climax comes and make sure that no intermediate action in any way detracts from it; remember that if the audience is to participate fully in the climax they must understand fully how it came about. To have to take recourse in explanations at the end of a play is disastrous.

The dialogue

Having arrived at an outline of the plot and characterisation, it is possible to begin on the dialogue.

There is no reason for this to be written down and adhered to word for word. It is usually far more satisfactory merely to decide on the content of the speech and allow the expression of it to be spontaneous, unless, of course, the dialogue is to be recorded.

How the outline of the script is arrived at depends on the individual. Some puppeteers just sit and write it; others believe that they obtain a more exciting result by asking a few friends or other members of the company to join in an impromptu session which is tape-recorded. Puppets should always be used for this, even if the puppets for the play in question are not yet made. It is not wise to use human acting as a basis for puppet acting: speech tends to become more important than action.

If the puppeteer himself is not to prepare the script, the writer should preferably be someone familiar with puppets and the requirements of the puppet play; and, as the play takes shape, the writer and producer should collaborate to ensure that all the necessary action can be accomplished by puppets.

Preparing a play through performance

It is perfectly possible to build up a play without working from an action outline. Obviously, such a script must spring from the puppets, so the set of characters to be used must already exist.

The first step is for the puppeteers to familiarise themselves with the puppets, which will begin to take on characters of their own as their limitations and capabilities become apparent.

The puppets are then ready to engage in conversation, each one speaking in the manner which the puppeteer feels is appropriate. Soon various ideas for dramatic situations will emerge. Conflict is the basic ingredient of all drama and we may be sure that, given two totally different puppet characters, conflict will soon appear. Now is the time to introduce a third character, and so the situation develops.

Having found a promising situation, continued experiments will produce more possibilities and the play will gradually develop and take shape; indeed, it may eventually take on a totally different shape from the original one. When, through practice and experiment, the final form of the play is arrived at, the dialogue can be written down, either word for word or in an outline, or recorded. As has already been stated, dialogue which is not learned by heart but is improvised on a basic structure is often more lively.

Music for the show

The function of music in the theatre is to enhance mood and atmosphere and to link scenes and bridge intervals so that these qualities are sustained. Music should never force itself upon an audience's notice.

It is usual to precede curtain-up with a short piece of appropriate feeling but music at the end of a performance is usually thought to detract from the effect of the final curtain. Sometimes, however, the dash and vigour of a variety finale can be given a final polish by a suitable piece being played after the curtain falls.

It pays always to listen to music with a critical ear, noting what certain passages suggest to you (and where they come on the record) and how certain pieces might be used. Such a reference book can save considerable time when music is needed.

Finally, always check peforming rights and royalties (See Appendices).

Rehearsal

Adequate rehearsal is essential for perfecting performing technique, developing confidence, smoothing out technical and production problems, discussing methods of presentation and considering all the aspects of design, lighting, sound, scenery and costume.

Allowance should always be made for the fact that construction usually takes much longer than one thinks it will. Rehearsal should never be rushed and a couple of hours at a time will usually prove to be as much as the performers can take.

The producer will find it helpful to draw up a schedule for rehearsals and try to keep to it. As a rough indication, a half-hour play could take a fortnight of evenings to rehearse after all the puppets, props, scenery and tapes are ready.

Usually the various scenes are prepared individually before they are put together and the play rehearsed as a whole. It is very important that the play should be sufficiently rehearsed as a whole.

The manipulators should know the play thoroughly before rehearsals begin. It helps considerably if the manipulators are also puppet makers. Understanding how the puppet is made gives a greater awareness of the possibilities of manipulation and movement.

First, the producer should work through the play with the manipulators in order to arrive at a general scheme for movement about the stage. At this point the producer is not concerned with the gestures of the individual characters but with the overall patterns of movement; with arranging groups and positioning individual puppets to the best visual and dramatic effect. Every move or series of moves that is fixed on should be noted in the master script and simple diagrams illustrating these drawn opposite the appropriate speeches.

The puppeteers' own movements should be worked out at this stage also—for example, how and when they must cross one another when manipulating—and off-stage positions fixed for the puppets so that they can be found without hesitation.

The next step is to decide on the basic actions of the individual characters, introducing their most important gestures and determining the cues for them. To this foundation details of action can be added and the complete pattern of the puppet's movement built up.

To make each puppet exciting to watch and convincing in his role, it is important to try to introduce as much variation of gesture as possible, within the limits of characterisation.

When exploring the range of movement and gesture, it is a very good plan to try to perform the play entirely in mime. The limitations of speechlessness often force a deeper exploration into the possibilities of conveying meaning through action. A far wider range of action and gesture is discovered and the resulting play has a good chance of being one in which the dialogue truly complements the action.

If the audience is to believe that the puppet is speaking, words and actions must synchronise and it must be possible to tell which puppet is speaking by other means than by recognising the voice. The art in this lies in subduing the actions of the figures that are silent (without allowing them to appear lifeless) so that all attention is focused on the speaking character. The silent figures can help in this with appropriately subdued gestures, such as nods of assent, directed towards the speaker.

A common weakness in puppet acting lies in the way the puppet takes and leaves the stage. Often this is out of character with the movement of the figure on the stage. In any type of performance the puppet must make an effective entrance. Faulty entrances and exits most frequently occur with marionettes, which are allowed to swing or drop down on to the stage. This immediately destroys the illusion. To be sure of a good entrance, the puppet should be in action before it comes into view.

Some puppeteers practise in front of a mirror; others maintain that it is dangerous to become too dependent on a mirror, for working without it is then difficult. In fact, one learns to tell when a puppet is not moving properly and dependence on a mirror may slow up the acquisition of this 'knack'.

On the other hand, the puppeteer must have some idea of the total stage picture; it is not enough for only the producer to see it. Performers often take turns sitting in the auditorium but even so they do not see their own manipulation and there is really no other way of achieving this except by using a mirror or a video tape recorder.

Almost as important as rehearsing the play is rehearsing the setting up and 'striking' (taking down) of the stage so that the whole operation becomes smooth and efficient. Setting out the puppets, the props and the scenery should all be practised until they become instinctive.

Another routine matter should be the checking of all equipment: examining all puppets, controls, strings, scenery and props before and after each rehearsal or show. Checking the packing of puppets, properties and other equipment when going to and when leaving a show is very much facilitated if a list is kept.

An emergency kit containing a small selection of tools, fuses, glue, tape, etc should always be kept handy (and tidy) for running repairs.

'Variety' shows

Until recently, shows consisting of variety or circus acts were, with few exceptions, the domain of the marionette. However, some of today's more imaginative puppeteers have shown that all types of puppet can provide first-class entertainment of this sort, although it is still the marionette that dominates the scene.

Puppet 'variety' is popular amongst puppeteers, especially solo performers who cannot present a play by themselves. It is also much in demand for children's parties, live variety shows and cabaret. The staging may be as elaborate, or as simple, as desired and most of the acts can be used for both adults and children with only a slight adaptation of the 'patter'.

The choice of material will depend partly on the puppeteer's skill in construction, partly on his skill in manipulation, but also on his own taste and the requirements of his audience.

A programme might well consist of a sketch or two and a number of acts involving tricks and 'transformations'.

The sketches need not be elaborate; it is the idea and its execution that matters. Albrecht Roser presents an act in which a clown plays with a balloon and the balloon ends up chasing the clown. The idea is simple but the precision timing and exquisite manipulation make it extraordinarily effective.

The following are some of the trick acts that might be used to make up the performance:

weight lifter
juggler
extending or collapsible puppet
acrobat
tumbler puppet
dual-controlled dancers
contortionist
stilt walker
lion and lion tamer
clown with collapsible chair
performing dog (or other animal)
Scaramouche (puppet with many heads, one inside the other)
puppet puppeteer
come-apart puppet (eg dissecting skeleton)

Many of these turns are traditional and have been performed for hundreds of years, notably by the Italian Fantoccini puppets. Each has to be fitted into an act and this requires some ingenuity and imagination. The dissecting skeleton cannot just walk on, come apart and walk off. If the puppet is to ride a monocycle, what is he to do whilst he is on it?

Animals are very popular with both adult and young audiences and can be used for many of the above acts (eg an acrobatic monkey or a bear on a monocycle). It is also possible to design one puppet so that it can perform many acts: a tight-rope walker can be a contortionist; a juggler can be an extending puppet.

Some puppets may simply perform to music; some may talk directly to the audience or to other puppets; some may perform whilst the puppeteer converses with the audience. All these techniques may be employed within the same show, depending on the acts. Where the show involves audience participation it is as well to have a few 'filler' acts prepared as it is impossible to gauge how protracted this will be.

Much of what has been said about the rehearsal of a play—particularly that which concerns puppet movement and gesture, practising with a mirror, setting up and striking the fitup and checking equipment—is relevant to variety. The attainment of speed and precision, however, is of supreme importance. Variety of all things must never be allowed to drag.

The performance

All the elements of construction and preparation are united in the performance; it is the moment when all aspects of the puppeteer's art are on show and it is essential that his work is shown off to the best advantage.

From that moment the performer arrives for an engagement he is on show. Often he has to erect his fitup in view of many fascinated eyes. To accomplish this efficiently is also part of his art.

Frequently, during erecting and striking the fitup, puppeteers have interruptions from interested adults and children. Some puppeteers are prepared to let the public back stage after the show, whilst others choose to maintain the illusion that they create and not to divulge their secrets. Into whichever category the puppeteer falls, he should always be patient with, and polite to, the enquirers. He need not allow them back stage after the show but he might spare a few minutes to talk and answer general questions which do not involve his trade secrets. A puppeteer who does not like inquisitive children and adults is in the wrong business for, if his show has any merit, it will naturally arouse curiosity and interest.

During the show, there must be complete silence back stage. Even whispers can carry and spoil the illusion that is being created.

If an interval is introduced during a play, it must be arranged at such a point that there is enough interest at the end of the first half to carry over into the second. Moreover, the interval must not be too long.

It is always a debatable question among puppeteers whether the performers should allow themselves to be seen after the show— assuming that they have not been working in the open. Some come forward to take a bow, some come forward with one of the puppets, others prefer to remain unseen: the question remains as to whether the magic and illusion of the puppet would be destroyed by the appearance of the performers.

After the first few performances of a new production, the puppeteer should pause to take a fresh look at the whole show, to reassess it in the light of how the audiences received it and reacted to it. If there are any improvements that can be made, he should make them, not be satisfied with anything less than his best. Every effort should always be made to improve the standard of any production. The show reflects and represents months of work but it is by the finished production that the puppeteer's work is judged.

I Puppetry organisations

The British Puppet and Model Theatre Guild

Founded in 1925 as the British Model Theatre Guild, this organisation subsequently became the British Puppet and Model Theatre Guild. It is the oldest existing puppetry organisation in the world.

Enquiries to: Mr. G. Shapley (Hon. Secretary), 18 Maple Road, Yeading, Nr Hayes, Middlesex.

The Educational Puppetry Association

This organisation was formed in 1943, to present and develop the full educational possibilities of puppetry as a creative and dramatic activity. It also encourages experimental work in puppetry in the education of retarded, subnormal and maladjusted children, and in adult rehabilitation.

Enquiries to: Hon. Secretary, Educational Puppetry Association, The Puppet Centre, The Battersea Town Hall Community Arts Centre, Lavender Hill, London SW 11

The Puppet Centre

The recently formed Puppet Centre Trust has established its headquarters, The Puppet Centre, in the new Battersea Town Hall Community Arts Centre, to serve the general interests of puppetry. It is a charitable organisation which aims at stimulating interest in puppetry through lectures, demonstrations, exhibitions and performances; there are also workshop facilities and an information service.

Enquiries to: The Puppet Centre, The Battersea Town Hall Community Arts Centre, Lavender Hill, London SW 11

The Puppeteers of America

Founded in 1937, this is a large organisation with a membership in many countries. It aims at the improvement of the art of puppetry in all its forms.

Enquiries to: The Executive Secretary, The Puppeteers of America, Post Office Box 1061, Ojai, California 93023

UNIMA (Union Internationale de la Marionnette)

The international puppetry organisation founded in 1929 and reconstituted in 1957. It has members in more than fifty countries and 'unites the puppeteers of the world'.

British membership enquiries to: Mr W. Meacock (Membership Secretary, Br UNIMA) 66 Devonshire Road, Harrow HA1 4LR, Middlesex

American membership enquiries to: Mrs Mollie Falkenstein, 132 Chiquita Street, Laguna Beach, California 92651

II Museum Collections

Performing Arts Collections a catalogue published by Editions du Centre National de la Recherche Scientifique, Paris 1960, contains information about all theatre collections throughout the world and includes puppets. It is especially useful as it lists not only the museums, libraries, etc. which contain collections, but also details of the type and amount of material in each.

Great Britain

The Bethnal Green Museum, London
The British Museum, Department of Ethnography, London
The Horniman Museum, London
The Pitt Rivers Museum, University of Oxford
Pollock's Toy Museum, Scala Street, London
The Victoria and Albert Museum, London
The Toy Museum, Rottingdean, Sussex*
The Museum of Childhood, Edinburgh, Scotland*
* These museums have small but growing selections of puppets.

United States of America

Detroit Institute of Arts: the major American collection of all types of puppet and related information
American Museum of National History
Cooper Union Museum for the Arts of Decoration, New York
Brooklyn Museum, New York
Museum of Fine Arts, Boston

Austria

Austrian National Library (Theatre Collection): contains Richard Teschner's unique *Figurenspiegel* theatre and puppets

Czechoslovakia

Musée International de la Marionnette (MIM), Chrudim: opened in 1971 and is building up a collection of contemporary exhibits and will continue to follow this policy. Thus today's modern exhibits will become tomorrow's archives.

France

Musée International de la Marionnette, Lyons
Musée de l'Homme, Paris

Germany

The Museum of Munich (Puppentheatersammlung der Stadt München)
one of the major world collections
Theatre Museum of Köln University (Institut für theaterwissenschaft)

Greece

The Museum of Folk Theatre of Shadows, Amaroussion, Athens, is
due to be opened in the near future by E. Spatharis, the Karaghiosis
puppeteer.

Russia

The State Central Puppet Theatre, Moscow: has a museum attached
to the theatre.

III Copyright regulations

Copyright laws protect musical, literary, dramatic and artistic works,
recordings and films. Protection is given to the form an idea takes,
not to the idea itself; thus, if an idea that has already been used is
presented again in a completely different way, there is no infringement
of the law of copyright. Anything printed or even written (it need not
be published) is automatically protected by copyright whether or not
it is deemed of any literary value. The normal period of copyright is
for the life of the author and for another fifty years after his death.

Sound recordings

Copyright of sound recordings covers their use for fifty years after
publication. Unless the puppeteer uses records which are specially
produced by certain firms and not covered by copyright, he must
obtain a licence for any music used, whether on record or tape-recorded
from records. It is illegal to tape-record from radio or television.

Phonographic Performance Ltd issues the licences for the use of
nearly all records released.

The Performing Rights Society Ltd collects the royalties for the
public performance of copyright musical works (but not dramatic
works such as operas or musical plays).

The use of copyright material

The puppeteer who wishes to use copyright material must obtain
permission from the owner of the copyright. It should be in writing,
but in certain circumstances may be 'implied from conduct'. The owner
of the copyright may require a fee in return for this licence. If consent

is given without a fee being asked, the owner retains the right to withdraw his consent at any time.

IV Safety precautions and regulations

The law imposes certain requirements upon most public and some private entertainments, mainly for the purposes of safety. The regulations are quite complex and the requirements vary, depending on the licensing authority, so it is wise for the puppeteer to consult his local authorities.

There are certain precautions which are a matter of common sense, most of which are required by law.

1   The use of flameproof material wherever possible. Materials not flameproofed in the manufacture may be rendered non-flammable by using one of the following solutions:

a. 15 oz Boric Acid, 10 oz Sodium Phosphate, 1 gallon water

b. 10 oz Borax, 8 oz Boracic Acid, 1 gallon water

Both solutions are suitable for scenery and coarser fabrics. The second is more suitable for delicate fabrics. *The solutions should be tested on a small piece of the fabric to be used* as they may affect the colours of some materials. After applying the solutions, the material should be dried without being rinsed.

Note Flameproofing is not permanent: the treatment should be repeated periodically.

2   It is advisable to carry a small fire extinguisher with the equipment and keep it in a prominent place. The type now made for cars is adequate and comparatively cheap.

3   Electrical appliances should all be earthed.

4   All electrical wiring should be of the type that has a protective rubber or PVC covering. Twisted flexible, or other unsheathed, wiring should not be used.

5   For occasional performances, any wires that must run at floor level to mains sockets should be so placed that they are not likely to be damaged or to trip up anybody back-stage. Any leads that may be too long for the premises in which they are being used should be carefully coiled and tucked out of the way, not allowed to trail around the floor.

V Where to buy materials

Most of the materials mentioned in the text are readily available from art and craft or model shops, chemists (drug stores), electrical and photographic shops, Woolworths (U.S. 5 and 10c. Stores) and large department stores—particularly in haberdashery, soft furnishings and dress materials, stationery, hardware and tools departments. Suppliers of materials not so readily obtained are listed below.

Books See Bibliography

All toy theatre materials Pollock's Toy Museum, 1 Scala Street, London W. 1.

No. 18 carpet thread Rope, twine and string manufacturers and merchants; cord and line manufacturers and merchants; in certain areas, chandlers, sports and handicraft shops; some department stores.

Celastic 'Celastic' is a trade name which has become, in puppetry circles, the standard term to describe all brands of this material. It is sold in a number of thicknesses. Suppliers are: *Britain* Adrian Merchant Ltd, Princes Road, Kingston, Surrey. *U.S.A.* Creegan Distribution Co., 273 Belleview Boulevard, Steubenville, Ohio 43952.

There is also a brand of this material known as 'Samcoforma' supplied by Samco Strong Ltd, P.O. Box 88, Clay Hill, Bristol BS99 74R

Fibre Glass (or Glass Fibre) Now available from many do-it-yourself shops, and motor accessory shops have kits (intended for car body repairs) as well as sheets of matting. To buy larger quantities, contact: Alec Tiranti Ltd, 72 Charlotte Street, London W1. Bondaglass Ltd, 53-55 South End, Croydon, Surrey.

Polystyrene (Styrofoam) Use self-extinguishing, expanded polystyrene. It is sold in standard block sizes by: *Britain* Vencel Products Ltd, West Street, Erith, Kent. *U.S.A.* Innerman and Sons, 1903 Euclid Avenue, Cleveland, Ohio. Magnus Craft Material, 108 Franklin Street, New York. Star Band Co., 800 Board Street, Portsmouth, Va.

Latex Rubber *Britain* Type A443W* Latex (* stands for white; pink is also available) from Macadam and Co., 5 Lloyds Avenue, London EC3. Dunlop's Liquid Rubber ('Soft Toy Mix'); for the address of nearest stockist write to Dunlop Rubber Co. Ltd., Chester Road, Birmingham 24. *U.S.A.* Pliatex Casting Rubber from The Sculpture House, 38 East 30th Street, New York 16. No. L200 Casting Rubber from Cementex Co. Ltd, 336 Canal Street, New York 13.

Dexion (slotted metal angle) Available in kits and separate lengths from do-it-yourself shops. In case of difficulty Messrs General Iron Foundry Ltd, 156 Bermondsey Street, London SE1 deliver throughout Britain and are very helpful with enquiries.

Stage Lighting Equipment Including lights, stands, dimmers and coloured acetates: *Britain* Rank Strand Electric Ltd, 29 King Street, London WC2. W. J. Furse and Co. Ltd, 9 Cartaret Street, London SW1. *U.S.A.* Times Square Lighting, 318 West 47th Street, New York. American Stage Lighting Co., 1331c North Avenue, New Rochelle, New York 10801. Capitol Stage Lighting Co., 509 West 56th Street, New York 10019. Also for coloured acetates: I. A. Friedman, 25 West 75th Street, New York. Arthur Brown and Bros. Inc. (see below)

Other useful suppliers

Britain Atlas Handicrafts, High Street, Manchester 4. Dryad Handicrafts Ltd, Northgates, Leicester. George Rowney and Co. Ltd, 10 Percy Street, London W1. Nottingham Handicraft Co., Hetton Road, West Bridgeford, Nottingham. Reeves and Sons Ltd, Lincoln Road, Enfield, Middlesex.

U.S.A. American Handicrafts Co. Inc., 20 West 14th Street, New York, N.Y. Arthur Brown and Bros. Inc., 2 West 46th Street, New York, N.Y. 10036. Bergen Arts and Crafts, Box 6895A, Salem, Massachusetts O1970. Creative Hands Ltd, 4146 Library Road, Pittsburg, Pennsylvania 15234. J. L. Hamett Co., 290 Main Street, Cambridge, Mass.

New York Central Supply Co., 62 Third Avenue, New York, N.Y.
Triarco Arts and Crafts, Dept. 4410, Box 106, Northfield, Illinois 60093.
The Puppetry Store (of the Puppeteers of America), 5013 S. Union,
Ashville, Ohio. Supplies a wide range of useful materials and books.

VI Bibliography

The bibliography includes some texts now out of print (marked by an
asterisk) but well worth reading. Often these texts can be obtained by
booksellers, the sales sections of the puppetry organisations or borrowed
from public libraries. Most are available either for loan or reference to
members of the puppetry organisations.

K. R. Drummond, 30 Hart Grove, Ealing Common, London W5
(telephone 01-992 1974) stocks all puppet books in print and can search
for others out of print. (Visitors by appointment only.)
The Puppetry Store of the Puppeteers of America is a useful source
of books in the U.S.A. (see previous section).

General

Tsurao Ando, *Bunraku: the Puppet Theatre*, Walker, New York 1970
Bil Baird, *The Art of the Puppet*, Plays Inc., Boston (remaindered by
    Collier-Macmillan London, New York) 1965
* Cyril Beaumont, *Puppets and Puppetry*, Studio, London 1958
* Olive Blackham, *Shadow Puppets*, Barrie and Rockliffe, London
    1960/ Harper, New York 1962
J. Bocek, *Jiří Trnka (Czechoslovak Puppet Master)*, Artia, Prague/
    Hamlyn, London 1963
Günter Böhmer, *Puppets Through the Ages*, Trs Gerald Morice
    Macdonald, London/ Plays Inc., Boston 1971
——, *The Wonderful World of Puppetry*, Macdonald, London/ Plays
    Inc., Boston 1971
* Jan Bussell, *The Puppets and I*, Faber, London 1950
* ——, *Puppets Progress*, Faber, London 1953
* ——, *Through Wooden Eyes*, Faber, London 1956
* J. Chesnais, *Histoire Generale des Marionnettes*, Bordas, Paris 1947
* J. P. Collier, *Punch and Judy*, Prowett, London 1828, Bell, London
    1881 etc.
M. R. Contractor, *Puppets of India*, Marg Publications, Bombay
    (obtainable from Educational Puppetry Organisation)
C. J. Dunn, *The Early Japanese Puppet Drama*, Luzac, London 1966
* P. Ferrigni, *Storia dei Burattini*, Bemporade, Rome 1902
Peter Fraser, *Punch and Judy*, Batsford, London 1970
* A. C. Gervais, *Marionnettes et Marionnettistes de France*, Bordas,
    Paris 1947
Franz Hadamowsky, *Richard Teschner und sein Figurenspeigel*, Edward
    Wancura, Vienna and Stuttgart 1956
Ann Hogarth, *Look at Puppets*, Hamish Hamilton, London 1960
Lothar Kampmann, *World of Puppets*, Evans, London 1972
Donald Keene, *Bunraku: the Art of the Japanese Puppet Theatre*,
    Ward Lock, London/ Kodansha, Tokyo

Gottfried Kraus, *The Salzburg Marionette Theatre*, Residenz Verlag, Salzburg 1966

* Charles Magnin, *Histoire des Marionnettes en Europe*, Paris 1862
* Ernest Maindron, *Marionnettes et Guignols*, Paris 1900

Jan Malik, *The Puppet Theatre in Czechoslovakia*, Orbis, Prague 1970

Paul McPharlin, *The Puppet Theatre in America*, Plays Inc., Boston 1969

Sergei Obraztsov, *The Chinese Puppet Theatre*, Faber, London/ Plays Inc., Boston 1961

* ——, *My Profession*, Foreign Languages Publishing House, Moscow 1950

A. R. Philpott, *Let's Look At Puppets*, Muller, London 1966

——, *Dictionary of Puppetry*, Macdonald, London/ Plays Inc., Boston 1969

* ——, *Puppet Diary*, Macmillan, London 1952

* H. R. Purschke, *Puppet Theatre in Germany*, Neue Darmstädter, Darmstädt 1957

A. C. Scott, *The Puppet Theatre of Japan*, Prentice-Hall, London/ Tuttle, Rutland Vermont 1964

Sejiro, *Masterpieces of Japanese Puppetry*, Trs. R. A. Miller, Prentice-Hall, London/ Tuttle, Rutland Vermont 1964

Rene Simmen, *Le Monde des Marionnettes*, Editions Silva, Zurich 1973

* E. Siyavusgil, *Karagoz*, Turkish Press and Tourist Department 1955

Sotiris Spatharis, *Behind the White Screen*, Trs. Mario Rinvolucri, London Magazine Editions, London 1967

George Speaight, *Punch and Judy: a History*, Studio Vista, London/ Plays Inc., Boston 1970

* ——, *The History of the English Puppet Theatre*, Harrap, London 1955

——, *The History of the English Toy Theatre*, Studio Vista, London/ Plays Inc., Boston 1969

* ——, *Juvenile Drama*, Macdonald, London 1946

* Philip John Stead, *Mr. Punch*, Evans, London 1950

J. Tilakasiri, *The Puppet Theatre of Asia*, Department of Cultural Affairs, Ceylon 1970

UNIMA, *The Puppet Theatre of the Modern World*, Harrap, London/ Plays Inc., Boston 1967

——, *UNIMA Almanach No. 1*, UNIMA, Moscow 1969

Max Von Boehn, *Dolls*, Dover, New York 1973

——, *Puppets and Automata*, Dover, New York 1973

* Walter Wilkinson, *The Peep Show*
* ——, *Vagabonds and Puppets*
* ——, *Puppets in Yorkshire*
* ——, *A Sussex Peepshow*
* ——, *Puppets into Scotland*
* ——, *Puppets through Lancashire*
* ——, *Puppets through America*

All published by Geoffrey Bles, London, between 1927 and 1938

* ——, *Puppets in Wales*, Geoffrey Bles, London 1948

* A. E. Wilson, *Penny Plain, Twopence Coloured*, Harrap, London 1932

Puppetry in Education

Margaret Beresford, *How to Make Puppets and Teach Puppetry*, Mills and Boon, London 1966

David Currell, *Puppetry in the Primary School*, Batsford, London 1969

——, *Puppetry for Schoolchildren*, Branford, U.S.A. 1969

Educational Puppetry Association, *The Puppet Book*, Ed. A. R. Philpott, Faber, London/ Plays Inc., Boston 1966

Moritz Jagendorf, *Puppets for Beginners*, Edmund Ward, London/ Plays Inc., Boston 1971

Shari Lewis and Lillian Oppenheimer, *Folding Paper Puppets*, Muller, London/ Stein and Day, U.S.A. 1964

Laura Ross, *Finger Puppets*, World's Work, London 1973

(No author), *Puppet People*, Macdonald Educational, London 1972

Technical

Majorie Batcheldor, *The Puppet Theatre Handbook*, Harper, New York 1947

Helen Binyon, *Puppetry Today*, Studio Vista, London/ Watson-Guptill, New York 1966

Jan Bussell, *The Pegasus Book of Puppets*, Dobson, London 1968

E. Copfermann, *Marionnettes, Jeux et Constructions*, Editions du Scarabee, Paris 1970

Educational Puppetry Association, *The Puppet Book*, Ed. A. R. Philpott, Faber, London/ Plays Inc., Boston 1966

* Peter Fraser, *Introducing Puppetry*, Batsford, London/ Watson-Guptill, New York 1968

M. C. Green and B. R. H. Targett, *Space Age Puppets and Masks*, Harrap, London/ Plays Inc., Boston 1969

Sheila Jackson, *Simple Puppetry*, Studio Vista, London/ Watson-Guptill, New York 1969

Moritz Jagendorf, *Puppets for Beginners*, Edmund Ward, London/ Plays Inc., Boston 1971

Waldo S. Lanchester, *Hand Puppets and String Puppets*, Dryad, London 1937

* Desmond MacNamara, *Puppetry*, Arco, London 1965

* George Merten, *The Hand Puppets*, Nelson, London and New York 1957

A. R. Philpott, *Modern Puppetry*, Michael Joseph, London/Plays Inc., Boston 1966

——, *Let's Make Puppets*, Evans, London 1972

S. and P. Robinson, *Exploring Puppetry*, Mills and Boon, London 1967

Vikki Rutter, *Your Book of Puppetry*, Faber, London 1969

——, *A B C Puppetry*, Plays Inc., Boston 1969

Alan Stockwell, *Puppetry*, Collins Nutshell Books, London 1966

H. W. Whanslaw, *A Bench Book of Puppetry*

——, *A Second Bench Book of Puppetry*

* ——, *Animal Puppetry*

All published by Wells, Gardner and Darton, London 1957

* ——, *Everybody's Theatre*, Wells, Gardner & Darton, London 1934

Glove Puppets

C. Creegan, *Sir George's Book of Hand Puppets*, Follett, London 1966
Janet Evec, *Puppetry*, W. and G. Foyle, London 1950
Peter Fraser, *Punch and Judy*, Batsford, London 1970
Suzy Ives, *Making Felt Toys and Glove Puppets*, Batsford, London/
    Branford, U.S.A. 1971
Shari Lewis, *Making Easy Puppets*, Muller, London 1968
Brenda Morton, *Needlework Puppets*, Faber, London/ Plays Inc.,
    Boston 1964
Barbara Snook, *Puppets*, Batsford, London 1965
Philip John Stead, *Mr. Punch*, Evans, London 1950

Rod Puppets

Hansjurgen Fettig, *Glove and Rod Puppets*, Trs. John Wright and
    Susanne Forster, Harrap, London 1973

Shadow Puppets

* Olive Blackham, *Shadow Puppets*, Barrie and Rockliffe, London
    1960/ Harper, New York 1962
Louise Cochrane, *Shadows in Colour*, Chatto and Windus, London
    1972
E. Coleman and R. Bryan, *Making Shadow Puppets*, Search Press,
    London/ Herder and Herder, New York 1971
Lotte Reiniger, *Shadow Theatres and Shadow Films*, Batsford, London
    1970
Herta Schönewolf, *Play with Light and Shadow*, Studio Vista,
    London/ Reinhold, New York 1968
* H. W. Whanslaw, *Shadow Play*, Wells, Gardner and Darton,
    London 1950

Marionettes

Dorothe Abbe, *The Dwiggins Marionettes: a complete experimental
    theatre in miniature*, Harry N. Abrams, New York 1970
* Olive Blackham, *Puppets into Actors*, Rockliffe, London 1948
Eric Bramall, *Making a Start with Marionettes*, Bell, London 1960
Eric Bramall and Christopher Sommerville, *Expert Puppet Technique*,
    Faber, London/ Plays Inc., Boston 1964
* Douglas Fisher, *Wooden Stars: the Lanchester Marionettes*,
    Boardman, London and New York 1947
* Peter Fraser, *Puppet Circus*, Batsford, London/ Plays Inc., Boston
    1971
S. French, *Presenting Marionettes*, Studio Vista, London/ Reinhold,
    New York 1964
* George Merten, *The Marionette*, Thomas Nelson, London and
    New York 1957
* H. W. Whanslaw, *Everybody's Marionette Book*, Wells, Gardner and
    Darton, London 1948
* H. W. Whanslaw and V. Hotchkiss, *Specialised Puppetry*, Wells,
    Gardner and Darton, London 1948
* John Wright, *Your Puppetry*, Sylvan Press, London 1951

The Toy and Model Theatre

* Arthur B. Allen, *The Model Theatre*, Wells, Gardner and Darton, London 1950
Jan Bussell, *The Model Theatre*, Dobson, London 1968
Moritz Jagendorf, *Penny Puppets, Penny Theatre and Penny Plays*, Plays Inc., Boston 1967
M. Scaping, *The Toy Theatre*, Premier Publishers, London 1967
* H. W. Whanslaw, *Everybody's Theatre*, Wells, Gardner and Darton, London 1948/1959
* ——, *The Bankside Stage Book*, Wells, Gardner and Darton, London

Plays, Stories and Play Production

Peter Arnott, *Plays Without People*, Indiana University Press 1964
M. Batchelder and V. L. Comer, *Puppets and Plays*, Faber, London 1959
Hans Baumann, *Caspar and his Friends*, Phoenix House, London 1967
Bill Binzen, *Punch and Jonathon*, Macmillan, London/ Pantheon, New York 1971
Eric Bramall, *Puppet Plays and Playwriting*, Bell, London 1961
* Remo Bufano, *Show Book of Remo Bufano*, Macmillan, New York 1929
Educational Puppetry Association, *Eight Plays For Hand Puppets*, Ed. A. R. Philpott, Garnet Miller, London/ Plays Inc., Boston 1968
Lynette Feasey (Ed.), *Old England at Play*, Harrap, London 1955
D. John, *St. George and the Dragon and Punch and Judy*, a Puffin Book, Alan Lane, London 1966
* Miles Lee, *Puppet Theatre Production and Manipulation*, Faber, London 1958
* A. R. Philpott, *The Magic Tower and Other Plays*, Macmillan, London 1952
* ——, *Mumbo Jumbo and Other Plays*, Macmillan, London 1954
Violet Philpott, *Bandicoot and his Friends*, Dent, London 1970
Antonia Ridge, *The Poppenkast (or How Jan Klaasen Cured the Sick King)*, Faber, London 1958
George Bernard Shaw, *Shakes Versus Shav*, Privately Printed (Lanchester)

Miscellaneous

C. J. Alkema, *Masks*, Oak Tree Press, London/ Sterling, New York 1971
Douglas Houlden, *Ventriloquism for Boys and Girls*, Kaye and Ward, London 1968
Shari Lewis and Lillian Oppenheimer, *Folding Paper Masks*, Muller, London 1966
Barbara Snook, *Making Masks*, Batsford, London 1972
M. C. Skinner, *How to Make Masks*, Studio Vista, London 1973

Art and Craft in Education, Monthly. Published by Evans Bros., London.

Billboard, Weekly. Entertainment trade paper. Published by Billboard Publishing Co., 1564 Broadway, New York City.

Czechoslovak Puppeteer, Monthly. Published by Orbis, Prague.

Figuren Theater, Quarterly. Partly in English. Published by Deutches Institut für Puppenspiel, 463 Bochum, Bergstrasse 115, Germany.

Het Poppenspel, Five times a year. In Flemish, with a resumé in English. Published by Louis Contryn, Kredistbank 140-04091, Mechelin, Belgium.

Outlook, Journal of the British Children's Theatre Association.

Perliko-Perlako, Puppetry review edited and published by Dr. Hans R. Purschke, Frankfurt /m 21, Hadrianstrasse 3, Germany.

The Puppet Master. Official Journal of the British Puppet and Model Theatre Guild.

Puppet Post, Quarterly journal of the Educational Puppetry Association.

Puppetry Journal, Bi-monthly journal of the Puppeteers of America.

Stage, Weekly. Theatrical newspaper. Carson and Comerford, London.

Theatre Notebook, Quarterly. Concerned with the history and technique of British Theatre. Published by Ifan Kyrle Fletcher, 22 Buckingham Gate, London SW1.

UNIMA France, Journal of the French section of UNIMA. Published by UNIMA-France, 86 Rue Notre-Dame-des-Champs, Paris 6e.

Wij Poppenspelers, Bi-monthly. The Journal (in Dutch) of the Nederlandse Verenijing voor hat Poppenspel, Valkenboslaan 243, 'S-Gravenhage, Nederland.

Woodworker, Monthly. Published by Evans Bros. London.

World's Fair, Weekly. Showman's trade paper. Includes Gerald Morice's Column, 'Punch and Puppetry Pars'. Published by The World's Fair Ltd., P.O. Box 57, Union Street, Oldham.

ACKNOWLEDGEMENTS FOR PHOTOGRAPHS

(Bracketed figures refer to chapter numbers, the following figures to the numbers of the illustrations. All photographs not listed are by the author.)

Gretl Aicher, Courtesy Salzburg Marionette Theatre (2) 8, 9, 10
Ken Barnard (4) 23   Courtesy Dora Beacham (3) 10,11   Black Theatre
of Prague of Hana and Joseph Lamka (2) 30, 31   Eric Bramall, the
Harlequin Theatre, Colwyn Bay (8) 101   British Broadcasting Corporation, Courtesy Gordon Murray (2) 59   Bura and Hardwick,
Courtesy Gordon Murray (2) 62 (9) 11   Burmese Government (2) 40
Jan Bussell, the Hogarth Puppets (2) 53 (8) 102   J. Čisárik, Courtesy
Joy Theatre, Czechoslovakia (6) 40   John Coles, Courtesy Ronnie Le
Drew (4) 17   Courtesy Cultural Attaché, Austrian Embassy, London
(2) 5   Ray Da Silva, the Da Silva Puppet Company, Huntingdon (2) 63
H. Southwell Eades, Courtesy John Blundall, the Midland Arts Centre
Puppet Company, Birmingham (2) 57 (6) 11   Stephan Fichert,
Courtesy Ian Allen and John Thirtle, the Playboard Puppets, London
(2) 58 (4) 5 (5) 4, 6, 14 (8) 31, 34, 35, 78   Derek Francis (8) 37 72
John Garner, Courtesy Percy Press (2) 48   Richard Gill, Polka
Children's Theatre, London (6) 18   Graphotos Ltd, Courtesy Rank
Strand Electric Ltd (10) 3, 12, 18   K. A. Harnisch, Courtesy Frieder
Simon, the Larifari Theatre, DDR (2) 22, 23 (4) 10, 11 (5) 3   E. S.
Harold (6) 20   Edward Hartwig, Courtesy State Puppet Theatre Lalka,
Poland (2) 25 (6) 44   Hausmann, Courtesy Cultural Attaché, Austrian
Embassy, London (2) 6   Tom Howard, Courtesy British Puppet and
Model Theatre Guild (2) 11   Adam Idziński, Courtesy Marta Janic,
State Puppet Theatre Pinokio, Poland (2) 26, 27 (6) 23, 47   Incorporated Television Company Ltd and Century 21 Films (2) 60, 61 (9) 14
Japan Information Centre, London (2) 44   Mme Keleti, MTI,
Courtesy Hungarian State Puppet Theatre Allami Bábszinház (2) 20, 21
Waldo S. Lanchester, the Lanchester Marionettes (2) 47, 50 (8) 44
P. Lecoq, Courtesy André Tahon, France (2) 17, 18   Daniel Llords,
Llords International, USA (2) 1, 71 (8) 62   Albert Marrion, Courtesy
Eric Bramall, the Harlequin Theatre, Colwyn Bay (2) 55 (8) 79,
Majorie Batchelder McPharlin, USA (2) 66 (3) 5   W. Meacock,
Courtesy Jan Bussell and Ann Hogarth, the Hogarth Puppets, Egham
(2) 52 (8) 36   Nat Messik, Courtesy Bil Baird, USA (2) 68, 69, 70
Franciszek Myszkowski, Courtesy State Puppet Theatre Guliwer,
Poland (2) 28   National Theatre of Puppets and Actors Marcinek,
Poland (6) 24   Jane Phillips, the Caricature Theatre, Cardiff (2) 54

(9) 15   Violet Philpott, the Cap and Bells Puppet Theatre Company, London (2) 19, 43, 51 (4) 6 (5) 5, 12 (6) 19   Violet Philpott, from the Lucy Claus Bequest (2) 42   Photax (London) Ltd (10) 1, 11   Oliver Postgate (9) 12, 13   L. Postupa, Courtesy Naive Theatre, Czechoslovakia (6) 43   Lotte Reiniger (9) 10   Albrecht Roser, Stuttgart (2) 12, 13, 14 (8) 43   Vladislav Scholz, Courtesy the State Central Puppet Theatre, Prague (5) 26   R. W. Sheppard, Courtesy Rank Strand Electric Ltd (10) 5, 6, 8, 9, 13, 17   Courtesy Mme Lenora Shpet, State Central Puppet Theatre, Moscow (2) 33, 34, 35 (6) 39   V. Sirucek, Courtesy Milos Kirschner, the Spejbl and Hurvinek Theatre, Czechoslovakia (2) 32   Edwin Smith, Courtesy George Speaight (9) 9   Barry Smith, from the author's collection (3) 9 (4) 15 (5) 13 (6) 27 (7) 8 (8) 32, 33, 45, 57.1, 67, 71.2, 77.1, 80 (9) 1, 19.1, 19.2   Barry Smith, Theatre of Puppets (2) 41, 46, 64, 65 (6) 17, 48   Barry Smith, Courtesy Jan Bussell and Ann Hogarth, the Hogarth Puppets (2) 2, 15, 16, 24, 29, 36, 37, 38, 39, 45, 49 (7) 4   Barry Smith, Courtesy John Wright, the Little Angel Marionette Theatre (7) 7   E. Spatharis, Greece (2) 3, 4 (7) 10   David Stanfield, Courtesy John Wright, the Little Angel Marionette Theatre, London (2) 56 (4) 9   Fred Tickner (8) 100   Burr Tillstrom, USA (2) 67   Mary Turner, Courtesy Muriel and Judith Shutt, the Mejandes Marionettes, London (8) 42   Votava, Courtesy Cultural Attaché, Austrian Embassy, London (2) 7   John Waterman, Courtesy Rank Strand Electric Ltd (10) 4   J. Wolski, Courtesy H. Jurkowski, Poland (9) 22   Ron Wood, Courtesy Gordon Staight, Gordon's Puppets, Plymouth (8) 71.3, 77.8, 81.